LIONS UNDER THE THRONE

FRANCIS BACON wrote in 1625 that judges must be lions, but lions under the throne. From that day to this, the tension within the state between parliamentary, judicial and executive power has remained unresolved. *Lions under the Throne* is the first systematic account of the origins and development of the great body of public law by which the state, both institutionally and in relation to the individual, is governed.

STEPHEN SEDLEY practised at the English Bar from 1964 to 1992 before serving as a judge of the Queen's Bench division of the High Court from 1992 to 1999 and as a Lord Justice of Appeal from 1999 to 2011. He has also sat as a judge ad hoc of the European Court of Human Rights and the Judicial Committee of the Privy Council. Over time, he specialised increasingly in the developing field of public law, and, in his role as visiting professor at Oxford University between 2011 and 2015, delivered the series of lectures which form the basis of this book.

LIONS UNDER THE THRONE

Essays on the History of English Public Law

STEPHEN SEDLEY

 **CAMBRIDGE**
UNIVERSITY PRESS

CAMBRIDGE
UNIVERSITY PRESS

University Printing House, Cambridge CB2 8BS, United Kingdom

Cambridge University Press is part of the University of Cambridge.

It furthers the University's mission by disseminating knowledge in the pursuit of education, learning and research at the highest international levels of excellence.

www.cambridge.org
Information on this title: www.cambridge.org/9781107559769

First published 2015

A catalogue record for this publication is available from the British Library

Library of Congress Cataloguing in Publication data
Sedley, Stephen, author.
Lions under the throne : essays on the history of English public law / Stephen Sedley.
pages   cm
Includes bibliographical references and index.
ISBN 978-1-107-12228-4 (Hardback) – ISBN 978-1-107-55976-9 (Paperback)
1. Public law–England–History.   2. Civil rights–England–History.
3. Rule of law–England–History.   I. Title.
KD3930.S43 2015
342.42′009–dc23   2015013726

ISBN 978-1-107-12228-4 Paperback

Let judges also remember that Solomon's throne was supported by lions on both sides: let them be lions, but yet lions under the throne; being circumspect that they do not check or oppose any points of sovereignty. Let not judges also be so ignorant of their own right as to think there is not left them, as a principal part of their own office, a wise use and application of laws.

Francis Bacon, Of Judicature, 1625

Newspapers have repeatedly said that there is a state of tension between the judges and the Home Secretary. The implication is that this is an undesirable state of affairs. That is a misconception. It is when there is a state of perfect harmony between the judges and the executive that citizens need to worry.

Lord Steyn, Administrative Law Bar Association
Lecture, 1996

To my grandchildren

CONTENTS

CONTENTS

PREFACE

By 2011, when I retired from the Court of Appeal, I had spent eighteen years on the bench and before that twenty-eight years at the Bar. Over those years I had seen public law grow from a topic which was not even taught in law schools, except as a footnote to constitutional law, to a major area of legal practice and constitutional development. I had also had the luck to play a minor part in this metamorphosis.

The offer, following my retirement, of a post as visiting professor of law in the University of Oxford provided the opportunity and the stimulus to confront the incuriosity I had met everywhere in my profession, as well as to satisfy my own curiosity, about how the public law of England and Wales (and in practice of Northern Ireland too) has come to be what it is. There was no way at my age to catch up on what should have been a lifetime's research. Working on these essays, while it has been for me an education, has repeatedly reminded me how limited my knowledge is, for although practitioners in a common-law system sometimes have to deploy historical material, its use tends to be goal-oriented and to lack context. The book, accordingly, is primarily for judges, practitioners and students, though I hope that academic lawyers, legal historians and political scientists will also find things in it to think about.

***

With the support of the Law Faculty, I delivered the twelve lectures which form the core of this book between 2012 and 2014. To them I have added two further papers delivered in the same period: one on the neglected public law of the Interregnum, initially delivered as the 2013 Sir Henry Hodge memorial lecture; the other, delivered in 2014 as the inaugural Rule of Law lecture for the Justice Institute of Guyana, on the influence of Dicey.

I wish in particular to acknowledge the support I have had from Anthony Bradley QC, emeritus professor of constitutional law in the

University of Edinburgh and for many years a colleague, mentor and friend, whose encouragement and guidance have piloted me through numerous reefs and shoals of English public law and its complicated history.

Among the many other debts of gratitude which I owe, one is to Professor Paul Craig FBA, QC for having suggested that I come to teach in Oxford and for his support, together with that of Dr Aileen Kavanagh, Professor Liz Fisher and the Dean, Professor Timothy Endicott, for my work there. I owe a special debt to Professor Sir Keith Thomas for casting an eye over a draft of Chapter 4 and, with what he called "a few pedantic notes", saving me from some embarrassing errors. And I have had indispensable research assistance from two able and upcoming lawyers, Sepideh Golzari, LLB, LLM, and Bianca Venkata, LLB, BCL.

Stephen Sedley
Oxford

Introduction

The first part of this chapter sketches the early growth of English public law. The second part tries to describe what it was like to be involved in the modern take-off of public law as it roused itself from its long sleep.

It seems surprising, given the modern prominence of judicial review of governmental acts, that no panoptic history of the public law of England and Wales exists.[1] By public law I mean the body of law, embracing both administrative and constitutional law, by which the state is regulated both institutionally and in its dealings with individuals.[2] This book does not fill that large space: it is, rather, a series of test drillings into a landmass. The vertical drillings are thematic attempts to trace their topic from early days to the present. The horizontal ones (which are not sequential) take a stratum of time and examine developments in public law within it.

The public law of Scotland does not form part of the history which this book examines. Neither the union of the two crowns in 1603 nor the union of the two states in 1707 brought the English and Scottish systems together. Rather than risk trivialising or misrepresenting Scottish public law, these essays treat it with a respectful silence.[3]

---

[1] Such a history is, however, coalescing in the still-emerging volumes of the *Oxford History of the Laws of England*: see, at the date of writing, vol. II (871–1216), Ch. 31; vol. VI (1483–1558), Chs. 2, 3 and 4; vol. XI (1820–1914), Part II. After the unification of England and Wales by the statutes of 1536 and 1543, the public law of the two countries was effectively uniform until the passage of the Government of Wales Acts 1998 and 2006.

[2] Cf. the definition in M. Loughlin, *The Idea of Public Law* (2003), p. 1: "the constitution, maintenance and regulation of governmental authority".

[3] A full account of Scottish public law can be found in the Stair Memorial Encyclopaedia, A. W. Bradley and C. M. G. Himsworth (eds.), *The Laws of Scotland*, vol. I, Part IV, "Administrative Law" (2000 reissue). Since the partition of Ireland in 1921, the public law of Northern Ireland has generally tracked that of England and Wales but from time to time has moved ahead of it.

HISTORY AND LAW

The distinction between the writing of legal history and the making of it was astutely described by Geoffrey Wilson:

> [T]he courts do not operate on the basis of real history, the kind of history that is vulnerable to or determined by historical research. They operate on the basis of an assumed, conventional, one might even say consensual, history in which historical events and institutions often have a symbolic value.[4]

That seems a harsh thing to say about a profession which sets great store by the accurate citation of precedent, but I think it is true. From Magna Carta[5] to *Anisminic*[6] by way of *Entick* v. *Carrington*,[7] the common law and the constitutional culture of which it forms part have adopted not the letter of the law but the meanings which it has become appropriate to find in it. The zeitgeist is at least as potent as the scholar.

History has neither beginnings nor endings, but in tracking the history of English public law it is difficult not to be struck by the modernity of the later Elizabethan and the early Jacobean judges, Edward Coke prominent among them,[8] and by the depth, breadth and – in the long term – continuity of the river of jurisprudence which flows from them to us. Elizabeth's reign saw a major increase in the volume of litigation and the emergence of an unprecedentedly high proportion of lawyers in the population.[9] But the late Tudor state was

---

[4] Postscript to M. Nolan and S. Sedley, *The Making and Remaking of the British Constitution* (1998), pp. 128–9

[5] See Ch. 4   [6] See Ch. 1   [7] See Ch. 3

[8] Although Coke (pronounced "Cook") features in this book in a generally favourable light, he had and still has many critics. He is the subject of a classic biography, *The Lion and the Throne* (1957) by Catherine Drinker Bowen. A scholarly account of the controversies between Coke, Ellesmere and Bacon, and the background to them, can be found in three articles by the former chief justice of New South Wales, James Spigelman, under the running title "Lions in Conflict": (2007) 28 *Aust. Bar Review* 254; (2008) 30 *Aust. Bar Review* 144; (2013) 38 *Aust. Bar Review* 1.

[9] "In the long history of the relationship between law and society in England, the later sixteenth century must be reckoned one of the most dynamic . . . It is not surprising that the first fifty years of the life of Sir Edward Coke . . . coincided almost exactly with the period from the accession of Edward VI to the death of Elizabeth, or that his law reports reflect so much of the social and economic life of middle England": C. W. Brooks, *Law, Politics and Society in Early Modern England* (2008), p. 93; see ibid. Chs. 4 and 7. The period has also been hailed as a high point of non-litigious dispute resolution: see D. Roebuck, *The Golden Age of Arbitration: Dispute Resolution under Elizabeth I* (2015).

itself the product of centuries of change. Its judges, heirs of a legal culture reaching back to and beyond early modern England, were sensing the first tremors of the constitutional earthquake which, by the end of the seventeenth century, was not only to settle into the foundations of the modern British state but to gestate ideas of individual rights and lawful governance which have helped to shape the modern world.

Although the radicals of the Civil War associated monarchical and aristocratic oppression with what they called the Norman yoke, counterposing it to the home-grown laws of the Anglo-Saxons, the Norman kings had in fact taken care to adopt and continue the Anglo-Saxon system of law.[10] Alfred's and Aethelstan's codes had been made not autocratically but on the advice of their counsellors.[11] Canute's code, four decades before the Conquest, undertook "to secure the whole people against what has hitherto oppressed them", including royal exactions. Such legislation can be intelligibly seen "not as expression of royal will but as royal concession".[12]

The continuity of this process with Magna Carta (and, at least formally, with modern legislative practice) is readily seen, though it may not be how successive monarchs and their ministers saw it. Chief Justice Fortescue in the mid-fifteenth century described the kings of England as ruling politically as well as regally, so that they were without power to tax their subjects without the latter's consent.[13] It was a continuity which, although disrupted by the anarchy of Stephen's reign, was severed neither by Henry VIII's autocratic conduct, which paradoxically depended on repeated Parliamentary endorsement,[14] nor by the Interregnum, which initiated reforms that took centuries to restore and consolidate.[15]

The laggard in this continuity has been democracy itself.[16] A parliament of knights of the shire and burgesses, or of merchants

---

[10] J. Hudson, *The Oxford History of the Laws of England,* vol. II , p. 487; D. Roebuck, *Early English Arbitration* (2008), Ch. 10.

[11] Hudson, *The Oxford History of the Laws of England,* vol. II, pp. 21 ff; pp. 498–9.

[12] Ibid., p. 25

[13] Fortescue, *De Laudibus Legum Angliae* (c. 1470, pubd. 1541), Ch. IX: "A king of England cannot, at his pleasure, make any alteration in the laws of the land, for the nature of his government is not only regal but political" – a principle traced by Brooks, *Law Politics and Society,* p.24) to Book III of Aristotle's *Politics.*

[14] See Ch. 11.   [15] See Ch. 4.

[16] Not an unusual sequence: see Ch. 9, n. 11. But in a remarkable moment of history, though one not to be repeated, the so-called Good Parliament of 1376 had asserted its supervisory power over the King's ministers by impeaching four of them before the House of Lords for corruption and incompetence: see Ann Lyon, *The Constitutional*

and landowners, elected by a narrow and generally corruptible electorate, had little claim to the representative quality ringingly but
vainly demanded by Colonel Thomas Rainborough at Putney in
1647:

> [T]he poorest he that is in England hath a life to live as the greatest he;
> and therefore truly, sir, I think it's clear that every man that is to live
> under a government ought first by his own consent to put himself under
> that government.[17]

Almost two centuries after the slow process of electoral reform was
initiated in the United Kingdom, and more than a century after the
Parliament Act 1911 announced itself as the first step in setting up an
elected upper chamber, this is a road we are still travelling down with
little in the way of maps or compasses.

The other jaw of the pincer which slowly closed on the monarchical
power of making law and dispensing justice began to take shape in the
twelfth century, when Henry I appointed a number of "justiciars of
the whole of England" to whose judgment, according to William of
Malmesbury, he entrusted "the administration of justice throughout the
realm, whether he himself was in England or detained in Normandy".[18]
While England remained administratively divided into Wessex, Mercia
and the Danelaw, each with its own customs enforceable at the level of
shire, hundred or borough, the *Leges Henrici* boasted that "the king's
court ... keeps its usages and customs always and everywhere with
singular immutability", and commentators now spoke of "the law of
the land"[19] – a common law both in the sense that it was no longer the
King's law and in the sense that it was the same wherever the King's
courts sat.

It was the Angevin kings who, attempting to bring order to a sometimes ungovernable state, brought the beginnings of an independent

---

History of the United Kingdom (2003), pp. 105–6. It was by deputing Sir Peter de la
Mare to speak for them in presenting the bill of impeachment that the Commons
inaugurated the office of Speaker.

[17] A. S. P. Woodouse (ed.), *Puritanism and Liberty (The Army Debates 1647-9)*, (1938),
p. 58. Major-General Ireton, a lawyer in civilian life, whose regard for private property
had prompted Rainborough's call for a universal male franchise, turned Leveller ideology
back on its proponents by asserting that the property-owning franchise itself predated the
Conquest. "If you make this the rule," he pointed out, "I think you must fly for refuge to
an absolute natural right." In the event, that is what the Levellers did.

[18] Hudson, *The Oxford History of the Laws of England*, vol. II, p. 262

[19] Hudson, *The Oxford History of the Laws of England*, vol. II, p. 491

system of justice into being. The process may with hindsight appear as one of progressive reform, but in its time was regarded as one of consolidation and restoration.[20] Nevertheless, wittingly or unwittingly, the change came.

> Final concords record at least seventy [men] sitting at the Exchequer as justices between 1165 and 1189 ... The chief justiciars and twelve other justices account for roughly two-thirds of the named appearances. Thus a core group of justices had emerged ... The group's influence on the court and its law must have been considerable.[21]

From 1176 the occasional dispatch of justices to try important cases regionally was succeeded by their routinely travelling out in eyre – that is to say on circuit – having first taken an oath to do the King's justice to everyone.[22] By the end of the twelfth century, sheriffs were barred (though not always effectively) from sitting as justiciars in their own shrievalties. By the end of the thirteenth, all the judges had served their time as professional lawyers, and justice was on the way to becoming an independent function of the state.[23]

---

[20] See D. Roebuck, *Mediation and Arbitration in the Middle Ages* (2013), pp. 17–18, esp. n. 4. Roebuck makes the point that "reform" did not acquire its modern connotation of progress or innovation until the end of the Middle Ages; indeed Raymond Williams, *Keywords:A Vocabularly of Culture and Society* (2014), allocates the change in usage to the eighteenth century. Its original meaning was repair or restoration – a return to a more orderly past.

[21] Hudson, *The Oxford History of the Laws of England*, vol. II, p. 503. Roebuck, *Mediation and Arbitration in the Middle Ages*, p. 23, cites a contemporary account of a royal justiciar of the early thirteenth century "so sedulous and practised" that his colleagues "are overpowered by the labour of Pateshull, who works every day from sunrise until night", making other justiciars redundant. Such judges still exist.

[22] Hudson, *The Oxford History of the Laws of England*, vol. II, p. 505

[23] It was not until much more recent times, however, that the administrative and judicial functions of local justices of the peace were separated from one another. For centuries JPs administered most of the Elizabethan Poor Law (with the consequence, according to E. G. Henderson, *Foundations of English Administrative Law: Certiorari and Mandamus in the Seventeenth Century* (1963), p. 143 that "much of the early development of modern administrative law is to be found in the cases on the poor law"). From the Statute of Artificers 1562 until the late nineteenth century JPs were empowered to fix wage rates and punish workers for absenteeism or substandard work, as well as to redress certain grievances against employers. Until the reform of municipal corporations in 1835, much of the government of the shires was conducted at their quarter sessions: see W. R. Cornish and G. de N. Clark, *Law and Society in England 1750–1950* (1989), pp. 19–21; S. Anderson, *The Oxford History of the Laws of England*, vol. XI, pp. 454–61. JPs continued to license pubs and betting shops until the late twentieth century.

Law as reported

It has been suggested more than once that in the sixteenth century the training of lawyers in the Inns of Court, dependent as it was on the oral transmission of legal doctrine, did not furnish a stable basis for the development of a precedent-based system. It was supposed that a void in law reporting was astutely filled by Coke with his reports, in large part recording his own decisions and giving him an undeserved influence on the development of the common law. Modern scholarship[24] questions the premise: it is now known that a considerable variety of printed and manuscript reports of cases supplemented the oral transmission of the common law both before and in Coke's time. The Year Books, blackletter reports of cases in law French, ran from the early fourteenth century to the mid-sixteenth, and Chaucer's serjeant-at-law, in the late fourteenth century, owned both statutes and law reports.[25] In such a context Coke's most significant decisions are legitimately regarded both as weathervanes of legal history and as a source of constitutional principle. Coke had a chequered career,[26] both in and out of royal favour, but he did not plough a lone furrow.

The growth of public law

The developments I have touched on were not simply the conditions from which public law, as part of the common law, was to emerge. They were themselves public law developments, restructuring the state and the individual's relation to it as drastically as anything in the succeeding centuries to which the essays in this book relate. They may have initially changed little, but they created the conditions for change.

---

[24] See J. Baker, *The Oxford History of the Laws of England*, vol. VI, Ch. 26.

[25] "In termes hadde he caas and doomes alle
  That from the tyme of kyng William were falle" (*Canterbury Tales, Prologue,* Folio edn, p. 20).

[26] See Bowen, *The Lion and the Throne.* He also has a chequered reputation, principally because of the venom with which, as Attorney-General, he prosecuted Sir Walter Raleigh on what was without doubt a trumped-up charge of treason: "Thou art a monster! Thou hast an English face but a Spanish heart ... Thou viper! ... I will prove thee the rankest traitor in all England." But one wonders whether Coke's rancour was any worse in its time and place than that displayed in 1972 by Governor Reagan's special prosecutor, Albert Harris, towards the young university teacher Angela Davis: "Not only is there enough evidence to send this case to trial, there is enough to take this young woman and lock her in a green gas chamber and drop cyanide pellets into the acid and put her to death."

> [I]f we look closely at fifteenth-century England, we see a social world in which the rule of law as we know it played a relatively small part. The major common law courts were generally under-used ... Private disputes were settled either by resort to violence or by informal arbitration, and there was no very highly developed public law to which constitutional disputes could be referred. By comparison, if we turn from the fifteenth to the mid-seventeenth century, there at first sight appears to be abundant evidence of change. .... [T]he common law and common lawyers were deeply involved in many of the constitutional disputes of the early Stuart period.[27]

It is with that metamorphosis that most of the history examined by this book begins. It is a story with no clean breaks or fresh starts. The endeavours first of monarchs and then of their ministers to reserve legislative and judicial powers to themselves form a recurrent theme in it. But so does their eventual acceptance of the hard fact that they could not raise taxes or govern without the advice and consent of those who controlled land and trade, nor administer consistent law and justice except through a professional judiciary, nor themselves stand aside from or above the law.

Inhabiting and permeating these changing structures and institutions have been the substantive principles of public law. By the mid-seventeenth century a practice manual was able to say of what was now the Upper Bench:

> This Court hath authority to Quash Orders of Sessions, Presentments, Endictments &c made in inferior Courts, or before Justices of Peace or other Commissioners if there be cause, that is, if they be defective in matter or form ... But this Quashing is by favour of the Court, for the Court is not tyed Ex Officio to do it ...[28]

These and other principles of judicial review have waxed, waned, slumbered and woken, but in the long term matured in response to continuing change in the society and polity which law inhabits. By the beginning of the eighteenth century the reactive interventionism of the late Tudor

---

[27] Christopher W. Brooks, *Law, Politics and Society in Early Modern England* (2008), pp. 8–9

[28] Style, *Practical Register* (1657), quoted in Henderson, *Foundations of English Administrative Law*, p. 107. The King's Bench was renamed the Upper Bench during the Interregnum. Styles' account of the judicial review jurisdiction highlights two important facets of it: (a) the focus on judicial proceedings, which, until *Anisminic*, drove courts to look for quasi-judicial functions in order to render decisions justiciable, and (b) the discretionary character of relief.

judges was being developed and nuanced, notably by Chief Justice Holt, who, in a case decided in 1700 on the amenability to judicial review of Welsh justices of the peace who had been granted statutory powers for the upkeep of Cardiff bridge, said:

> [T]his court will examine the proceedings of all jurisdictions erected by Act of Parliament. And if they, under pretence of such Act, proceed to incroach jurisdiction to themselves greater than the Act warrants, this Court will send a certiorari to them, to have their proceedings returned here.[29]

In the centuries since then public administration has changed massively, and public law has changed with it. Whether it will be allowed to go on doing so is one of today's great questions.

AUTOBIOGRAPHY AS HISTORY

My own walk-on part in the more recent phase of this process has posed a problem in writing these studies. While it has been the stimulus for the entire exercise, it has also inexorably affected my view of events. As a barrister, although I sometimes acted for public authorities, the bulk of my public law work was bringing challenges on behalf of individuals to uses and abuses of state power. As a judge, I must have decided as many cases and applications in favour of public authorities as against them, though I have not counted. But it would be idle to claim that any judge goes into court with a blank mind (an open mind is something entirely different), any more than does a historian sitting down to write, and it would be disingenuous for me, as I believe it would be for any judge, to pretend that my own experience had no bearing on my thinking and my decision-making. But the bearing is rarely linear, and that is what makes both litigation and adjudication interesting.

It is also why, in delivering the lectures which form the basis of this book, I resorted from time to time to anecdote. It helped, or so I hoped, to make the content a little more vivid and the topics a little more immediate. In editing them for publication I have eliminated most of

---

[29] *R* v. *Glamorganshire Inhabitants* (1700) 1 Ld. Raym. 580. See also *Groenvelt* v. *Burwell* (1700) 1 Ld. Raym. 454; Henderson, *Foundations of English Administrative Law*, pp. 101–16; W. Wade and C. Forsyth, *Administrative Law* (10th edn), pp. 509–21.

these minor vanities or relegated them to footnotes. In place of them, there follows here, segregated from what I have attempted to make a reasonably objective set of historical essays, an anecdotal sketch of my encounter with public law as it began, in the last three decades of the twentieth century, to stir into life after two generations of torpor. These were my formative years.

They were also, as it turned out, the formative years of the modern body of common law by which the machinery of state is still both regulated and guarded – for, as I have stressed elsewhere, public law is as much concerned with the protection and validation of good administration as it is with controlling abuses of power. A checklist of these developments, to a number of which I had the good fortune to contribute either at the Bar or on the bench, would include the duty to give reasons for decisions, the enforcement of policies which have generated legitimate expectations, the injection of fair procedures into public consultation, the recusal of decision-makers for apparent bias, the justiciability of decisions for error of fact, the proportionality of decision-making, the expansion of standing for public interest challenges – none of them dreamed of in the philosophy of *Wednesbury*.[30]

My present topic, however, is not these developments, nor the handful of high-profile cases which form the epistemic framework of modern public law – *Ridge* v. *Baldwin, Anisminic, Padfield, British Oxygen, O'Reilly* v. *Mackman* – but the largely unnoticed groundswell of judicial review applications heard from the early 1970s in the Queen's Bench Division of the High Court, and more rarely the Court of Appeal and the House of Lords, which filled the many spaces around the leading cases and gave shape and substance to today's public law jurisprudence.

The lion stirs

When I was called to the Bar in 1964, public law was not taught except as a footnote to constitutional law, and was not a recognised field of practice. Public law briefs went, if anywhere, to the town and country planning Bar, who at least had some knowledge of the workings of local authorities.[31] Challenges to central government or to statutory bodies were a novelty and a puzzle to most of the legal profession. Nevertheless,

---

[30] See Ch. 1.

[31] For a striking example, see the account of the genesis of *Bromley LBC* v. *GLC* [1983] AC 768 (H. B. Sales and A. W. Bradley, "The '*Fares Fair*' Case" [1995] PL 499).

the atmosphere at ground level was beginning to change. Three things, I think, were playing a part.

One was legal aid. The 1949 Legal Aid and Advice Act was a major element of the welfare state. In addition to paying for legal advice, it provided public funding for anybody who had a viable claim or defence but could not afford a lawyer. High street solicitors, the first stop for potential litigants, were surprisingly slow to recognise legal aid as a respectable source of income, but by the 1960s local firms were beginning to make use of it and the Bar was beginning to benefit from the briefs it generated. As a result, in my first few years at the common law Bar, publicly funded work for tenants paying excessive rents for substandard accommodation formed a significant part of my practice. Because only unfurnished tenants had Rent Act protection, how little furniture could deprive a tenancy of protection became a crucial question[32] in private law. But both the introduction of a statutory fair rent regime for unfurnished tenancies[33] and the innovative use of public health legislation to secure repairs to badly neglected private and council lettings[34] began to demonstrate how porous the frontier between public and private law was. Here too legal aid was able to help.

In 1968 the Society of Labour Lawyers published a slim book, *Justice for All*, which encouraged the setting up of law centres – non-profit legal practices funded by a combination of local funding and legal aid fees, and directed specifically to the needs of people who ordinarily had little or no access to law or lawyers. The law centres, of which the first was set up in North Kensington in 1970 and which within a decade had come close to fifty in number, were a second catalysing element in the revival of public law. Their work was backed up by voluntary bodies such as the Child Poverty Action Group, whose in-house lawyers operated at a high level of expertise.[35] Much of my work at the Bar in and after the 1970s came from law centres and specialist advice centres.

The years after 1968 saw a third phenomenon which contributed to the revival of public law: newly qualified lawyers who wanted to do socially useful work. The availability of local authority grants to enable students from less affluent backgrounds to enter universities or

---

[32] See *Woodward* v. *Docherty* [1974] 1 WLR 966.   [33] Rent Act 1965
[34] See *GLC* v. *LB Tower Hamlets* (1984) 15 HLR 54.
[35] See the entry in the *Oxford Dictionary of National Biography* on Henry (later Mr Justice) Hodge, the CPAG's first in-house solicitor. As the entry records, government eventually co-operated, to its own benefit, in selecting test cases to resolve complicated questions of benefit entitlement.

professional training played a part in this. So did the political atmosphere, which at times encouraged a dangerous sense that personal com-
mitment was a substitute for competence. The established profession was
quick to stigmatise what it dubbed the Alternative Bar, but the generation
which followed mine into the profession has changed the profession's
own sense of what is worthwhile. Today, pro bono advocacy is a well-
regarded stratum of practice at the Bar, and the major City solicitors'
firms today compete for prestigious pro bono work.

∗∗

With these springboards, the take-off of public law in the last quarter of
the twentieth century – a recurrent aspect of the themes traced in the
second part of this book – was owed at least as much to the unsung cases
which from the 1970s began to bring elements of justice to some of the
obscurer corners of public administration as to the great landmark cases
which all modern students know.

The problems of low-income tenants, for example, were as much due to
the neglect of their statutory duties by local authorities as they were to
rack-renting on the part of private landlords. But while tenants had by
definition a contractual relationship with their landlords, they had no
private law relationship with the local authorities which had a statutory
duty to monitor disrepair and structural danger, or with the rent tribunals
and rent officers whose duty was to set fair rents. How then did one go
about dealing with a council which left rented houses running with damp,
or a rent officer who had refused to adjourn a hearing which the tenant
was prevented by illness from attending? The answer to the first question
lay as often as not in little-known and little-used enforcement provisions of
the Public Health Acts, to which I will come. The answer to the second, if
there was one, had to lie in a public law obligation on the part of the rent
officer to act fairly. But how did you enforce such an obligation? It had to
be by the use of the prerogative writs or orders which my generation had at
best glimpsed on the constitutional law course.

So it was that, in a state not far from terror, I found myself rising to my
feet in the court of the Chief Justice, Lord Parker, who in those days took
the entire judicial review list – the Crown Office list – in the course of a
half-day pause in a week of criminal appeals,[36] to apply for an order of

---

[36] By the time Parker's successor, Lord Widgery, retired in 1980, the list had become badly
backlogged. Lord Justice Donaldson was given the task of clearing it, which he did before

certiorari to quash an entry made in the rent register in the tenant's absence, and an order of mandamus requiring a hearing which the tenant could attend. The three judges listened politely to my argument ("Tell us where the shoe pinches," Lord Parker would say when you were about two minutes into your case) before taking up their pens and turning to the Treasury Devil: "Yes, Mr Bridge?" I still recollect the elation of hearing Nigel Bridge concede the claim and realising that I had won a case.

Then there was the case of Charles Bullen. As a condition of drawing unemployment benefit Mr Bullen was required to be available for work. Since he was a poet by profession, not a lot of work was available. His prolonged unemployment triggered a statutory power to have him sent by a tribunal to what was in effect a labour camp, where the long-term unemployed were required to do menial and repetitive work for minimal remuneration. On the day of the tribunal hearing, however, Mr Bullen had secured a job interview with Woolworths. You might have found it hard to think of a better reason for an adjournment; but in Mr Bullen's absence the tribunal ordered him to a labour camp. The High Court quashed their decision, holding that the question was not the metaphysical *Wednesbury* question whether any tribunal in its right mind could have failed to adjourn, but simply whether what they had done was plainly unfair.[37]

More public law issues than you might have expected were fought out in the criminal courts. We successfully prosecuted several local authorities under the public health legislation as landlords of houses in a state so prejudicial to health as to constitute a statutory nuisance.[38] On other occasions prosecutions brought by local authorities or the police arose out of public law provisions. I spent a good deal of time in the mid- and late 1960s defending Kentish travellers who had been driven on to roadside verges through the methodical use by local authorities of their new power to fence and ditch the commons on which gypsies had

being appointed Master of the Rolls. Widgery's successor as chief justice, Lord Lane, stopped presiding in the Queen's Bench divisional court (i.e. a court of two or more judges), and the divisional court itself gave way, following the passing of the Supreme Court Act 1981 (now renamed the Senior Courts Act), to the specialist panel of single judges who now compose the Administrative Court.

[37] *R v. SW London Supplementary Benefits Appeal Tribunal, ex p Bullen* (1976) 120 Sol. Jo. 437

[38] *R v. Newham Justices, ex p Hunt; R v. Oxted Justices, ex p Franklin* [[1976] 1 All ER 839 (Held: a private citizen, in contrast to a local authority, could prosecute for statutory nuisance under s. 99, Public Health Act 1936, without first serving an abatement notice.) In the great majority of these cases I was instructed by local law centres and advised by a knowledgeable public health inspector, David Ormandy.

traditionally camped, without using the concomitant power to open proper caravan sites in lieu, even when the power was made a duty.[39]

Yet other prosecutions arose out of public law disputes. One was the prosecution helpfully brought by Hounslow council against the campaigner Erin Pizzey, alleging that her Chiswick Women's Refuge, the first in the country, was a house in multiple occupation for the purposes of the Housing Act 1961 with consequent restrictions on its occupancy. By the time she was prosecuted for breaking the limit of thirty-six occupants which the council had set, seventy-five desperate women and their children, for whom local authorities had done nothing, were living in the house. The defence that the house was in the collective occupation of a single fluctuating community, not of multiple households, was accepted by the local magistrates. The council's appeal reached the House of Lords,[40] where a not unsympathetic panel included two former Lord Chancellors, Dilhorne and Hailsham. Half way through my submissions Hailsham looked hard at Dilhorne and asked:

> If my noble and learned friend were to invite me to his country house for the weekend, would I cease to be the head of my own household and become a member of his?

At the lunch adjournment the court reporter came over to me and explained the bizarre intervention: Dilhorne had never invited Hailsham to his country house,[41] and Hailsham didn't mind who knew it.

***

One of the rewards of doing public law cases in the renaissance years was the occasional chance to push a new boat out. It had to be done tentatively and not to travel too far from shore, but if the facts were right

[39] Caravan Sites and Control of Development Act 1960, ss. 23 and 24; Caravan Sites Act 1968. For the history, see R v. *Lincolnshire County Council, ex p Atkinson* (QBD, 22 September 1995) [1997] JPL 65, cited by ECtHR in *Chapman* v. *United Kingdom (27238/95)*. The breaches of duty proved largely non-justiciable because the Act directed all complaints to the Department of the Environment, which consistently failed to deal with them.

[40] *Simmons* v. *Pizzey* [1979] AC 37: "Neither 36 nor 75 is a number which in the suburbs of London as they exist at the present time can ordinarily and reasonably be regarded as a single household" (per Lord Hailsham).

[41] Dilhorne a rather humourless man, was a descendant of Sir Edward Coke. Given the task of advising on who should succeed Harold Macmillan as prime minister in 1963, he had sidelined the extrovert Hailsham in favour of the lacklustre Sir Alec Douglas-Home (see *ODNB*, cap. Buller).

it could be done. When Brent Council in 1984 set about merging two of its schools after a perfunctory public consultation, parents considered that they had been ignored and that closure and merger had been a *fait accompli*. I spent a long Sunday in my chambers preparing the case (one of many reasons for not being a barrister) and persuaded Mr Justice Hodgson next day that Brent had failed to meet the legitimate expectation of the parents that they would be given grounds for the proposals in sufficient detail and in sufficient time to allow a considered response. That the set of criteria on which we succeeded have become part of the common law has been one of the real rewards of the job.[42]

So by 1988 the High Court was examining the business of government with rather more knowledge and acuity than before. When Derbyshire County Council decided to close one of its secondary schools, the Secretary of State's approval, which was required by law, was slow in coming. Finally, however, an official in the Department of Education phoned the county council to say that a letter approving the closure would shortly be in the post. She asked that this be kept confidential until the letter arrived, with the predictable consequence that within hours the local press knew about it and were on the phone to London to ask the local MP for a comment. The MP (who had children at the school and was a member of the party in government) stormed into the Department of Education and pointed out to the Secretary of State that closure of the school could cost him his seat. The letter giving permission was retrieved from the departmental out-tray, and when the replacement letter arrived it refused permission to close the school. Derbyshire contended that it was of no effect: permission to close the school had already been given by phone. The parents, for whom I was acting, contended that there was only one valid decision, and that was the letter of refusal.

Towards the end of the first day's argument in the divisional court, Lord Justice Watkins asked why the departmental file, which plainly formed a key part of the relevant history, was not in court.

---

[42] *R v. Brent LBC, ex p Gunning* (1985) 84 LGR 168, 189, approved *R (Moseley) v. LB Haringey* [2014] UKSC 56. At about this time I was grumbling that the innovative work of some of the first-instance judges was being "frustrated by the Court of Appeal, which distributes its work among judges not all of whom have much acquaintance with administrative law. It is becoming axiomatic that if you are going to win a public law case on civil rights you have got to win it at first instance" ("What Next?", in J. Cooper and R. Dhavan (eds.), *Public Interest Law* (1986), Ch. 18).

"Files of this kind concern the formation of policy at the highest level, my lord" said counsel for the Secretary of State. "They are never produced in court."

"On my desk by 10 tomorrow morning," said the judge,[43]

and the court rose. Next day, there was the departmental file on the school. Pinned to the front of it was a memo which read:

"Minister. The local authority and politicians of all colours are pressing for an early decision. If you are content to approve I will, of course, speak to [the local MP] on Monday. Approve?"

Alongside the last word was a handwritten tick, identified as his personal tick by the minister in an affidavit which went on to assure the court that it had been administered only after studying the entire file.

The outcome was a judgment which held the letter of refusal to be the single valid decision:

Here the LEA, and in due course the objectors, were entitled as a matter of good administration, of fairness and in fulfilment of a legitimate expect- ation to have from the Secretary of State that which would in law be regarded as an approval (or, as the case may be, a rejection or a modifica- tion) of the LEA's proposals, not a mistaken, unauthorised and confiden- tially expressed telephone message. That seems to us to be good common sense too.[44]

As I have said, public law is about good administration as well as bad.

✳✳✳

I mention these cases because, although many of them were obscurely reported, if reported at all, and are barely referred to in the textbooks, they reflect the substantive change in legal culture and reasoning which, with a following wind from the high-profile cases, began to shake public law out of the long sleep which forms part of the history traced in this book. They were, to be sure, islands of success in a sea of frustration; but the mood of the common law was changing from quiescence to vigilance. Principles which in earlier cases had been forgotten or abstractly pro- claimed were now being applied in response to the merits of real cases, and new principles were being developed.

---

[43] Tasker Watkins, who had won a VC in the war, usually got his way.

[44] *R v. Secretary of State for Education and Science, ex p Hardy* (CO/354/88; 27 July 1988) DC (Watkins LJ and McNeill J)

Daylight in prisons

The slow but accelerating movement of legal history was nowhere clearer than in relation to the prison system, on which up to the 1970s public law had made no impact at all. The senior judges had sent out a message that prisoners, by definition undeserving, must put up with whatever conditions were their lot. They could not come complaining to the courts.

> "If the courts were to entertain actions by disgruntled prisoners," said Lord Denning, "the governor's life would be made intolerable."[45]

But by 1979 the Hull prison riots had driven the courts, confronted with some serious denials of due process, to hold that the boards of prison visitors, when adjudicating on disciplinary charges, were obliged to proceed fairly.[46] This, however, left intact the inner bastion of prison discipline, governors' adjudications. The Court of Appeal, likening them to decisions of a military commander in the field or of a ship's master at sea, went on holding them immune to legal challenge, however unfairly they were conducted.[47]

The Joshua whose trumpet brought this wall down was a prisoner named Mark Leech, then both a professional con artist and an expert barrack-room lawyer, subsequently a reformed character running a charity for ex-prisoners. It was on Leech, as luck would have it, that a deputy governor chose to practise a textbook denial of natural justice. Having heard a prison officer read out the details of a disciplinary charge, the governor announced that he found the case proved.

> "Excuse me," said Leech, "You haven't heard my defence."
> "I'm not interested in your defence," said the deputy governor.

With this on the record (in those days a prison officer used to make a written note of disciplinary proceedings), the only possible answer was non-justiciability. But one of the strengths of public law litigation is

---

[45] *Becker* v. *Home Office* [1972] 2 QB 407. My own first encounter with Lord Denning was when I tried, in the same year, to compel the board of visitors to hear counsel on behalf of Frankie Fraser, the Kray brothers' enforcer, who was facing a charge of mutiny: *Fraser* v. *Mudge* [1972] 1 WLR 1132; see S. Sedley, *Ashes and Sparks* (2011), Ch. 20.

[46] *R* v. *Board of Visitors, Hull Prison, ex p St Germain (No 1)* [1979] QB 425; *(No. 2)* [1979] 3 All ER 545

[47] *R* v. *Deputy Governor Camphill Prison, ex p King* [1985] QB 735

that government does not fight to win at all costs: it will sometimes recognise that to win a particular point in a particular case may distort the law, and Treasury counsel will modify their arguments accordingly. So it was that in Leech's case counsel for the Home Office, John Laws, made it clear that they did not wish to protect the governor's position by rolling back the Hull prison decision on the justiciability of board of visitors' decisions. Governors' adjudications had to be, if anything, an exception to what was now the rule.

The main problem for the Home Office's argument that prison discipline would collapse if prisoners could challenge governors' adjudications was that the events which gave rise to the pair of cases which eventually came before the House of Lords were comically out of kilter with the solemnity of the argument. Leech had been charged with having a biro adapted for smoking cannabis concealed in the ceiling of his cell. His co-appellant, Prevot, had a glamorous French wife who had arrived for a visit wearing a fur coat, under cover of which he was alleged to have enjoyed some marital comfort in breach of the Prison Rules. The governor had refused to let him call his wife, or any of the sixteen other prisoners in the visiting room at the time, to support his indignant denial that any such thing had occurred. The sight of Nigel Bridge, now the presiding law lord, trying to keep a straight face as I opened the facts was an object lesson in the relevance of merits. The law lords unanimously allowed the two appeals.[48]

The daylight that Leech's case and a series of other cases let into the prison and parole systems,[49] intensified (not initiated) when the Human Rights Act came on stream in October 2000,[50] formed an important element in the reawakening and renewal of English public law. It did not acquire a high public profile, but it formed part of the groundswell of jurisprudence which was able, as the culture of judicial abstentionism receded, to turn principle into practice.[51]

I have argued in the past, and still believe, that the test of a civilised system of law is not how it treats the respectable and the virtuous but whether it can apply an equal standard of justice to the marginal,

---

[48] *Leech* v. *Deputy Governor, HMP Parkhurst*; *Prevot* v. *Deputy Governor, HMP Long Lartin* [1988] AC 533.

[49] See generally T. Owen and A. Macdonald, *Prison Law* (4th edn, 2008).

[50] See *Daly* v. *Home Secretary* [2001] 2 AC 532. [51] See further Ch. 10 and Ch. 12.

the unrespectable and the undeserving. Public law in England and Wales, at its best, has in my lifetime shown itself able to do this.

MAKING HISTORY

At least one other occasion sticks in the memory. One morning in 1967 I was waiting for a case in which I was briefed to be called on in the Divisional Court while judgment was delivered on a claim that had been heard a few weeks earlier about the amenability of the criminal injuries compensation scheme to judicial review. The scheme had no statutory foundation: it consisted simply of a White Paper setting out the circumstances in which compensation would be paid *ex gratia* to victims of violent crime. Mrs Lain, a policeman's widow, was contending that she came within the scheme; the government was contending that whether she did or not, the court had no power to construe or enforce the scheme – it was a pure exercise of the royal prerogative and not justiciable.

> "The Board," submitted Treasury counsel, "is subject to control by the Crown, by whom it has been constituted, and not by this court."

It was when Lord Justice Diplock, in his customary monotone,[52] began delivering the second judgment, rejecting the Crown's claim that it stood above or outside the law, that it dawned on me that I was listening to legal history in the making.

It was not for another seventeen years that *Ex parte Lain*[53] received Lord Scarman's accolade[54] as a case as important in its day as the *Case of Proclamations*[55] had been three and a half centuries before. In turn, a few years later, I was able to build on it in preparing and arguing

---

[52] Diplock, when in the Court of Appeal, used to read his judgments almost inaudibly from a manuscript which he would then pass to the shorthand writer. His manuscripts, the shorthand writer told me many years later, were as illegible as his delivery was inaudible. It was only when he came to correct her typed drafts that Diplock's sharp and lucid prose emerged. Once in the House of Lords, all his judgments were delivered in print.

[53] *R v. Criminal Injuries Compensation Board, ex p Lain* [1967] 2 QB 864. See further p. 140 below.

[54] *Council of Civil Service Unions v. Minister for the Civil Service* [1985] AC 374, 407

[55] (1611) 12 Co.Rep. 74

M v. *Home Office;*[56] and again, some years after that, in deciding *Pankina* v. *Home Secretary.*[57]

These are the roads and bridges which make history practical and practice meaningful.

---

[56] [1992] QB 270 (CA). See further Ch. 3, and Sedley, *Ashes and Sparks*, Ch. 28, "The Crown in its Own Courts".

[57] [2010] EWCA Civ 719 (CA) (upheld on alternative grounds by the Supreme Court [2012] UKSC 33)

PART I

Histories

1

Lions in winter: public law in the twentieth century

Why did public law, at the height of its powers as it entered the twentieth century, go into prolonged hibernation? What brought it back to life?

The Wednesbury Gaumont

Once upon a time – in 1947 to be exact – in a small town in the west Midlands which has now vanished into the Birmingham conurbation, a sabbatarian group secured a majority of seats on the local council. One of their aims was to halt the growing disregard of Sunday as a day of rest and prayer and the use of the sabbath for secular entertainment. So, when the chain which owned the local Gaumont cinema applied to the council for permission to open on Sundays, the councillors granted the application (probably because they had been advised that they could not adopt a blanket policy of refusal), but made it a condition that the permission was not to include the admission of children under fifteen. For the sabbatarians this was a very satisfactory condition because it meant, in the days before universal television, that parents would not be able to go to the cinema on Sundays either, unless they were prepared to leave their children unsupervised in the house. Effectively the councillors had succeeded in keeping the Gaumont closed on Sundays.[1]

The Sunday observance laws had for centuries forbidden Sunday entertainments. But by the 1930s cinema had become a mass entertainment medium. To enable picture houses to open on a Sunday, the one day when most working people were able to go, Parliament in 1932 passed the Sunday Entertainments Act, allowing local authorities to lift the ban on Sunday entertainments on such conditions as each authority thought fit to impose. This was the power which the Wednesbury councillors were using

---

[1] For a fuller account of the background to the case, see Michael Taggart, "Reinventing Administrative Law", in N. Bamforth and P. Leyland (eds.), *Public Law in a Multi-Layered Constitution* (2003), pp. 313ff.

when they purported to allow the cinema in Walsall Street to open on Sundays provided no children were admitted. It was not surprising that Associated Provincial Picture Houses, who had spent a fortune upgrading the Walsall Street cinema to a state-of-the-art Gaumont picture palace, took exception to this and went off to the High Court to challenge it. The argument was straightforward enough: if, as was uncontested, it was appropriate to let the Gaumont open on Sundays, it was a misuse of the statutory power to annex a condition which meant that the permission granted with one hand was being taken away with the other.

The long sleep

Everyone knows what Lord Greene MR said about the law; but not everyone remembers the outcome: the cinema proprietors lost in the High Court and lost again in the Court of Appeal.[2] Not for the first or last time, the court set out a shining set of principles on which it would unhesitatingly correct public law errors, and then declined to apply them to the facts before it.

In its time and place, this was unsurprising. For reasons which I hope to explore in this chapter, judicial review of governmental action, which had been developed and refined by the Victorian judges,[3] had fallen into a long, if fitful, sleep from which it awoke only in the later twentieth century.[4] In the course of it, a succession of challenges to the way in which the liberalising power created by the Sunday Entertainments Act was being deployed or manipulated by local authorities had come before the courts, and effectively all of them had failed. So atrophied had public law become that the *Wednesbury* case itself was brought not by application for a prerogative writ but by a civil action for a declaration that the resolution was *ultra vires* and unreasonable. The judicial response, well exemplified by the decision, was that both central and local government were to be left to get on with their job without an over-nice regard to the legality of what they were doing, so long as they did not behave like the Poplar councillors and frighten the horses.[5]

---

[2] *Associated Provincial Picture Houses Ltd* v. *Wednesbury Corporation* [1948] 1 KB 223
[3] See Ch. 2.
[4] For a survey of the interaction of law and politics in these years, see J. A. G. Griffith, *Judicial politics since 1920: A Chronicle* (1993).
[5] In 1921 Poplar borough council, which had resolved to pay all its workers a living wage and to pay women the same as men, refused to collect rates which fell disproportionately heavily on the poor. Thirty councillors, after marching with banners and a brass band to

The borough of Wednesbury in the fullness of time became part of the borough of Sandwell; the cinema chain was sold and the Gaumont in Walsall Street became a bingo hall. The Court of Appeal's decision too has merged into history: it is unlikely that any modern court of judicial review would allow such a resolution to stand. It might be held to be vitiated by the council's attempt to enforce a view of how young persons should spend their Sundays which lay beyond its remit and was outside the policy and objects of the legislation, or because of the annexure of a condition which made the permission itself all but worthless. Whether these features needed to be classed as irrelevant considerations in order to get into Lord Greene's taxonomy of unreasonableness[6] would not detain the court. Today it is widely accepted that the defining question in modern public law is not whether what has happened fits into a predetermined slot of technical error, taking it outside the body's formal authority (though this can happen), but whether it represents an abuse of power.[7] The main reason why the *Wednesbury* judgment continues to be cited in court is the state's perennial desire to get the genie back into the bottle and to confine challenges to Lord Greene's tick-boxes.[8] But when

---

the High Court, were gaoled for contempt of court. They were released after six weeks of widespread protest. See N. Branson, *Poplarism 1919–1925: George Lansbury and the Councillors' Revolt* (1979), and n. 35 below.

[6] "It is true that discretion must be exercised reasonably. Now what does that mean? ... [A] person entrusted with a discretion must, so to speak, direct himself properly in law. He must call his own attention to the matters which he is bound to consider. He must exclude from his consideration matters which are irrelevant to what he has to consider. ... Similarly, there may be something so absurd that no sensible person could ever dream that it lay within the powers of the authority." Lord Greene then used the *reductio ad absurdum* (picking on people with red hair) used by Warrington LJ in *Short* v. *Poole Corporation*, a case which prefigured the supine jurisprudence of *Wednesbury*: see sub-head "Judicial acquiescence" and n. 33 below.

[7] See the sources cited in M. Fordham, *Judicial Review Handbook* (6th edn, 2012), §45.2.3, 45.3.3; cf. 45.2.1. See also Ch. 7.

[8] In 1993 Professor J. A. G. Griffith wrote to me: "In late 1951 Harry Street and I published the first edition of *The Principles of Administrative Law*. In the section on judicial review we paid particular attention to the *Wednesbury* decision. No one else did. Later it became fashionable, as we know. In early 1982 I surveyed the decisions in the Law Reports." In the ten years following the Court of Appeal's decision he found precisely two references to the case. By 1977 references were averaging five a year; by 1981, twelve. Since then, of course, citations of *Wednesbury* have become countless – a simple function, Griffith went on to surmise, of the growth of judicial review itself. Where I part company with him is his closing remark that the decision "has been used by the courts to expand judicial review ... Lord Greene would be most surprised by some of the uses to which his words have been put". On the contrary, much of the development of modern public law has been a struggle to escape from Lord Greene's straitjacket.

Lord Diplock in the *National Federation of the Self-Employed* case[9] warned that no case decided before 1950 should now be regarded as authoritative, he was not picking an arbitrary date: he was seeking to bring down the shutters on *Wednesbury*.

What had happened?

The initial change of gear in public law is conventionally traced to a case argued in 1914, *Local Government Board* v. *Arlidge*.[10] *Arlidge's Case* concerned an issue not far removed from the one which had goaded the Court of Common Pleas into action in *Cooper* v. *Wandsworth Board of Works*:[11] official interference with private property for social ends. Local authorities now had power to make closing orders on houses which were unfit for human habitation, but there had first to be a public local inquiry. Mr Arlidge had submitted to the board of inquiry an expert's report denying that the house of which he was landlord was unfit for human habitation, but he had chosen not to exercise his right to be heard by the inquiry inspector and had not thereafter been allowed to see the inspector's report to the Board, nor therefore been able to make further submissions on it. He had then done some repairs and asked the local council to rescind the closing order. The council had refused because it considered that the repairs were inadequate, with the result that the Board were compelled to hold a second public inquiry into the refusal. This time Mr Arlidge turned up with a battery of lawyers and experts to argue his case. The inspector evidently agreed with the council because the Board, having asked Mr Arlidge if there was anything else he wanted to submit, again found against him. His case therefore turned on the Board's refusal on both occasions to let him see and contest an inspector's report which had been composed after a hearing at which Mr Arlidge had had a full opportunity to put his case.

A High Court judge found nothing wrong with this procedure. The Court of Appeal, by a majority, took an opposite view. On the Board's further – and successful – appeal, the judicial committee of the House of Lords, all five of whom had been Liberal politicians, now with Lord Haldane in the chair, did not decide the case on the simple ground that Mr Arlidge (unlike Mr Cooper in the *Wandsworth* case) had been free to

---

[9] [1982] AC 617, 639–40: see "The princess wakes" below, p. 39.
[10] [1915] AC 120. The historical context of the case is discussed in Ch. 8
[11] (1863) 14 CB (NS) 180: see Ch. 2.

make his case, had he chosen to do so, at the public inquiry.[12] Instead, Haldane looked to the development over the previous hundred years of legislative inroads into private rights:

> Parliament, in what it considers higher interests than those of the individual, has so often interfered with such rights on other occasions that it is dangerous for judges to lay much stress on what a hundred years ago would have been a presumption considerably stronger than it is today.

He might as easily have said "five years ago" as "a hundred years ago"; but it was the long-term change in the legislative atmosphere, driven by the need for effective slum clearance powers which he went on to describe, that carried him and the other law lords to the view that the policy of the 1909 Housing and Town Planning Act was not to accord property owners more procedural rights than had been accorded to Mr Arlidge. Lord Loreburn's principle[13] – that the duty to hear both sides was a duty that rested on everyone who decides anything – was not in issue: the issue was how it applied to the working of the 1909 Act.

It is worth looking at the detail of *Arlidge's Case* because merits can influence lawmaking. Mr Arlidge's self-righteous preparedness to litigate with money that he was not prepared to spend on making his property habitable will not have endeared him to the courts, particularly when on both statutory appeals he had had the opportunity of a full hearing before the inspector. Given this not very stirring background, it would be hard to see much of a jurisprudential change in the law lords' decision.[14] But, in the oblique way in which law develops, it may have set the tone for the years of judicial quiescence which were to follow.

The law reports for the period of the war record little in relation to individual rights beyond decisions that internment without charge or trial of naturalised enemy aliens was within the statutory power to make wartime regulations for the defence of the realm,[15] and that the Crown in

---

[12] He had submitted to the Board some expert reports which concluded that the house was habitable, but he had not attended the inquiry.

[13] *Board of Education* v. *Rice* [1911] AC 179; see Ch. 8.

[14] Compare Wade's excoriation of *Arlidge* as "a turning point, in which the law failed to keep abreast of the standard of fairness required" (W. Wade and C. Forsyth, *Administrative Law* (10th edn, 2009) p. 409) with Robson's view that in *Arlidge* "issues of far-reaching constitutional importance" had been interpreted in a "generous and broad-minded spirit" by the House of Lords (*Justice and Administrative Law* (2nd edn, 1947), p. 385).

[15] *Zadig* v. *Halliday* [1917] AC 260; but see the dissent of Lord Shaw of Dunfermline, prefiguring that of Lord Atkin in *Liversidge* v. *Anderson* [1942] AC 206.

wartime had prerogative as well as statutory powers to appropriate land without paying compensation.[16] But both the Divisional Court and the Court of Appeal rejected a xenophobic application to declare two naturalised German-born citizens ineligible for office as privy counsellors, and in so doing enlarged the rules of standing.[17] And the law lords, sitting as the judicial committee of the Privy Council in 1916,[18] rejected the Crown's claim to a prerogative power to declare a captured vessel to be prize regardless of whether it was prize in law.

> "The idea that the King in Council, or indeed any branch of the executive, has power to prescribe or alter the law to be administered by courts of law in this country," said Lord Parker of Waddington,[19] "is out of harmony with the principles of our constitution."

A Victorian judge would have said that this was business as usual. A modern judge would say the same.

The change

What then changed the atmosphere in the years between the wars? It is understandable that the courts in wartime would have considered it unpatriotic to obstruct the business of government; but no decision in the years of the Great War approaches the judicial abdication of World War II. What had happened in between was less visible but more durable. Beneath it lay two fundamental shifts. One was the slow enlargement of the regulatory Victorian state into the modern welfare state. The other was the consolidation of a now professionalised civil service into a *corps d'élite* more competent and experienced than its transient ministers and in many respects more powerful than Parliament. These changes presented the judiciary with a choice: to go on asserting and exercising their control of executive government in a new and unfamiliar context, or to step back and let a professional administration run the country, keeping judicial review for marginal cases. Their choice of the second of these courses was neither conspiratorial nor possibly even conscious, but in retrospect it is readily discernible.

---

[16] *Re a Petition of Right* [1915] 3 KB 649
[17] *R v. Speyer and Cassel, ex p Makgill* [1916] 1 KB 595 (DC); upheld on appeal [1916] 2 KB 858: see Ch. 12.
[18] *The Zamora* [1916] 2 AC 77   [19] at 90

The welfare state

In 1906 a Liberal government had been elected with a massive majority. By the time it was re-elected in 1910 it had initiated legislation for a system of old-age pensions and national insurance against unemployment and illness, financed out of taxation of the better-off. The refusal of the hereditary peers who composed the House of Lords – five hundred men, said Lloyd George, chosen randomly from among the ranks of the unemployed, and six out of seven of them Tories – to pass the necessary finance bill gave the Liberals their chance at parliamentary reform. With a fresh electoral mandate enabling them to pack the upper house if necessary with newly created Liberal peers, and amid scenes of parliamentary hysteria,[20] they forced through the first Parliament Act, forbidding the Lords to reject any bills passed by the Commons or to delay money bills.[21]

Part of the significance of the 1911 Parliament Act lay in its affirmation of one dominant sovereignty – that of the Commons – within the constitutional sovereignty of Parliament as an entity. The traditional relationship of the Commons, the third estate of the realm, to the second estate, the peerage, along with the first estate, the clergy, had become inverted: the slow march of democracy had finally made the Commons the first estate of the realm. This in turn eased the passage of legislation which transferred decisive powers to ministers and through them to the civil service.

Judicial protest

The effect of this process on the judiciary was oddly ambivalent. On the one hand there was protest. In 1929 the Lord Chief Justice, Lord Hewart, took the extraordinary step – extraordinary even by modern standards of judicial openness – of publishing a book called *The New Despotism*[22]

---

[20] See J. Field, *The Story of Parliament* (2012), pp. 232–3. There was a precedent: in 1832 the Lords had dropped their opposition to the Reform Bill when William IV agreed to Grey's request to create enough peers to force the bill through the Upper House.

[21] The Parliament Act 1911 bore a preamble: "It is intended to substitute for the House of Lords as it at present exists a second Chamber constituted on a popular instead of a hereditary basis." A century later, this had still not happened.

[22] Ernest Benn (1929). Many readers must find Hewart's prose leaden and pompous, but Tom Bingham in *The Rule of Law* (2010), p. 48, generously calls it "a powerful and very readable polemic". Hewart's argument was supported by Sir Carleton Kemp Allen in *Bureaucracy Triumphant* (1931).

in which he fulminated against what he argued, with some justification, was a new and dangerous mode of governance: the creation by Parliament of powers which gave ministers and their departments legislative functions beyond the control of either MPs or the courts.

Hewart, who had begun life as a journalist and leader-writer, had entered Parliament as a Liberal politician in 1913 and by 1919 was Attorney-General. In 1922 the post of Lord Chief Justice became vacant,[23] enabling him to claim the office by conventional right. Were it not for his celebrated, if circumlocutory, dictum that "justice must not only be done but manifestly and undoubtedly be seen to be done",[24] Hewart's long tenure as chief justice might have passed almost unnoticed. But his book created an understandable stir, arguing as it did that Parliament was now in the habit of repeatedly surrendering elements of its sovereignty to an unaccountable bureaucracy.[25] Some of his examples, from the late nineteenth century, were no more than instances of subordinate rule-making powers. But Hewart was also able to point to the use from 1918 onwards of what have become known as Henry VIII clauses, giving ministers authority to legislate. He instanced, among others, an act of 1925[26] which empowered the minister to deal with "any difficulty" in the functioning of the act by doing anything he considered "necessary or expedient", including amending the act itself. In reality, Henry VIII's short-lived Statute of Proclamations 1539[27] had done no more than assert the monarch's power to issue proclamations with the force of law "for the good order and governance" of the state.[28] What Hewart

---

[23] The vacancy was engineered for Hewart's benefit. Lloyd George in 1921 had appointed A. T. Lawrence to the post (as Lord Trevethin) in return for an undated letter of resignation. The first Trevethin knew of his own resignation was when he read about it in the *Times*.

[24] *R v. Sussex Justices, ex p McCarthy* [1924] 1 KB 256

[25] Hewart's book is strikingly silent about his own role in this process, first as a parliamentarian and then as a law officer.

[26] Rating and Valuation Act, 1925, s. 67(1). The senior civil servant who briefed the parliamentary draftsman on the formulation of this measure probably treated himself to a small celebratory sherry at the Athenaeum (see below). Hewart also justifiably instanced the Trade Boards Act 1918, the Animals (Anaesthetics) Act 1919, the Gas Regulation Act 1920 and the London Traffic Act 1924.

[27] 31 Hen. VIII ch. 8; repealed 1 Edw. VI c.12; see Ch. 9. Although Tudor monarchs went on ruling by proclamation after its repeal, Coke's ruling in the *Case of Proclamations* (1611) determined that the practice was unlawful.

[28] A prerogative power still possessed by the Crown in relation to colonial dependencies: see *R v. Foreign Secretary, ex p Bancoult (No 2)* [2007] EWCA Civ 498; [2008] UKHL 61.

had identified in the modern state was something more radical: a rolling transfer of sovereignty from MPs, and hence the legislature, to ministers, and thus the executive.[29]

Judicial acquiescence

The other, seemingly contradictory, phenomenon was the absence of any serious judicial resistance to this process. The remedy prescribed by Hewart for the new despotism was simply better parliamentary scrutiny. True, a Diceyan loyalty to Parliament's prescriptions was a serious inhibition; but public law in the nineteenth century[30] had displayed the resilience and inventiveness of the common law when challenges were posed by legislation to some of its values. Neither during nor after Hewart's tenure as Lord Chief Justice from 1922 to 1940 is there evidence of a serious judicial endeavour to resist the undermining of constitutional values.

This is not the same thing as saying that there was little or no judicial review of governmental action in the same period. Instances of tribunals and officials acting outside their powers, or of judicial or quasi-judicial bodies failing to behave fairly, continued to come before the courts, and a respectable proportion of them were decided against the state.[31] But these were for the most part orthodox judicial responses to orthodox public law issues[32] (though they appeared to commentators such as Professor Griffith[33] to be suspiciously weighted in favour of property-owners). The question is why for half a century the common law failed to use its intrinsic inventiveness and its treasury of precedent to halt or slow the advance of bureaucratic power without accountability. One has also to ask why, even in cases not involving the central state, the common law seemed to be going backwards – for example in *Short* v. *Poole*

---

[29] For a startling recent instance of its continued use, see Ch. 11, n. 70.   [30] See Ch. 2.

[31] See Susan Sterett, *Creating Constitutionalism?* (1997). I have found no figures for the 1920s and 1930s, but Sterett (pp. 52–3) records that from 1946 to 1967 public law challenges to the exercise of statutory powers other than taxation were successful in between 15 and 44 per cent of cases; this in a caseload rarely totalling more than 100 a year. There is no reason to think the pre-war years were very different.

[32] E.g. *Errington* v. *Minister of Health* [1935] 1 KB 249, quashing a slum clearance order for want of due process in the prior inquiry; *R* v. *Minister of Health, ex p Yaffe* [1931] AC 494, holding that a provision deeming delegated legislation to be part of the statute did not immunise it against a *vires* challenge (cf. *Institute of Patent Agents* v. *Lockwood* [1894] AC 347). See Wade and Forsyth, *Administrative Law*, pp. 409–12.

[33] J. A. G. Griffith, *Judicial Politics since 1920* (1993), p. 33

Corporation,[34] where Romer J in the High Court had struck down a local authority resolution that women teachers who married should be automatically dismissed, because the resolution had nothing to do with the efficient provision of education but was a piece of social engineering which lay beyond the council's powers – the exact ground on which a year earlier in *Roberts* v. *Hopwood*[35] the law lords had excoriated the Poplar councillors for resolving to pay both female and male employees a living wage. The Court of Appeal, taking a literal *ultra vires* approach and ignoring the Poplar decision, overturned him.

Political instability

Part of the reason may lie in a judicial reluctance to become embroiled in an increasing range of complex statutory procedures.[36] The decision in *Arlidge* lends some weight to this explanation, but by itself it cannot account for fifty years of abstentionism.

A second part of the reason may lie in the rapid turnover of governments and ministers. Lloyd George's National government which had overseen the eventual victory over Germany, leaving the country economically on its knees, was succeeded by two Conservative administrations before, in 1924, the first Labour government took office, only to be brought down within a year with the help of a fabricated political scandal.[37] The Conservative government which followed it had to cope with Britain's first and only general strike. When the great depression struck in 1929, the Labour government which was returned to office mutated within two years into a series of miniority governments and coalitions which, under successive prime ministers, the last of them Winston Churchill, saw the country into and through World War II. In 1945, emerging once again victorious and exhausted, the British people elected a Labour government with a radical programme of social and economic reform which it set about carrying into effect with the aid of a civil service by now habituated to

---

[34] [1926] Ch. 66

[35] [1925] AC 578. The decision, overturning a strong court of appeal, included "one of the most outspoken political judgments ever to come from their Lordships", that of Lord Atkinson (Griffith, *Judicial Politics since 1920*). See also fn. 5 above.

[36] See Ch. 13.

[37] The "Zinoviev letter", a forgery containing supposed instructions from Soviet Russia, was passed by the Foreign Office to the *Daily Mail* with the aim and the effect of undermining the Labour vote in the upcoming election.

the exercise of uncontested authority. It is here that the third part of the reason may lie.

The judicial lion

The long sleep of public law from the First World War to the 1970s is all the more striking because of the confidence with which the judiciary had stridden into the twentieth century. For two full centuries the Act of Settlement had placed the judges beyond the reach of ministerial reprisal. Since 1835 the senior judges had been on salaries of £5,000 a year,[38] an income which not only put them, as it was intended to, beyond corruption but which made them wealthy men; even wealthier, in real terms, during the deflationary years of the 1870s and 1880s; so wealthy that it was not until 1953 that the salary had finally to be increased.

From their Olympian position the Edwardian judges, as confident in their juridical supremacy as Britain was in its imperial supremacy, felt able to direct withering fire upon government:

> "If ministerial responsibility were more than the mere shadow of a name," thundered Lord Justice Farwell in 1910, denouncing an objectionable taxation procedure, "the matter would be less important, but as it is the courts are the only defence of the liberty of the subject against departmental aggression."[39]

Why then did the next generation of judges, despite Hewart's angry protests, let public law go to sleep? Why did they not pull down the fences between quasi-judicial and administrative functions and require all of them to be carried out fairly?[40] Why did they defer repeatedly to ministerial and departmental decisions with minimal regard to their legality? Why did they tolerate the continued growth within the state of power without accountability?

---

[38] As long ago as 1714 the salary had been set at £1,500; by 1800 it was £3,000 net of taxes; in 1810 it was raised to £4,000, and in 1825 to £5,500 before being reduced to a steady £5,000 in 1835.

[39] *Dyson v. Attorney-General* [1911] 1 KB 410, 424

[40] Atkin LJ's judgment in *R v. Electricity Commissioners* [1924] 1 KB 171, seemingly limiting intervention to judicial (and hence quasi-judicial) functions, was not cleared up until *Ridge v. Baldwin* in 1964: see the account in Wade and Forsyth, *Administrative Law*, pp. 514–17.

The executive

It was not only the judges who now stood tall. By 1914 the chief inspectors of the regulatory bodies and the permanent under-secretaries in departments of state were on salaries of £1,000 a year or more, putting them on a par with successful professionals in other walks of life. More importantly still, the career entrants who took the highest places in the new civil service examinations were now some of the brightest classics graduates from Oxford and Cambridge. They came frequently from prosperous and well-connected families, and while they never forgot that they were the Crown's servants, these first incarnations of Sir Humphrey Appleby[41] could hold their own with ministers and MPs, many of whom were now their social equals, others their social inferiors. In as class-conscious a society as Britain's, moreover, the prospect of an eventual place in the civil honours list played its part in the recruitment and retention of top-flight public administrators.

So the courts, by abstaining, were not leaving a void. While at Westminster politicians came and went, in Whitehall a capable and experienced career civil service, its leaders now drawn from the same public schools and universities as the judges, was in charge. The executive to which the judges were ceding command of the state possessed a confidence in its own ability to govern which the judges will for the most part have endorsed.

The Northcote-Trevelyan élite

Who constituted this new élite?

The social historian Beatrice Webb was a member of the committee chaired by Lord Haldane[42] on the machinery of government. Reporting in 1918, the committee advised a streamlining of the departments and services which had grown up organically and piecemeal over the previous hundred years. Haldane, who had been at the centre of government for

---

[41] The suave and ruthless permanent secretary in the 1980-4 BBC television series *Yes, Minister!* and *Yes, Prime Minister!*

[42] Richard Burdon Haldane, 1856-1928, scholar, statesman, lawyer and philosopher. A prominent QC, he sat as MP for East Lothian from 1885 to 1911. He was an outstanding Secretary of State for War from 1905 until hounded from office in 1912 by the right-wing press for alleged pro-German sympathies (he had read Hegel in the original). He was Lord Chancellor 1912-15 as a Liberal, but in 1924 became the first Labour Lord Chancellor.

many years, based his model of efficient government on two institutions: the cabinet and the civil service, with ministers serving as the conduit between the two. The report did lip-service to the constitutional role of Parliament, but Beatrice Webb noted in her diary that, although she tried to keep the issue of democratic control on the committee's agenda, Haldane, Murray and Schuster were "forever insisting that the working of Parliament makes sensible, leave alone scientific, administration impracticable"[43] – in other words, that democracy got in the way of government.

Who then were Murray and Schuster? They were two of the new breed of permanent secretary: academic high-flyers, recruited by competitive examination and earmarked for promotion and eventual honours. Sir George Murray, educated at Harrow and Christ Church, Oxford, had begun his career at twenty-four in the Foreign Office, moved to the Treasury and became successively chairman of the Board of Inland Revenue, secretary of the Post Office (a grander position than it now sounds), and in 1903 permanent secretary to the Treasury. Sir Claud (later Lord) Schuster was educated at Winchester and New College, Oxford, and rose as a career civil servant to the position of permanent secretary to the Lord Chancellor, a post he held from 1915 to 1944. In that period he served ten different Lord Chancellors under as many different governments.

For all practical and political purposes, dealing with the Lord Chan-cellor meant dealing with Schuster. When in 1933 some of the judges, pointing out that they were not civil servants, protested to the Lord Chancellor at the proposal to include them in statutory public service pay cuts, Schuster sent instructions to the parliamentary draftsman:

> Begin with a recital, which should be as long and pompous as possible, asserting the independence and all the rest of it ... Then declare that notwithstanding all this they are affected by the cut.[44]

Of the many other self-confident high-flyers who in the inter-war years populated and ran the civil service, one can take Sir John Anderson, who eventually became Viscount Waverley. Anderson graduated in science from Edinburgh University and in 1905, at twenty-three, came top in the civil service exams. From the Colonial Office he moved between

---

[43] Quoted in P. Hennessy, *Whitehall* (1989), p. 295.
[44] Quoted in R. Stevens, *The Independence of the Judiciary* (1997), p. 61.

departments, including a spell during the Troubles in Dublin,[45] becoming in 1922 permanent secretary at the Home Office (which for the next ten years he ran, according to Peter Hennessy "almost as a personal fiefdom"[46]), and then, in 1932, governor of Bengal.[47] From here he moved into politics, entering Parliament in 1938 as an Independent. Within a year he was Home Secretary (where he acquired immortality as the defendant to Mr Liversidge's lawsuit) and then Chancellor of the Exchequer. By the end of the war Anderson's standing was such that he was nominated by Churchill to run the country should Churchill and his Foreign Secretary, Anthony Eden, both perish.[48]

Although nothing was done formally by Parliament to implement Haldane's scheme of government, the civil service set about reorganising itself along the lines he had proposed. The Treasury's dominant relationship to other departments was systematised, departments appointed establishment officers to supervise their personnel, and policy research councils were initiated.[49] There is general agreement among political scientists and historians that the civil service in the inter-war and post-war years reached a pinnacle of power which it had never previously attained and, for well-attested reasons,[50] has since lost. Executive government consequently entered the 1950s with a sense that, provided it remembered to doff its cap to the rule of law and the supremacy of Parliament, it could do pretty much what it wanted. What it wanted to do was driven by departmental policies in which ministers might have the first say but not always (thanks to Sir Humphrey Appleby) the last.

The Athenaeum

Thus the men (and the handful of women) brought into the upper tiers of the civil service by the Northcote-Trevelyan reforms[51] were drawn by

---

[45] Where he was a ruthless administrator, known as Black-and-Tan Anderson.

[46] Hennessy, *Whitehall*, p. 561

[47] Where he displayed an alarming penchant towards European fascism: see M. Carritt, *A Mole in the Crown* (1985), pp. 154–5. Carritt found him "uncouth and dour", a picture confirmed by Hennessy, *Whitehall*.

[48] Hennessy, *Whitehall*, pp. 559–60. Anderson, when permanent secretary to the Ministry of Shipping, had told the Haldane Committee that sniping at civil servants in Parliament and the press devalued the constructive civil servant who "kept his minister out of trouble and had a smart answer to an awkward question" – the prototype of Sir Humphrey Appleby and the model which, after World War I, progressively took charge.

[49] Hennessy, *Whitehall*, p. 299   [50] See Hennessy, *Whitehall*, Part 4.   [51] See Ch. 2.

and large from the same social and educational backgrounds as a judiciary which was still appointed by the Lord Chancellor after private consultation with, among others, his own permanent secretary. Some – Schuster himself for example – were members of the Inns of Court and might perfectly well have become judges. Not only the backgrounds but the social milieux of the two groups were now much the same.

Sir Herbert Cozens-Hardy, who was Master of the Rolls from 1907 to 1920, used to write to every newly appointed High Court judge who was not already a member of the Athenaeum, encouraging him to join.[52] Since the point of joining a London club was (as it still is) to socialise with other "clubbable" individuals in conditions of familiarity and confidentiality, it was to be expected that many of Whitehall's current and upcoming permanent secretaries would also be members. Sure enough, between a third and a half of the top civil servants in the inter-war years[53] belonged to the Athenaeum. There they will have encountered many of the Chancery and King's Bench judges, a number of Lords Justices of Appeal, the Master of the Rolls (though not Lord Hewart), the Attorney-General (later Lord Chancellor) Sir William Jowitt and most of the law lords.[54]

This is not to suggest that deals were done over brandy and cigars: both groups must have steered scrupulously clear of individual cases or issues, and not only because talking shop was bad form. What will have been engendered was a new mutuality of confidence.

World War II and after

Although the political climate changed radically with the 1945 election, and governmental policy with it, two things stood reasonably firm: the loyalty of the civil service to its political masters and its self-assured conduct of their government. Even so, the judges might have been provoked into intervention by the radicalism with which the commanding heights of the economy – the mines, the railways, the docks – were

---

[52] "All the judges, without exception, are members of the Athenaeum, and I presume you will wish to be a member." Cozens-Hardy to Lord Buckmaster LC, 26 May 1915, quoted by R. F. V. Heuston, *Lives of the Lord Chancellors 1885–1940* (1987), p. 269.

[53] Sample taken from Hennessy, *Whitehall*, Ch. 2, "Welfare, War and Peace".

[54] Data derived from *Who Was Who* for (a) senior civil servants named by Hennessy, *Whitehall*, and (b) the higher judiciary sampled for 1930. Brooks, the Reform and the United Universities Club also had members in both groups: for example, Lord Greene and Sir John Anderson were members of Brooks.

being taken into public ownership and vast new institutions – a national health service, a proactive town and country planning system and much else – brought into being. But, at least for a time, they held off. In the early 1950s Sir Raymond Evershed, the Master of the Rolls, gave a lecture in Australia in which he acknowledged that in the light of past events many people had believed that social welfare or other collectivist legislation passed by the 1945 Labour government would be emasculated by the courts; but, he said, this had not happened – the judges had not sabotaged the welfare state.[55]

In fact by the post war years the judges had all but abdicated in favour of the executive. In 1942 they had surrendered even the rudimentary oversight of ministerial powers which the law afforded them: they held in *Liversidge* v. *Anderson*[56] that whether the Home Secretary had "reasonable cause to believe" someone to have hostile connections depended on whether the cause seemed reasonable to the Home Secretary, so that the courts had no power of scrutiny or review whatever. Lord Atkin's dissenting opinion, accusing his colleagues of being "more executive-minded than the executive", was a solitary ray of light in what Professor Wade later called "a dreary catalogue of abdication and error" – the denial of a fair hearing before cancellation of a licence on which livelihood depended;[57] a rigidly literal reading of privative clauses so as to exclude even cases of fraud;[58] a Crown veto on disclosure of documents in civil actions;[59] refusal to quash an order made by a minister who had announced in advance of consultation that his mind was made up;[60] and, of course, the exclusion of children on Sundays from Wednesbury's cinemas.

It is possible that the post war continuation of this mindset had in part to do with a fear of legislative reprisal. Many of the leaders of the Labour party were old enough to remember the battles before World War I between the labour movement and a judiciary which appeared determined to sabotage the growing industrial and political effectiveness of trade unions.[61] Aneurin Bevan, Attlee's Minister of Health, who remembered those events from his childhood in the Welsh valleys, issued a

---

[55] Leslie Zines, *Constitutional Change in the Commonwealth* (1991), p. 36
[56] [1942] AC 206   [57] *Nakkuda Ali* v. *Layaratne* [1951] AC 66
[58] *Smith* v. *East Elloe DC* [1956] AC 736   [59] *Duncan* v. *Cammell Laird* [1942] AC 624
[60] *Franklin* v. *Minister of Town and Country Planning* [1948] AC 87
[61] See W. R. Cornish and G. de N. Clark, *Law and Society in England, 1750–1950* (1989), pp. 336–45.

public warning to the judges not to undermine his government's reforms. By now, in any case, abstention was an acquired judicial mindset which was going to be slow to change: Lord Justice Devlin in 1956 told an academic audience that the common law had irrecoverably lost the power to control the executive.[62] But change it did.

The princess wakes

When in 1981 Lord Diplock surveyed the rules of standing in public law, he took the opportunity to say something of wider import – for Diplock never said anything without some carefully thought-out purpose.

> The rules as to standing for the purpose of applying for prerogative orders, like most of English public law, are not to be found in any statute. They were made by judges, by judges they can be changed; and so they have been over the years to meet the need to preserve the integrity of the rule of law despite changes in the social structure, methods of government and the extent to which the activities of private individuals are controlled by governmental authorities, that have been taking place continuously, sometimes slowly, sometimes swiftly, since the rules were originally propounded. Those changes have been particularly rapid since World War II. Any judicial statements on matters of public law if made before 1950 are likely to be a misleading guide to what the law is today.[63]

Few of the senior judges of the 1950s and 1960s, least of all Lord Diplock, were candidates for the role of Prince Charming, but it was their jurisprudence which woke English public law from its long sleep and set it on the path it remains on today. Once scrutiny of all public law adjudications and decisions for both legality and fairness had become the acknowledged role of the higher courts, refinements could follow: legitimate expectation, first procedural, then substantive; the legal propriety of the content of policy and the fairness of its application; public interest standing; and much else, including proportionality. So could the

---

[62] 'The Common Law, Public Policy and the Executive" (lecture to the Bentham Club, 28 February 1956) [1956] CLP 1; Patrick Devlin, *Samples of Lawmaking* (1962), Ch. 6, esp. pp. 104–5. Devlin was appointed a law lord in 1961. By the time he retired prematurely, the House of Lords had decided *Ridge* v. *Baldwin* and the gap was beginning to close. See K. J. Keith, "*Ridge* v. *Baldwin* – Twenty Years On" (1983) 13 VUWLR 239.

[63] *R* v. *IRC, ex p National Federation of the Self-Employed* [1982] AC 617, 639–40

conceptualisation of public law's generic concern as the abuse of public power rather than the corporate analogy of *ultra vires* activity.

Some of the pressure for change came from outside the courts. In 1955 the Inns of Court Conservative and Unionist Society published a pamphlet, *Rule of Law*, arguing that state interference with individual freedom had reached a point at which it needed to be rolled back, and proposing a general right of appeal to (not merely review by) an Administrative Division of the High Court.[64] Its immediate outcome was the Franks Committee.[65]

Probably the first harbinger of the change had been the *Northumberland Compensation Appeal Tribunal* case.[66] Argued and decided in December 1951, it stands just on the right side of Lord Diplock's watershed. Rejecting the obsequies that had been pronounced during public law's long sleep on the justiciability of errors on the face of the record,[67] a court of appeal which included Lord Justice Denning held that error on the face of the record was alive and well as a ground for quashing an administrative decision, and that the record nowadays included all the documents constituting the proceedings, together with the decision itself, but not anything – for example biased behaviour or extraneous motives – which needed to be separately proved. It is not without relevance that the *Northumberland* case concerned the computation of compensation for a hospital board clerk's loss of office on the introduction of the NHS: there is a perceptible sense in the judgments that the managerial state was not going to be allowed to trifle with individuals' established entitlements.

Here, at least, was a window capable of letting in the light upon errors of law whether or not they went to jurisdiction and whether or not the tribunal making the error was quasi-judicial. But only quasi-judicial decisions were now regarded as requiring fair procedure,[68] and errors of law in lower courts and tribunals could be challenged, absent statutory rights of appeal, only where they went to jurisdiction.

---

[64] For a well-informed account of what followed in Whitehall, see J. Jacob, *The Republican Crown* (1996), pp. 174 ff. The authors of the pamphlet included the future Lord Simon of Glaisdale.

[65] See fn. 73 below.

[66] *R v. Northumberland Compensation Appeal Tribunal, ex p Shaw* [1952] 1 KB 338

[67] See *R v. Nat Bell Liquors* [1922] 2 AC 128, esp. per Lord Sumner at 159; cf. *R v. Greater Manchester Coroner, ex p Tal* [1985] QB 67.

[68] *R v. Electricity Commissioners* [1924] 1 KB 171

Filling the gaps

The first of these gaps, which had already been recognised as an embarrassment in two leading Privy Council cases,[69] was stopped in 1963,[70] when the chief constable of Brighton, Charles Ridge, who had been dismissed by the local watch committee without a hearing, took his case to the House of Lords and won.[71] Since Mr Ridge had had a very full hearing before the judge and jury who cleared him of conspiracy to obstruct the course of justice, after which the judge had commented acidly on his leadership of the Brighton constabulary, and since Mr Ridge's solicitor had thereafter been allowed to try to persuade the watch committee to change its mind, and since Mr Ridge had then been able to appeal directly to the Home Secretary, the case might have been regarded as rather weaker than Mr Arlidge's half a century earlier. In fact it was so regarded first by the High Court and then by a unanimous Court of Appeal. But the atmosphere was changing: the House of Lords by four votes to one held that the watch committee's failure to give him notice of the case against him and a chance to answer it rendered their dismissal of Mr Ridge a nullity. Due process in relation to dismissal from an office for cause, they held, was a fundamental right, and it was irrelevant to ask what difference a hearing could have made. Lord Reid in the leading speech demolished the long-standing supposition that there could be decisions which, although they affected the tenure of public office, escaped the principles of fairness because they were merely administrative decisions. The very fact that such office was at risk brought in an obligation to act fairly: the justice of the common law, as Mr Justice Byles had called it a century earlier,[72] would always be there to fill the gaps.

---

[69] *Ceylon University* v. *Fernando* [1960] 1 WLR 223, and *Kanda* v. *Government of Malaya* [1962] AC 322

[70] The dismissal occurred in 1957, following an Old Bailey prosecution arising out of corruption allegations centring on a nightclub called the Bucket of Blood. The civil proceedings, issued in 1958, reached the House of Lords in late 1962; judgment was given in March 1963, one month short of the centenary of *Cooper's Case*.

[71] *Ridge* v. *Baldwin* [1964] AC 40. No reliance whatever seems to have been placed by counsel for the watch committee on *Arlidge*. Lord Reid (at 72) referred to it simply for the proposition that ministers could act through surrogates. Lord Morris (at 124) referred to it, perhaps tongue in cheek, for Lord Haldane's endorsement of Lord Loreburn's formula in *Rice*.

[72] *Cooper* v. *Wandsworth Board of Works* (1863) 14 CB (NS) 180: see Ch. 2.

The second gap was partly stopped by Parliament when in 1958 it legislated to give effect to the Franks Report[73] by requiring most tribunals to give reasons for their decisions, with a right of appeal from them to the High Court.[74] For those tribunals which could still be challenged only by way of judicial review, the 1958 Act repealed the generality of Parliament's no-certiorari clauses;[75] but it ring-fenced decisions of the Foreign Compensation Commission against the repeal and thereby changed the course of history.[76]

The courts in the course of the nineteenth century had developed a technique for controlling lower tribunals, even where they were shielded by no-certiorari clauses, by holding that a decision made without jurisdiction was no decision at all. This approach, which had the virtue of theoretical clarity and the vice of practical unpredictability, left many decisions which were bad in law standing on the basis that any error which infected them lay within the jurisdiction of the deciding body.[77] The law lords forming the majority in Anisminic v. Foreign Compensation Commission purported to respect this distinction: but by reasoning which came close to intellectual sleight of hand,[78] they held that no tribunal had jurisdiction to get the law wrong, with the result that every material error of law went to the tribunal's jurisdiction. At least, this was what Lord Diplock was later to conclude that they had held. In a carefully worded passage some years afterwards[79] he explained that the distinction between the two forms of error had "for practical purposes" been abolished by Anisminic, with the result that any decision reached by way of an error of law was a nullity.

---

[73] Committee on Administrative Tribunals, Cmnd. 218, 1957; Tribunals and Inquiries Act 1958.

[74] Tribunals and Inquiries Act 1958, s.12, s.9, Sch. 1. This had the effect of making error on the face of the record of the scheduled tribunals redundant.

[75] Tribunals and Inquiries Act 1958, s. 11(1)

[76] Tribunals and Inquiries Act 1958, s. 11(3); Anisminic Ltd v. Foreign Compensation Commission [1969] 2 AC 147. An appeal from the Commission on points of law was later introduced.

[77] See Ch. 2.

[78] The majority decision is sharply criticised in T. Endicott, Administrative Law (2009), Ch. 9, both as an unexplained departure from precedent and for internally inconsistent reasoning. But see the judgment at first instance of Browne J [1969] 2 AC at 223 ff., reasoning from extant authority and first principles to the same conclusion: "[I]f the commission wrongly construes subparagraphs 4(1)(a) or (b) [of the Order in Council] as requiring them to consider something which on their true construction those subparagraphs do not require to be considered . . ., they act without jurisdiction . . ." (255).

[79] Re Racal Communications [1981] AC 374, 382–3

Lord Reid's formulation of the escape-route was in fact a masterpiece of equivocation:

> [The tribunal] may in perfect good faith have misconstrued the provisions giving it power to act *so that* it failed to deal with the question remitted to it and decided some question which was not remitted to it.[80]

The provisions which "give a tribunal power to act" are those which create its constitutive jurisdiction[81] – that is to say its power to sit and decide anything. For example, a tribunal which is required to have a lawyer presiding cannot proceed without one. By contrast a tribunal which answers the wrong question is making a mistake in its adjudicative jurisdiction, which had historically been review-proof in relation to all decisions that enjoyed legal finality.[82] The sleight of hand consisted of conflating these two things by the phrase "so that". But, as became clear in the years that followed, this was not just about getting round the Foreign Compensation Commission's decision. There was a more radical judicial agenda: to establish the courts as the sole arbiter of all questions of law, closing down any inherited or nascent culture of administrative law distinct from lawyers' law.[83]

"Into something rich and strange"

It was this sea-change in its culture, rather than *ex cathedra* citations of the law lords' decisions, that fed the steady growth of public law through the 1970s and 1980s. It became received wisdom that all adjudications had to be fairly conducted whatever the nature of the proceeding, and that any material error of law by a lower court or tribunal was now justiciable.[84] Despite the eccentric ways in which this had come about, these inclusive doctrines set public law on a new plateau.

---

[80] At 171; my italics.

[81] The distinction between constitutive and adjudicative jurisdiction is explained in *Watt* v. *Ahsan* [2005] EWCA Civ 990, §16,§81; on appeal, see [2007] UKHL 51, § 30.

[82] See e.g. *Moses* v. *Macferlan* (1760) 2 Burr. 1005 (Lord Mansfield CJ). See further Ch. 2. It is even arguable that the Commission's error, if error it was, was one of fact.

[83] See Ch. 13. See in particular H. W. Arthurs, *Without the Law* (1985).

[84] The reception and impact of *Anisminic* illustrate Geoffrey Wilson's contention (see Introduction) that the courts tend to adopt "an assumed, conventional, one might even say consensual, history" of their own law. One critical factor in those years was Treasury Counsel's principled reluctance to limit or undermine *Anisminic* in order to restore the former distinctions.

What then about the gap that Hewart in the 1920s had identified but had done nothing about – the devolution of great areas of apparently unreviewable power to the executive? It took the rest of the twentieth century for the law to develop a principled approach to the use of policy and discretion, refashioning its concepts of both legality and fairness in order to do so. This complex story – the doctrines of public consultation and legitimate expectation are merely two facets of it – is touched on later in this book.[85]

Another explanation?

Having said all this, it is necessary to enter a caution against my own explanation of the reawakening of public law and, by extension, of the long sleep which preceded it. The emergence of English public law from hibernation was replicated in the second half of the twentieth century in a variety of forms throughout the common law world: in India, Australia, Canada, New Zealand and the United States, to name the major players. Although its procedures differed, Scotland's substantive public law in these years broadly corresponded with that of England. What happened in each of these jurisdictions requires its own study, but it does suggest that some kind of jurisprudential zeitgeist was at large in the common-law world[86] and that neither the long sleep nor the reawakening was a uniquely English phenomenon.

---

[85] See esp. Chs. 5 and 7.
[86] And possibly beyond it: there was a parallel expansion of judicial review of decisions of the Council and Commission by the European Court of Justice during the 1970s and 1980s: see P. Craig, *UK, EU and Global Administrative Law* (the 2014 Hamlyn Lectures).

2

The dark satanic mills: the Victorian state

When William Blake, in a prefatory verse to the epic poem *Milton* which he etched between 1804 and 1808, asked whether Jerusalem had been "builded here Among these dark Satanic Mills", he was looking back in time. But when in the next stanza he called for his bow of burning gold and his arrows of desire and promised to fight on "Till we have built Jerusalem In England's green & pleasant land", he was speaking for the generation which was to bring about the administrative and legal changes that did much to shape modern public law.

The Industrial Revolution

Great Britain's massive commercial, industrial and imperial takeoff in the nineteenth century was unanticipated, unprecedented, unplanned and pretty much uncontrolled. We have learnt to call it the Industrial Revolution,[1] but the Victorians saw the spectacular growth of their trade and industry as progress rather than revolution. In a sense they were right. It was the conditions of the people which were most obviously revolutionised, as hundreds of thousands of displaced rural workers and famine-stricken immigrants swarmed into Britain's conurbations. The consequent proliferation of pollution, waste, disease, injury, poverty and unplanned development drove the more farsighted members

---

[1] It is often claimed that the expression "Industrial Revolution" originated with Arnold Toynbee in his 1884 Oxford lectures (see Tristram Hunt, *Building Jerusalem: The Rise and Fall of the Victorian City* (2004), p. 16); but Raymond Willams, *Keywords: A Vocabulary of Culture and Society* (1976), gives multiple earlier uses of this and similar phrases, especially among French commentators, who were quick to see the analogy with the political revolution of 1789. Cf. the events of 1688–9, which were instantly christened the "Glorious Revolution" to distinguish what was in reality a *coup d'état* from the Cromwellian revolution which had preceded it and was named the "Puritan Revolution" by the Victorian historian S.R. Gardiner.

of the political class into action and the courts from time to time into reaction.

This chapter looks at three interlocking elements of this teeming story: the use by Parliament of primary legislation to regulate commerce and industry, principally by hugely expanding executive and devolved powers; the deployment of these powers by central and local government and official bodies; and the use by the judiciary of old and new legal tools to keep public administration within the bounds of legality as the judges understood it. It was in the course of this multi-faceted process that much of what we have learned to regard as modern public law took shape. Why another generation of judges let it go to sleep for the first half of the twentieth century, and how in the latter half of that century it rose from what seemed to be the grave, are the two main questions addressed in the previous chapter.

Political reform

The French Revolution had scared the English ruling class badly. Although it was England's soldiers and sailors who had finally defeated him, it is evident from the popular song and literature of the time that Napoleon was regarded as a heroic figure and a potential liberator from some of the most repressive governments this country had or has ever seen. The fact that Jacobinism had little support in Britain, and that the radical Corresponding Societies were numerically small, did not dampen the imaginations of Home Office informers or calm the nerves of those in power.

The slow but inexorable build-up of the movement for a universal adult male franchise (votes for women took longer still) brought about the first Reform Act in 1832, reached its first climax in the People's Charter of 1838 and achieved a wider property-based franchise in the great Reform Act of 1867. But behind it lay dramatic events like the massacre of pro-democracy demonstrators in St Peter's Fields, Manchester, in July 1819 and the conviction and transportation in 1834 of seven Methodist farm labourers from Dorset, the Tolpuddle Martyrs, who had committed the crime of trying to form a trade union. The widespread anger which followed Peterloo, and the public agitation which resulted in the commutation of the Dorset labourers' sentences, made it clear to the political class that it was going to have to come to terms with popular discontent. But the longer-sighted politicians and public administrators, as the century wore on, saw that a well-managed state could accommodate change without surrendering power. The growth and consolidation of public law during the nineteenth century is testimony to the skill and foresight with which the Victorians set about accomplishing this.

Religion

One of the principal achievements of the French and American revolutions at the close of the eighteenth century had been the constitutional separation of state and religion. Religion was to be a private matter; the state was to be agnostic. The pervasive role of organised religion in nineteenth-century English society, by contrast, is hard to imagine today. When in 1797 the Proclamation Society brought a successful prosecution for blasphemy against the bookseller Thomas Williams for publishing Tom Paine's *The Age of Reason*, the judge, Mr Justice Ashhurst, directed the jury:

> [A]ll offences of this kind are not only offences against God but crimes against the law of the land ... inasmuch as they tend to destroy those obligations by which civil society is bound together; and it is upon this ground that the Christian religion constitutes part of the law of England.[2]

But within Christianity were powerfully conflicting tendencies. The Constitutional Association and the (unfortunately named) Vice Society used the common law crimes of blasphemy and criminal libel to prosecute both freethinkers and republicans.[3] They had the support of conservative moralists like William Wilberforce, but they were increasingly resisted by other evangelical Christians, like Stephen Lushington, a vocal opponent of capital punishment and slavery, who in Parliament denounced the Vice Society as "a set of cowardly pusillanimous hypocrites, who prosecute the poor and helpless but leave the great and noble unmolested"[4] – a form of class discrimination which characterised much Victorian legislation for the enforcement of morals.

Utilitarianism

Beneath these cross-currents lay the philosophical divide between the *laissez-faire* idealists who found, or claimed to find, support in Adam

---

[2] *R v. Williams* (1797) 26 St. Tr. 654, 716–17

[3] Of the many episodes of principled resistance to oppressive governments in the early nineteenth century, a vivid instance is that of William Hone: see S. Sedley, *Ashes and Sparks* (2011), Ch. 38, pp. 391–4.

[4] W. Cornish *et al.*, *The Oxford History of the Laws of England (1820-1914)*, vol. XI, p.147

Smith for their claim that regulation was contrary to the natural and prosperous order of things, and utilitarians and pragmatists who, taking their cue from the influential work of Jeremy Bentham, argued that the greatest happiness of the greatest number required calculated and determined state intervention. The historian Eric Hobsbawm remarked of the earlier nineteenth century:

> There is no doubt whatever that among the British middle classes ... the Protestant pietists greatly and increasingly outnumbered the minority of agnostic radicals. But a Bentham moulded the actual institutions of their age far more than a Wilberforce.[5]

Parliament

Against this background the history of public and constitutional law in the nineteenth century is in significant part the history of the use of the Parliamentary process to achieve changes which combined economic and social management with religious and philanthropic ideals.

Even so, and contrary to what one might have expected, the volume of primary legislation did not significantly increase in the course of the nineteenth century. Where in 1800 Parliament had passed 109 public general Acts, the number rose only slightly – to 116 – in 1850, and in the 1900–1 session fell to 42. What changed was the content of the statutes, which increasingly eschewed detail and instead created large powers and duties for executive and local government. A modern history of Parliament describes the shift:

> Between 1832 and 1850 most legislation became public, of general application. To initiate it, governments had to exercise increasing control over the parliamentary timetable. The volume of legislation was enormous, not only in the urgent addressing of social and economic problems such as public health, mines, the prison system, merchant shipping and factory inspection, but also in the explosion of railway building. In the 1840s, as many as forty different Bills a day were being scrutinised by committees. Standing committees were established; questions to ministers allowed; parliamentary sessions lengthened to cope with the workload. Parliament was changing from a club into a workplace ...[6]

---

[5] Eric Hobsbawm, *The Age of Revolution, 1789–1848*, (1988), p. 243
[6] John Field, *The Story of Parliament* (2002), p. 199

In 1879, to take a single year, Disraeli's Parliament passed acts to deal with alcoholism, industrial schools, shipping casualties and salmon fisheries, all of them requiring new administrative machinery.

The reform movement

The frequently ferocious opposition which the reform movement encountered, both in and outside Parliament, reflected a corresponding mix of public piety and private interest.

Three lives may help to illustrate the process. Lord Shaftesbury, Edwin Chadwick and Samuel Plimsoll were all privileged philanthropists with access to the levers of political power as well as grassroots support. What distinguished them was not simply that they were moved by conscience but that they grasped, and by degrees got others to grasp, that in its own long-term interests British society, and in particular its mercantile economy, needed enforceable controls on its activities and their by-products if it was not to collapse under the weight of its own growth.

Bentham and Chadwick

If in this way, and in this sense, the Victorian state can be seen as a beneficiary of the rationalism of the eighteenth-century Enlightenment, the conduit between the two was Jeremy Bentham. It was Bentham's disciple and friend Edwin Chadwick, born in 1800, who turned his polymath's mind to disease prevention and control, preventive policing, the administration of the Poor Law, the exploitation of children in factories, the liability of employers for industrial accidents, the control of alcohol, public recreation and state-funded pensions, and who in the course of a long life, despite hostility and obstruction, achieved remarkable successes.

Reform came hesitantly and piecemeal, but the reformed Parliament of 1832 made a start; and with the election in 1846 of a Liberal government headed by Lord John Russell, the door was pushed open. In Russell's first year of office Parliament passed Chadwick's Baths and Washhouses Act and the Nuisances Removal and Diseases Prevention Act, part of a new model of social legislation. In place of the hundreds of local enabling Acts, each secured at its own expense by a different municipality to allow it to drain or light its streets or to build a library, a single statute now gave municipalities the power, with central supervision and support, to promote personal and local safety and cleanliness.[7]

These pioneering Acts were followed by the bill which, in the teeth of ferocious localist opposition, became the great Public Health Act of 1848. The Act gave every municipality the powers it needed to promote and protect public health, either through the town corporation or through an elected local Board of Health, with power to ensure that the local water supply was clean and the local sewerage efficient, that roads, parks and burial grounds were hygienic, and that all new builds had proper toilets and drainage. The system was to be paid for either out of the rates or by secured borrowing. But it was not to be entirely voluntaristic: a General Board of Health was brought into being, with power to compel localities to set up boards of health if either a tenth of the ratepayers petitioned for it or if the local death rate reached 23 per thousand. By 1858, 219 municipalities had adopted measures under Public Health Act powers.[8]

The political and journalistic invective with which Chadwick's great measure was met – "a covert plan for despotism" and so on – had some effect. The City of London managed to get itself exempted from the legislation, leaving London with a chaos of public health bodies which was only incompletely brought under control by the 1855 Metropolis Management Act. But the combination of central empowerment and local initiative snowballed: by 1864 a further 268 towns had decided to establish boards of health, whether out of civic pride or out of fear of becoming insanitary backwaters,[9] but partly too – or so one historian suggests – out of admiration for the wholesale transformation of Paris which was being driven through by Haussmann across the Channel.[10]

---

[7] The idea itself was not new: it had been used to replace private enclosure Acts by a consolidating Inclosure Act in 1801 and a General Inclosure Act in 1845, creating a template which local landowners could adopt. It had also been used in the Lighting and Watching Acts of 1830 and 1833 to enable two-thirds of a parish's ratepayers to secure a local constabulary.

[8] There is no space here to describe Chadwick's numerous other projects – registration of deaths and their causes, a professional civil service with entry by competitive examination, street drainage, a cheap postal telegraphy system, making the railways a public enterprise, and much else – nor the abrasive manner which lost him many supporters but probably gained him many of his victories.

[9] The general belief until the later nineteenth century that miasma was the main vector of disease also created a fear that airborne disease would spread from the slums to the respectable suburbs.

[10] Hunt, *Building Jerusalem*, Ch. 7, p. vii

Shaftesbury

Chadwick's work was paralleled by that of his contemporary, the Earl of Shaftesbury, an evangelical Christian where Chadwick was a rationalist, and, as a hereditary peer, in a position to promote his own legislation. This he famously did, once again opposed by the clamour of economic liberalism, in order to secure the passage of the Climbing Boys Act, the 1833 Factories Act (the "Ten Hours Act") and the Mines and Collieries Regulation Acts – another tally of measures designed at one level simply to stop some of industrial capitalism's most inhumane practices, but at another to ensure that the system was protected from itself in its own long-term interests.

It would be a mistake to think that these measures came simply from the top down. The Ten Hours Act, for example, was the legislative echo of intense popular and industrial agitation for a ten-hour working day which long antedated it and to which Shaftesbury and others were responding.[11]

Plimsoll

The Plimsoll line which runs round cargo vessels to delineate their maximum load may look simple and uncontroversial, but its story lies on the dark side of the Victorian state. Samuel Plimsoll,[12] who had made his money as a coal merchant, in 1868 became the MP for Derby, a constituency so far from the sea that he had little to fear electorally from any maritime interests. He was incensed by the loss of lives in unseaworthy merchant vessels which regularly sank through overloading or structural weakness, and whose owners could then collect insurance payouts while the families of the drowned seamen went hungry. His campaigning in and outside Parliament for a maximum load met with ferocious opposition. Repeatedly threatened with lawsuits, and denounced and insulted by the shipowners and their supporters, Plimsoll was buoyed up by popular acclaim as well as the support of philanthropists like Shaftesbury.

The Merchant Shipping Act of 1854 created an inspectorate to enforce legislative standards, but while these included things like lifeboats they

[11] See J. L. and Barbara Hammond, *The Bleak Age* (1934), Ch. XI.
[12] For a readable account of Plimsoll's life, see E. S. Turner, *Roads to Ruin: The Shocking History of Social Reform* (1950), Ch. 7.

did not include the elementary provision of a load-line – something that the government of India had already done by simply legislating for three inches of freeboard for every foot of immersion. The powerful British shipping interests succeeded for years in blocking Plimsoll's legislation, blinding the Royal Commission which reported in 1874 with pseudo-science and intimidating the Board of Trade inspectors who were given the task of enforcement when eventually, in 1876, legislation provided for cargo vessels to bear a load-line.

The difficulties thrown in the way of Plimsoll's campaign for maritime safety, even when he had secured the principle through legislation, are a reminder that concerted self-interest was capable of halting, slowing, diverting or even sabotaging the juggernaut of Victorian reform.

Executive and local government

Some of the legislation I have touched on lay plainly in the field of public law – for example the 1848 Public Health Act. Much of it, by contrast, regulated private law relationships, typically contracts of employment. But all of it is relevant, because all of it involved regulatory supervision by the central or local state.

It is worth recalling how massive and deep-seated the issues were. In 1832 a pioneering surgeon, Charles Turner Thackrah, extrapolated from his finding that in Leeds alone 450 people a year were being killed in industrial accidents to an estimate that the national figure probably exceeded 50,000. In the course of the 1840s, with no increase at all in the amount of available accommodation, the population of the poorer parts of the great cities doubled. In 1847, people were found to be living forty to a house in St Giles in central London – luxury compared with the twenty people to a room found by the Royal Commission on handloom weavers.[13] Rural squalor was more often than not replaced by urban squalor as speculative builders crammed back-to-back dwellings into narrow streets and alleys, frequently with a single privy to serve up to twenty houses.[14]

Because of the chaotic state of public administration in the early part of the century, it was on urban land owned by some of the more forward-thinking members of the aristocracy that proper building standards

---

[13] Hunt, *Building Jerusalem*, p. 29
[14] *Report of the Commission on the Health of Towns, 1844–5*, cited in J. L. and Barbara Hammond, *The Bleak Age*, Ch V.

began to be set and enforced. Lord Stamford, who owned Ashton-under-Lyne, Sir John Ramsden, who owned Huddersfield, and the Duke of Norfolk, who owned Glossop, all required solid buildings (not jerry-built walls half a brick thick) laid out in streets of a decent width. But the absurd window tax, first introduced in 1696 as a temporary measure, still penalised the owners of houses with more than eight windows.[15] By the time it was repealed in 1851 the window tax had caused untold harm in the design and construction of hundreds of thousands of artisans' houses.

One reason why these conditions were able to be debated and acted on was the Victorian appetite for facts and statistics. One thing governments could do and repeatedly did, using the royal prerogative, was set up Royal Commissions of inquiry. Over four hundred were set up in the course of the nineteenth century. The cost was colossal (it used to be said that the first task of a Royal Commission was to lay down a decent cellar), but the information assembled by them was encyclopaedic and their recommendations for reform were often dramatic. The General Register Office, set up in 1837, documented Britain's horrifying mortality rates, while Chadwick's Poor Law commissioners assembled a detailed survey of the association of poverty with illness.

In terms of working people's health and living conditions, the early and mid-nineteenth century saw Britain going backwards.[16] To the extent that it became the great object of public law in the middle and later parts of the century to halt and where possible to reverse this decline, and to bring domestic conditions more nearly into line with Britain's imperial prosperity, it was to executive and local government that the task fell of making it happen.

The civil service

Parliament had neither the resources nor the desire to manage the systems which it set up. But it had at its disposal a well-educated middle class from which dependable commissions, boards and inspectorates

---

[15] According to the Hammonds, *The Bleak Age*, p. 55, it averaged 8s. 3d a year – far more than most working people could afford.

[16] In Manchester, Liverpool and Glasgow by 1841 life expectancy in a child's first year was between twenty-six and twenty-eight years. The Glasgow expectancy had been thirty-five in the 1820s, a figure which was not regained until the 1860s. Both the drop and the recovery are a measure of the impetus to reform.

could be appointed to enforce standards set and rules made under delegated powers. The establishment and management of these was ordinarily delegated to "one of Her Majesty's principal Secretaries of State" – in other words, to a department of the civil service.

By 1800 the essential structure of modern departmental government – the Home Office, the Foreign Office and the Treasury[17] – was in existence. Tax farming – the privatised system of tax collection – had resulted by the mid-eighteenth century in a body of about 14,000 freelance officers, but they did not constitute a civil service. The main executive agency with which Britain entered the nineteenth century was Customs and Excise, managed by Crown commissioners and staffed by excisemen who policed both the manufacturers whose products were dutiable and the coasts and ports through which contraband of every sort was smuggled. While the Excise was subject in principle to judicial review, litigation seems to have been rare,[18] probably because abuses of its constabulary powers, if they occurred, could be raised by way of defence in the course of prosecutions. In 1827, in regulatory mode, the disparate statutory provisions for levying taxes on goods and products were consolidated by Act of Parliament.[19]

Even so, by the beginning of Victoria's reign in 1837 there remained a yawning gap between the need of government for an efficient cadre of skilled and independent officials to staff the great departments of state, and the continuing amateurism of ministerial government. It became increasingly obvious that the lack of accumulated experience and political independence in public administration was a major impediment to the development and implementation of policy and ultimately to Britain's stability and success. The closing of this gap by the professionalising of its civil service in the second half of the nineteenth century was one of Britain's most remarkable achievements.

The one existing department which could be used as a model and hence as an argument for modernisation was the Board of Trade,[20] the

---

[17] Refounded after the Restoration with the aid of Dutch accounting systems brought in by the efficient and ruthless Sir George Downing.

[18] W. Cornish et al., The Oxford History of the Laws of England (1820–1914), vol. XI, p. 344, n. 10

[19] Excise Management Act 1827

[20] Peter Hennessy, Whitehall (1989), describes the Board of Trade's nineteenth-century role (or at least its intended role) as "running the blockade in the Napoleonic war and coping with the dislocation of trade; overseeing the British merchant marine and the condition of the seamen working in it; assisting in the abolition of the slave trade; relaxing the

lineal descendant of the Committee for Trade and Plantations set up in 1621 by James I to monitor the twin processes of colonisation and exploitation, and the progenitor of the modern Department of Trade and Industry. The Board had acquired, because it needed them, a body of efficient and non-political civil servants (a name originally adopted by the East India Company to distinguish them from the company's military servants), who could provide continuity of policy and informed advice in the course of repeated changes of government and the comings and goings of variably capable ministers.

The historic report by Sir Stafford Northcote and Sir Charles Trevelyan on the future of the civil service, commissioned by Gladstone as Chancellor of the Exchequer and published in 1854, attracted snowballing support for its proposal to professionalise and depoliticise the entire civil service.[21] There is plenty of evidence that the report's highly placed supporters, from Gladstone to Jowitt, had more than efficiency in view. They saw that the continuing popular movement to enlarge the franchise and to improve the democratic process might one day put a radical government in office. Trevelyan had written to the Lord Chief Justice:

> The irresistible tendency of the times is to bring into activity the political power of the lower classes of society.

If by the time that happened public administration had been professionalised and insulated from party politics, the aspects of the state which mattered most could probably be preserved.

So it was that by 1900, when the Labour Party was founded, what Peter Hennessy calls "the country's first true meritocracy, a genuine aristocracy of talent"[22] was already settled into office. Where the public administration of the Stuarts had been conducted by use of the prerogative, and that of the Hanoverians by the use of patronage, Gladstone intended the public administration of the Victorians to be based on virtue.[23] The proposed changes, in his view, would also "strengthen and multiply the

---

Navigation Acts; and supervising the railway boom" – as well as spearheading the movement for free trade which in 1846 secured the repeal of the Corn Laws.

[21] The *Report on the Organisation of the Permanent Civil Service* was opposed by conservatives like James Fitzjames Stephen because it would create a tribe of secure and undeserving jobsworths. But the Indian civil service had in 1853 been opened to entry by competitive examination and was thriving.

[22] Hennessy, *Whitehall*, p. 31

[23] H. G. G. Matthew, *Gladstone, 1809–1874* (1986), quo Hennessy, *Whitehall*

ties between the higher classes and the possession of administrative power". In Jowitt's estimation, they would "give us" – that is the Oxford élite – "another root striking into a new soil of society". As we have seen in the previous chapter, their ambition proved even truer than they anticipated.

The regulatory state

By 1914 Parliament had created, among other authorities, inspectorates of factories, mines, explosives, prisons, police, reformatory and industrial schools, aliens, anatomy, animal welfare and inebriate retreats, all of them requiring Home Office support and supervision,[24] and most of them staffed by inspectors (a striking proportion of them women) of an intellectual calibre comparable with that of the Oxbridge elite now running the Home Office itself. They provided a fund of expertise which the generalists at the centre, however brilliant, lacked, and which gave the latter's advice a solidity which it could not otherwise have had.

It was the first phase of parliamentary activism, following the electoral reforms of 1832, which saw the establishment of the factory inspectorate (pursuant to Chadwick's and Shaftesbury's 1833 Factories Act), in addition to the Poor Law commission (thanks to Chadwick's work) and the tithe commission,[25] each deriving its authority directly from statute rather than through a minister. One beneficial effect of this pattern was that opportunities for day-to-day political manipulation or control were slight. These bodies were, as the *Law Magazine* spotted as early as 1853, "governments in miniature". True, the obligation resting on some of them to report to Parliament exposed them instead to the risk of losing their funding or their mandate if they displeased the current legislative majority. But the factory inspectors faced no such handicap. They were given power to make regulations and to adjudicate summarily on infractions of them, and they were to report not to Parliament but to the Home Secretary.[26] They were also protected by a no-certiorari provision, a mechanism to which I will come.

At Chadwick's insistence, the Poor Law commissioners were similarly insulated by the 1834 Poor Law Amendment Act against direct political

---

[24] See J. Pellew, *The Home Office 1848–1914* (1982), Part III.

[25] Tithes Commutation Act 1836, starting the century-long process of abolishing the tithes which formed the basis of the Church of England's income.

[26] Who in the course of time directed them to cease acting as judges in their own cause and to adopt a uniform set of regulations.

control or interference, whether by Parliament or by ministers, to both of whom, however, they had to report. But they were exposed to litigation, both by an express provision that their acts were to be open to challenge by way of judicial review and by the requirement that their directions could only be enforced by obtaining orders of mandamus; the latter provision reflecting the fact that the people the commissioners supervised, the local Poor Law guardians, were themselves public officials.

The tithe commissioners were given powers that were more nearly judicial and accordingly, while protected by a no-certiorari clause, were plugged directly into the legal system by a right of appeal against their decisions both on fact and on law. This statutory recourse, as we shall see, did not prevent the courts also using their common law powers.

The model which became established was on one view more restrictive but on another view better adjusted to the rule of law. Newly established inspectorates were no longer given summary powers of enforcement. They were required to prosecute before the local magistrates or to seek injunctions from the higher courts, while the power of the factory inspectors to certify machinery dangerous was made challengeable by arbitration. These were requirements which had a potential both for good and for ill. Ironically, it may have been the model which looked least autonomous, that of the mines and alkali inspectorates, which was the most secure: by vesting enforcement powers in the secretary of state or a local authority in whose name the inspectors then acted, Parliament clothed them with greater invulnerability than some of their more independent peers. The Poor Law commissioners, with Chadwick at the helm, found eventually that without a minister to speak for them in Parliament they were defenceless against the political attacks which were eventually to undo them.

It was the Home Office on which the obligation fell to administer many of the new public authorities. In 1848 the Home Secretary's entire staff numbered twenty two; by 1870 it was still only thirty three. Despite the eventual adoption in 1873 of entry by competitive examination, the number of civil servants remained pretty steady: in 1913, below the permanent under-secretary, each of the six divisions of the Home Office was run by an assistant secretary and staffed by a handful of senior and junior clerks,[27] with a total establishment of less than thirty. What had mushroomed by then, however, were the inspectorates for which the

---

[27] A single division, with a staff of five, dealt not only with nationality and immigration but with byelaws, licensing and parliamentary Bills. See J. Pellew, *The Home Office 1848–1914*, Ch. 2.

Home Office was responsible: there were 229 factory inspectors, a tenth
of them women; ninety-two inspectors of mines; in total nearly
350 trained officials with powers of entry, investigation and prosecution.
The standing commissions for which the Home Office was responsible
were also throwing a growing burden on it. The 1877 Prisons Act, for
example, replaced local prison authorities with a central prison commission which the Home Office had to administer. By the 1880s senior
Home Office officials were complaining that they were having to take
work home.

Legal conflict

Much of public administration at the start of the nineteenth century was
still in the hands of the local justices of the peace. The great principle
established in *Entick* v. *Carrington* in 1765, that ministers of the Crown
had no investigatory or judicial powers, had not yet affected the local
magistracy, which had powers not only of adjudication and punishment
but wage-fixing and other regulatory functions. Since a large proportion
of them were landowners and employers, and since each local bench was
pretty much self-perpetuating, their decisions were frequently self-
interested and often corrupt.

This was why in 1833 the system of the earlier Factories Acts had been
abandoned. The 1802 Act had put enforcement in the hands of two
unpaid 'visitors' appointed by the local justices, one to be a clergyman,
the other a JP. The system was so ineffectual that no attempt was
thereafter made to build on it. Instead, in the pioneering Act of 1833,
an independent national inspectorate of factories was set up, with powers
of entry and inquiry and authority to make rules. The system was
rudimentary and lacked teeth because enforcement still depended on
securing a conviction before the local justices. But, as Arthurs points
out,[28] what was equally important was that Parliament had signalled an
acceptance of central government's responsibility for making the legislation work.

One major step in this direction was the inclusion in the 1833 Act of a
section[29] intended to bar judicial review of the actions of the inspectors.
Since the inspectors now had power to make rules with the status of

---

[28] H. W. Arthurs, *Without the Law* (1985), pp. 104 ff
[29] s.42: "... neither shall any Conviction, except [for forging documents] ... be removable
by Certiorari ... into any Court whatever."

subordinate legislation and enforceable by criminal sanctions, this was a radical insulation of administration from law, going beyond the provision in the 1825 Factories Act which had shielded local magistrates from review by the higher courts.[30] Such preclusive clauses were on the whole well meant: they were intended to prevent factory owners from obstructing enforcement by means of litigation. But they were also capable of insulating perverse and unjust decisions of justices of the peace from challenge – a serious problem when one recalls the composition of the local benches. The King's Bench had long before the nineteenth century established the availability of the prerogative writs to control any new body, albeit one established by statute.[31] The question now was whether and when they could be used.

The consequent tensions which racked public law in the course of the nineteenth century had four main elements. One was the desire of public administrators, and of the parliamentarians who backed them, that the new agencies should be able to carry out their mandate without judicial interference or obstruction. I have described some of the efforts which went into securing this. The second was the desire of those who were now subject to regulation, whether individuals, trade unions, corporations or local authorities, to be able to challenge the regulators before an independent judicial tribunal. The third was the judicial imperative to respect Parliament's prescriptions. The fourth, pulling in the opposite direction, was the judicial impulse to monitor the legality and fairness of public administration.

These elements were interrelated and complex. While many of those with objections to the actions of what would today be called quangos were propertied interests who resented interference with their activities, others were individuals who needed redress or protection and, often because of bias in the local justice system, were not getting it. Some, too, were local bodies, for example Poor Law guardians, who found themselves in conflict with the new central body, the Poor Law commissioners. These, and a good few others, wanted a court to turn to. But the judges, while historically responsible for invigilating the propriety of what the state

---

[30] For a stronger form of preclusive clause, see the Inclosure Act 1845, s. 166: "no Order, Adjudication, or Proceeding ... under the Authority of this Act ... shall be quashed for Want of Form, or be removed or removable by Certiorari or any other Writ or Process into any of Her Majesty's Courts of Record ..."

[31] *Smith's Case* (1670) 1 Ventr. 66 ("This court cannot be ousted of its jurisdiction without special words"); *Groenvelt v. Burrell* (1697) 1 Ld. Raym. 454, 469, per Holt CJ.

did, were also required to respect and maintain the ring-fences erected by Parliament around newly created administrative bodies.

Recourse to law

The prerogative writs, which are still the basis of judicial review,[32] were well established by the beginning of the nineteenth century. Although they had originated, as their name suggests, in the exercise of the Crown's power to control the acts of lower tribunals and official bodies,[33] the authority to issue them had always lain in the hands of the judges of the central courts. By the writ of certiorari (now called a quashing order) they could strike down a decision made without the power to make it; by the writ of mandamus (now called a mandatory order) they could compel a body or lower court to take action which it was failing to take; and by the writ of prohibition (now called a prohibiting order) they could forestall illegal action.

These writs were used to control what have always been rather demeaningly called inferior tribunals and bodies – that is to say public bodies subject to the supervisory jurisdiction of the courts which in the 1870s were reconstituted as the High Court of Justice. It did not go unremarked that the existence and extent of this jurisdiction were determined by the superior courts themselves. But it was a form of control which, said Lord Justice Farwell in 1910,

> is a necessary and inseparable incident to all tribunals of limited jurisdiction, for it is a contradiction in terms to create a tribunal of limited jurisdiction and unlimited power to determine such limit at its own will and pleasure.[34]

Manifestly, not all mistakes made by tribunals and quangos related to their jurisdiction. The distinction between error as to jurisdiction and error within jurisdiction had been clearly made by Sir Edward Coke CJ in the *Marshalsea* case in 1616.[35] There the court of King's Bench allowed a

---

[32] They were renamed prerogative orders by the Administration of Justice (Miscellaneous Provisions) Act 1938, and renamed "quashing orders", "mandatory orders" and "prohibiting orders" by the Civil Procedure (Modification of the Senior Courts Act 1981) Order 2004.

[33] See Edith Henderson, *Foundations of English Administrative Law* (1963).

[34] *R v. Shoreditch Assessment Committee, ex p Morgan* [1910] 2 KB 859, 880

[35] (1616) 10 Co Rep 68b. Headnote: "When a court has jurisdiction of the cause and proceeds ... erroneously, no action lies; but when the court has not jurisdiction of the

claim for assault and false imprisonment against officers who had acted on an order of the Court of the Marshalsea, the King's domestic court, when neither party was a member of the royal household and the order had therefore been made without jurisdiction. Had it been simply erroneous, Coke stressed, the court would not have intervened.

The reason why this approach became critical in relation to Parliament's no-certiorari clauses was that the courts had held, as long ago as 1759, that a no-certiorari clause in the empowering legislation did not protect a public body from judicial review of acts done without jurisdiction,[36] since such a decision was in law no decision at all. In case after case the no-certiorari clauses in the Victorian social legislation, along with the finality clauses favoured by eighteenth-century Parliaments,[37] succumbed to this doctrine.[38]

The line between decisions which actually related to the decision-maker's jurisdiction and those which, by contrast, lay within their jurisdiction but had simply been erroneous was not always easy to draw, but drawing it determined whether the court was going to intervene or not. In this situation the scope for judicial manipulation was plain. From a legal realist point of view it presents a perfect instance of a self-made opportunity for the judges to make findings which would generate the results they wanted. There are plenty of judgments in the course of the mid- and late nineteenth century which lend support to this view. But there were also wholesome statements of principle which went beyond the cases before the court and helped to shape modern public law.

Statutory bars on certiorari were not only readily circumvented in relation to jurisdictional questions: they did not in any event block

cause, the whole proceeding is *coram non judice* [i.e. before no judge], and an action will lie against them. . ."

[36] *R v. Derbyshire JJ* (1759) 2 Keny. 299: the King's Bench granted certiorari to quash an *ultra vires* order of quarter sessions requiring outgoing highway surveyors to make over their funds to an incoming surveyor, despite the prohibition in 3&4 W&M c.12, s. 23, against granting certiorari to quash "any order made by virtue of this Act", on the ground that this did not protect orders made without jurisdiction.

[37] E.g. the Land Tax Act 1797, 38 Geo. III c.5, s. 8 (cited C. Stebbings, *Legal Foundations of Tribunals in Nineteenth Century* England (2006), p. 236, n. 19): all decisions of the commissioners to be final "without any further Appeal, upon any Pretence whatsoever".

[38] The doctrine has become known as the *ultra vires* doctrine: as to its origins, see the postscript to Ch. 7. Cf. M. J. Detmold, *Courts and Administrators* (1989), p. 177: "Aesop's fable of the boy and the jar of philbert nuts is intended to illustrate the point that one who attempts too much runs the risk of ruining his whole enterprise . . . Our parliaments have often made the same mistake with their privative clauses."

applications for mandamus or prohibition. And in 1857 the Summary Proceedings Act gave a uniform right of appeal from magistrates' courts and quarter sessions on any point of law on which a case could be properly stated.[39] The upshot was that by mid-century there were few issues of public law which could not be brought before the higher courts, and from the last quarter of the century the Judicature Acts made the decisions of the High Court subject to two tiers of further appeal. Judicialisation, for good or ill, thus became one of the principal tendencies of the regulatory state.

Judicial input

The case most frequently cited as an example of judicial bias in interpreting social legislation is *Ryder* v. *Mills*,[40] an appeal by case stated (not a judicial review, and therefore unaffected by the no-certiorari provision) brought by a factory owner against the local factory inspector, in which the Court of Exchequer had to decide whether the historic ban, first imposed in the 1833 Factories Act, on employing children for more than ten hours a day could be circumvented by using them in shorter relays which exceeded ten hours in total.

> "The Act," said Baron Parke, "... must be construed strictly; that is, a man is not to be restrained from the liberty which he has of acting as he pleases, and rendered liable to punishment, unless the law has plainly said that he shall."

It looked very much, he admitted, as if Parliament had intended to limit children's shifts to ten hours in total:

> without question, it would most certainly prevent them from being overworked and secure to them more completely the benefit of some education in public schools which the legislature meant them to enjoy; . . .

---

[39] The procedure seems to have derived from an eighteenth-century statute providing for a case to be stated by the commissioners for house and window taxes. The Quarter Sessions Act 1849 enabled a case to be jointly stated for the opinion of the Queen's Bench, typically on liability to rates. The Summary Jurisdiction Act 1857 enabled the parties to bypass quarter sessions and require justices to state a case for the Queen's Bench (with a three-day time limit). In such cases certiorari was redundant. The procedure was in due course adopted by the Housing of the Working Classes Act 1890, and extended to closure and demolition orders under the Housing and Town Planning Act 1909.

[40] (1850) 19 LJ (NS) (pt 3) 82 (Exch.) According to D. Roberts, *Victorian Origins of the British Welfare State* (1960), p. 298, one factory inspector had already lost ten or eleven prosecutions of employers for operating an illegal relay system before this case was decided.

but then this result could only have been obtained by a larger sacrifice of the interest of the owners of factories, and we cannot assume that Parliament disregarded so important a consideration.

The court's decision to prioritise the interests of employers, although it was very plainly a policy choice, could be justified by a legal principle, in this case the principle of construing penal statutes restrictively. But exactly the same was true of the downside of the judgment: the marginalising of the interests of working children and the attenuation of their protection from excessive exploitation defied a clear legislative intent which the court was required to respect. The legal choice, in other words, was also a policy choice: there was no single principle of law to drive the court inexorably to its conclusion.

The frustration experienced by the factory inspectorate at decisions like these was replicated by that of other official bodies whose remit brought them into conflict with the law, not only when they were challenged by powerful interests but when they sought the help of the courts to get things done. The Poor Law commissioners, says Arthurs,[41]

> encountered debilitating delays whenever they sought mandamus to compel compliance by local officials; the Board of Health "did not consider common law prosecutions of nuisances worth the time or expense".

A Parliament in which both the legal profession and industrial interests were extremely well represented was not over-anxious to reverse this situation. The privative clause in the Coal Mines Inspection Act 1842 was dropped in the successor legislation of 1850 and not restored thereafter. But in one remarkable instance, Parliament incautiously judicialised a regulatory system and then had to retreat. The Railway and Canal Traffic Act 1854 set up a commission which was subject to direct appellate supervision by the Court of Common Pleas. Although the court was given power to appoint an engineer or barrister to take evidence on oath and to report, as well as power to commit company directors to prison for non-compliance with its injunctions, it did not relish its assigned role as, in effect, the upper chamber of a specialist tribunal. In 1873 the system was abandoned in favour of a new and more conventional railway commission with a power (and so implicitly a duty) to state a case for the superior courts on any question of law which confronted them.[42]

---

[41] *Without the Law*, p.159

[42] There is no space here to survey the massive impact on the legal system of the railways – the "only ... development in the nineteenth-century world of business and

In this and similar ways, as varying models and patterns of regulation evolved, judicial oversight evolved with them. One means by which the judges did this was the *ultra vires* doctrine – the emerging principle of company law that things done outside a limited company's articles of association were void in law. While in contract law the doctrine had the pernicious effect of allowing a corporation to renege on its debts and other obligations,[43] in public law it let the courts turn the clock back to midnight and to require a rethink wherever a statutory body went outside its remit.

Dicey and administrative law

Despite all this, Dicey felt able to announce in his *Law of the Constitution*[44] that in Britain, in contrast to France, there was no system of *droit administratif*. In this as in other things he was magnificently wrong.[45] By his time, as we have seen, Britain had a system of judicial supervision of public administration closely paralleling the jurisdiction of the French Conseil d'État, itself a powerful and independent tribunal, albeit constitutionally part of the administrative structure. To the extent that Dicey's point was that the common law applied to everyone equally, from the prime minister to the policeman, he was right to attribute the jurisdiction to the common law but wrong to suggest that it put citizen and official on an equal footing. What public law has always had to do is to adjust the imbalance of power between the citizen and a state which, uncontrolled, might commit a variety of wrongs against the public. The administrative law of both countries has as its central task the calibration of powers and rights between two inherently unequal parties.

Back to the future

Although it was in the course of the nineteenth century that much of modern public law took shape, it did so under a weight of formal and procedural handicaps.

---

technology … large, wealthy, invasive, and pervasive enough not only to engage the English legal establishment, but to reshape it" (R. W. Kostal, *Law and English Railway Capitalism, 1825–1875* (1994), p. 3). The regulatory legislation, Kostal suggests (p. 7), was "badly designed, poorly drafted, and weakly enforced", leaving regulators to work by suggestion rather than coercion. But the common law, he argues, had a largely unrecognised regulatory effect. See further p. 256.

[43] *Colman* v. *Eastern Counties Railway Co Ltd* (1846) 16 LJ Ch. 73; discussed in S. Sedley, *Freedom, Law and Justice* (the 1998 Hamlyn Lectures), pp. 26–7.

[44] First published in 1885; Ch. IV and XII.   [45] See Ch. 14.

I have touched on the development of the notion of error within and outside jurisdiction. The complexities to which this distinction gave rise in the era of the regulatory state were endless. A tithe commissioner's decision that the claimant's land was not exempt from the obligation to pay tithes, which on one view was exactly what the commissioner was there to decide, was struck down as a jurisdictional error.[46] By contrast, when magistrates evicted a man on the basis that he had been housed by the parish as a pauper, the King's Bench refused to let him show that he was a contractual tenant and so outside the justices' jurisdiction.[47] The elusive distinction was not resolved until, in the mid-twentieth century, the House of Lords in *Anisminic*[48] did away with it altogether in favour of a single justiciable category of error of law.[49]

Error of law, however, was itself a source of complexity in the nineteenth century. If the error did not appear on the face of the record, it was generally not open to challenge, though if it went to jurisdiction it could be established by affidavit evidence. It was once again only in the mid-twentieth century, in the *Northumberland* case,[50] that this problem was reconsidered and resolved by admitting pretty well all relevant documentation as part of the record and thereby opening it to scrutiny for error of law; although what amounts to an error of law, as opposed to an error of fact or a permissible exercise of discretion, is another legal hinterland which is still being explored today.

A third complication, again affecting jurisdiction, was whether the decision under attack was judicial (for example a conviction by magistrates), quasi-judicial (typically an administrative decision affecting property rights) or purely administrative. The right to be heard, ever since Sir Edward Coke's decision in *Bagg's Case*,[51] had been a jewel in the crown of the common law, but the Victorian courts were reluctant to apply it to what they regarded as administrative decisions made by the growing number of official bodies in the regulatory state, whatever their impact on individual interests.[52] This distinction too was to fade in the course of

---

[46] *Bunbury v. Fuller* (1853) 9 Exch. 111   [47] *R v. Bolton* (1841) 1 QB 66
[48] *Anisminic Ltd v. Foreign Compensation Commission* [1969] 2 AC 147
[49] See Paul Craig, *Administrative Law* (7th edn, 2012), § 16–022 ff. on this issue, and Ch. 2 for an excellent survey of the nineteenth-century state. See also Stebbings, *The Legal Foundations of Tribunals in Nineteenth Century England*, esp. Ch. 6.
[50] *R v. Northumberland Compensation Appeal Tribunal, ex p Shaw* [1952] 1 KB 338
[51] (1615) 11 Co.Rep. 93b
[52] An authority deploying all these possibilities is the decision of Coleridge J in *Re Constables of Hipperholme* (1847) 5 Dow. and L. 79, refusing to authorise certiorari

the twentieth century,[53] eclipsed by Lord Loreburn's dictum in 1911 that the duty to listen fairly to both sides "is a duty lying upon everyone who decides anything".[54]

The net result, while these distinctions persisted, was to allow the Victorian judges to a significant extent to choose where they were prepared to intervene. Where they declined to intervene, as they did initially, for example, in relation to the income tax commissioners,[55] public administration obtained the breathing space it desired. Where they did intervene, they applied and developed principles that have a familiar ring today. And intervene they increasingly did as the century passed and the perceived need to protect the individual from an over-powerful state grew. They held that any public law body with power to impose obligations[56] or interfere with common law rights[57] was answer-able to the superior courts for the legality of its actions. They enlarged the concept of a judicial body to include one with "administrative duties which need not be performed in court, but in respect of which it is necessary to bring to bear a judicial mind – that is, a mind to determine what is fair and just ...".[58] And they corralled administrative discretion by requiring it to be exercised both judicially and reasonably.

The terms in which these obligations were spelt out by the higher courts are interesting. In *Sharp* v. *Wakefield*[59] Lord Halsbury LC, holding

proceedings (a) because the appointment of constables by the local justices was an administrative and not a judicial function, and (b) because the record anyway showed no error on the face of the vestry resolution making the appointments; but (c) granting certiorari for the purpose of inquiring, on affidavit evidence, whether the justices had exceeded their jurisdiction.

[53] See W. Wade and C. Forsyth, *Administrative Law* (10th edn, 2009), pp. 407–8; but see also Ch. 1 above.

[54] *Board of Education* v. *Rice* [1911] AC 179

[55] See C. Stebbings, *The Victorian Taxpayer and the Law, a Study in Constitutional Conflict* (2009), Ch. 4.

[56] *R* v. *Local Government Board* (1882) 10 QBD 309, 321, per Brett LJ obiter: "... my view of the power of prohibition at the present day is that the court should not be chary of exercising it, and that wherever the legislature entrusts to any body of persons other than to the superior courts the power of imposing an obligation upon individuals, the courts ought to exercise as widely as they can the power of controlling those bodies of persons ...."

[57] *R* v. *Assessment Committee of St Mary Abbotts, Kensington* [1891] 1 QB 378: per Lord Esher MR: vestrymen appointed under statute to hear objections to the valuation list were not a court or tribunal but (per Fry LJ, concurring) had no power to limit the common law right to appear by a suitable agent.

[58] *Royal Aquarium* v. *Parkinson* [1892] 1 QB 431, 452 per Lopes LJ

[59] [1891] AC 173, 179

that an administrative discretion has to be exercised "according to the rules of reason and justice, not according to private opinion ...; according to law and not humour ... not arbitrary, vague and fanciful but legal and regular; and ... within the limit to which an honest man competent to the discharge of his office ought to confine himself", cited two early authorities for his propositions. One was *Rooke's Case*,[60] which as long ago as 1598 had determined that the commissioners of sewers were obliged by "the rule of reason" to distribute the cost of embankment repairs among all the neighbouring owners of land at risk of flooding, and could not use their discretion to impose them solely on the riparian owner. The other was *Wilson* v. *Rastall*,[61] a case decided a century earlier by the court of King's Bench, equating discretion with regularity and predictability in a sense now familiar in relation to the use of policy in public law.

As the century approached its end, a full divisional court of seven judges sat to consider the validity of a bylaw banning singing and music within fifty yards of any dwelling house. In the course of a judgment describing the limits of what was reasonable and therefore lawful in the exercise of the power to make such bylaws, Lord Russell of Killowen CJ included "such oppressive or gratuitous interference with the rights of those subject to them as could find no justification in the minds of

---

[60] (1598) 5 Co Rep 100a. Sewers were not simply foul-water drains: they were the flood control and watercourse works on which the recovery and preservation of agricultural land depended, and the commissioners' role in apportioning the cost of them was an important one. In *Rooke's Case*, however, they had levied the entire cost of repairing a river bank on the riparian owner, letting his neighbours benefit from the repair without contributing to its cost. It was said on their behalf – exactly as would be said today – that this was a matter for the commissioners' discretion, whatever the court might think. Not so, said Coke – "... notwithstanding the words of the commission give authority to the commissioners to do according to their discretions, yet their proceedings ought to be limited and bound with the rule of reason and law. For discretion is a science or understanding to discern between falsity and truth, between wrong and right, between shadows and substance ... and not to do according to their wills and private affections ..." The point of discretion, Coke wrote in his commentary on Littleton, "is to discern by the right line of the law, and not by the crooked cord of private opinion ..." (Co. Litt. 227b).

[61] (1792) 4 TR (Durnford and East) 753, per Kenyon CJ at 757: the court's discretion should be "confined within those limits within which an honest man, competent to discharge the duties of his office, ought to confine himself; and that discretion will be best exercised by not deviating from the rules laid down by our predecessors; for the practice of the Court forms the law of the Court."

reasonable men"[62] – a test in which it is not entirely fanciful to see the embryo of a doctrine of proportionality.

Much of this law was concerned with the substance of administrative decisions; but just as important was the process by which they were reached. Starting with *Bagg's Case* in 1616, the right to be heard became embedded in the common law.[63] You can witness its penetration into the public law of the Victorian regulatory state in the decision of the court of Common Pleas in *Cooper* v. *Wandsworth Board of Works*.[64] Social legislation had forbidden the erection of new buildings without prior notice to the local board of works. When Mr Cooper did just this, the board went in and pulled the partly finished building down, as the Act empowered them to do. But Mr Cooper won his claim for damages against them because, although the statute was silent about it, the common law gave him a right to be heard before any such decision was taken. "The justice of the common law", said Mr Justice Byles, "will supply the omission of the legislature."

Envoi

Looking back at the ways in which Queen Victoria's judges had established the nature and extent of their supervisory role, the *Oxford History of the Laws of England* comments:

> Perhaps the most significant feature of this narrative is that judges took for granted that principles of legality and fair procedure existed and that they should apply to new decision-makers, however exalted.[65]

I began with Blake's vision at the start of the nineteenth century of a new Jerusalem among England's satanic mills. I can end with the remark of Don Fabrizio, the Sicilian aristocrat in Lampedusa's *Il Gattopardo* (*The Leopard*) who has anxiously watched the rise of Garibaldi's republicanism but comprehends the need to accommodate it:

> If we want things to stay as they are, things will have to change.

Because the wiser of Don Fabrizio's English contemporaries understood this well, the old became the new as the nineteenth century rolled on,

---

[62] *Kruse* v. *Johnson* [1898] 2 QB 91. Everybody knew that the bylaw had been made to stop the Salvation Army holding street services which were often disrupted by opponents or hooligans.
[63] See Ch. 8.   [64] (1863) 14 CB (NS) 180   [65] Vol. XI, p. 521

and both in turn came to prefigure things that we are sometimes encouraged to believe were novel in the public law of the later twentieth century.[66] But change turned out, as it generally does, to be a long and rocky road, and one down which, although it has today broadened into a reasonably well-signposted highway, we are still travelling.

[66] "... the great development that has recently taken place in the law of judicial review whereby the courts have asserted a general jurisdiction to review the decisions of tribunals and inferior courts": per Lord Browne-Wilkinson, *R v. Lord Chancellor, ex p Page* [1993] AC 682, 700; cf. *Rooke's Case* (1598) 5 Co. Rep. 100a, n. 61 above; *Keighley's Case* (1609) 10 Co. Rep. 139.

3

New corn from old fields: the Hanoverian harvest

In the third quarter of the eighteenth century a series of governmental attempts to suppress public criticism produced a backlash which forced judges, juries and the law to take sides. They sided with personal liberty, with enduring consequences. This chapter looks among other things at how these developments have conditioned the extent and use of both ministerial and judicial powers.

The ministerial ascendancy

With somewhat artificial precision, Sir William Anson[1] picked 1714, the year in which George of Hanover ascended the British throne, as the point at which the Crown ceased to govern through its ministers and ministers began to govern through the Crown. But his point was an important one. The settlement of 1689 had constitutionalised the monarchy and had at least begun to make it the political servant of Parliament; but the statutory Protestant succession,[2] by placing on the throne a king who spoke no English and preferred to be in Hanover, decisively accelerated the transfer of political power from the monarch's personal secretaries of state to a political ministry deriving its authority from Parliament.

The rule of law

So too in the sphere of law, a full century before George ascended the throne, Coke in the *Case of Prohibitions*, had told James I that his judicial function was not his own: it was exercised in his name by his judges, and

---

[1] W. Anson, *The Law and Custom of the Constitution* (1908 edn), Vol. II, Part 1, p. 41
[2] Act of Settlement 1700, s. 3

had been since the Norman Conquest.[3] Historians[4] have characterised Coke's mind as "essentially mediaeval" and his institutional thinking as "rooted in the historical past"; but Coke wore this as a badge of honour:

> "Out of the old fields," he wrote, "must come the new corne."

Like other active jurists of the Jacobean years, Coke was able to reach back, past the autocratic regimes of the Tudors and the house of York, not only to Bracton in the mid-thirteenth century but to Henry VI's Chief Justice Sir John Fortescue who, writing in the mid-fifteenth century,[5] had said that it was "not customary for the kings of England to sit in court or pronounce judgment themselves; and yet they are called the king's judgments". Fortescue's nineteenth-century editor Andrew Amos made the significant point that this was prophetic not only of Coke's stance on the power of adjudication in the *Case of Prohibitions* but of the larger principle, which did not reach fruition until the eighteenth century, that "the king can do nothing in his public capacity without the agency of some responsible minister".

The Bill of Rights

The Bill of Rights (as Chief Justice Pratt was to point out in *Entick v. Carrington*) said nothing about departmental government or ministerial responsibility; nor, for that matter, about judicial independence. Nor was it necessarily within the logic of the 1689 settlement that ministers in carrying out the functions of government would be answerable to Parliament, of which they did not even have to be members, or to the judges who like themselves were surrogates of the Crown. But the logic of the settlement was that the expansion and division of governmental labour would continue, as it did;[6] and the security of judicial tenure accorded by the Act of Settlement[7] set the scene for a more confident constitutional jurisprudence than had been feasible under the post-Restoration Stuart dynasty.

It is against this fluid but slowly cohering background that one can most clearly see what was arguably the major constitutional development

---

[3] See Ch. 6.

[4] T. Plucknett, *A Concise History of the Common Law* (4th edn, 1948), p. 230; C. W. Brooks, *Law, Politics and Society in Early Modern England* (2008), pp. 427–8.

[5] *De Laudibus Legum Angliae*, Ch. VIII [6] See Ch. 11.

[7] Like much else, this had been anticipated by the Long Parliament: see Ch. 4, "The Courts".

of the eighteenth century: the understanding that the Crown's ministers were answerable politically to Parliament and legally to the courts – in other words, that sovereignty within the state was not triangular but bilateral.[8] It was the political upheavals of the 1760s which crystallised the distinction between power, which ministers were exercising energetically in the name of the Crown, and sovereignty, which resided elsewhere in the state. When Bacon in 1625 had warned the judges against checking or opposing "any points of sovereignty", the location of sovereignty was still contested. The events of the 1760s were violent, messy and complicated, and many of their consequences were unanticipated by any of the participants; but it was the constitutional law which emerged from them that established Parliament's sovereign entitlement to the final word on what the law was to be, the judges' sovereign entitlement to the final word on what the law was, and the subjection of the executive to both.

The Vicar of Bray

The political and religious history of the seventeenth and eighteenth centuries is too rich and too complex to be described here, but if you want a reasonably accurate, if cynical, overview of the vicissitudes that England went through between the Restoration and the Hanoverian succession, you could do worse than recall the ballad of *The Vicar of Bray:*[9]

> In good King Charles's golden days
> When loyalty no harm meant
> A zealous High Churchman was I
> And so I got preferment.
> To teach my flock I never missed
> Kings were by God appointed
> And cursed were they who dared resist
> Or touch the Lord's anointed
>
> And this is the law that I'll maintain
> Until my dying day, sir,
> That whatsoever king may reign
> I'll still be the Vicar of Bray, sir.

---

[8] "In our society the rule of law rests upon twin foundations: the sovereignty of the Queen in Parliament in making the law and the sovereignty of the Queen's courts in interpreting and applying the law": *X v. Morgan-Grampian Ltd* [1991] 1 AC 1, 48, per Lord Bridge.

[9] The authorship of the song is uncertain, but its protagonist was based on a real sixteenth-century Vicar of Bray in Berkshire who had managed to keep his living and his head through the successive reigns of Henry VIII, Edward VI, Mary Tudor and Elizabeth I.

When royal James possessed the crown
And Popery grew in fashion
The penal laws I hooted down
And read the Declaration.[10]
The Church of Rome I found would fit
Full well my constitution
And I'd have been a Jesuit
But for the Revolution.

When William was our king declared
To ease the nation's grievance
With this new wind about I steered
And swore to him allegiance.
Old principles I did revoke,
Set conscience at a distance,
Passive obedience was a joke,
A jest was non-resistance.

When gracious Anne became our queen,
The Church of England's glory,
Another face of things was seen
And I became a Tory.
Occasional Conformists base
I blamed their moderation
And thought the church in danger was
By such prevarication.

When George in pudding-time[11] came o'er
And moderate men looked big, sir
I turned a cat-in-pan[12] once more
And I became a Whig, sir;
And this preferment I procured
From our new faith's defender
And almost every day abjured
The Pope and the Pretender.

The illustrious House of Hanover
And protestant succession
To these I do allegiance swear –
While they can keep possession.
For in my faith and loyalty
I never more will falter

[10] Viz the royal Declaration of Indulgence of 1687 suspending the laws against Catholics and Nonconformists.
[11] In the nick of time.   [12] A turncoat (Fr. *côté en peine*).

And George my lawful king shall be –
Until the times do alter.

And this is the law that I'll maintain
Until my dying day, sir,
That whatsoever king may reign
I'll still be the Vicar of Bray, sir.

The Hanoverian harvest

The great lawsuits of the 1760s had four effects of historic importance. One was to inhibit the use of executive power to intimidate dissenters and suppress free expression, a development which has continued to resonate worldwide, from the first amendment to the Constitution of the United States to article 19 of the Universal Declaration of Human Rights. A second effect was to establish that ministers are answerable to the law. A third was to separate the administration of justice from executive government by denying ministers power to issue search or arrest warrants. The fourth, still relevant today,[13] was to invalidate general warrants – that is to say warrants which allowed the officers executing them to choose where to search and whom to arrest.

Wilkes and liberty

John Wilkes, at least in the severe eye of history, though not in the eyes of the Georgian crowd, had very little to commend him. A rake who had married money, he was a gifted demagogue to whose lips the word "freedom" readily sprang but whose principles extended little further than repeatedly advocating war with France and with Spain. In 1757 he secured election to Parliament by the customary means of bribing the 40-shilling freeholders who were Aylesbury's only voters, a process which he complained had cost him some £7,000. In 1762, with Charles Church-ill, Wilkes founded and began to co-edit the *North Briton*, a periodical counterblast to the Bute administration's weekly journal, the *Briton*, which was being edited by Tobias Smollett. The *North Briton* ran to forty-five issues between June 1762 and April 1763. It was issue no. 45 which led to the closure of the paper and changed the course of history.

[13] See n. 17.

The *North Briton*, like Wilkes himself, was short on policy but long on vituperation of the government, of Lord Bute personally and of the Scots he had brought into his administration. When Bute resigned in April 1763, it looked as if issue no. 44 of the *North Briton*, which had come out nine days earlier, was going to be its last. But a week after Bute's resignation the King opened Parliament with a speech, written (as it still is) by his ministers, which aroused the ire of Wilkes and his friends by its support for the terms of peace which were being negotiated with France. The leading article (its authorship is still uncertain, though it may well have been Wilkes' work) took care to attribute the King's speech to his ministers but went on to denounce

> the most odious measures and the most unjustifiable public declarations from a throne ever renowned for truth, honour and an unsullied virtue.

This was too much for the new prime minister, George Grenville, and his Secretary of State Lord Halifax. With the advice of the Treasury Solicitor, Philip Carteret Webb, they decided that the publication was a seditious libel and set out to close the *North Briton* down by issuing a warrant for the arrest of its authors, printers and publishers – a general warrant, in other words, of a kind which appears until then to have been issued regularly by ministers *ex officio*. Having issued it, the ministers ordered the King's Messengers to arrest George Kearsley as the publisher and Dryden Leach and Richard Balfe as the successive printers of the paper. Interrogated before the Home Secretary, they named Wilkes as the editor of issue no. 45. The Law Officers advised that if Wilkes was also the author of the article he would not be protected by parliamentary privilege, and he was accordingly arrested.

The usefulness of a general warrant to an irritated government was now plain. In all, forty-five arrests were made under the *North Briton* warrant. It enabled limitless speculative searches to be undertaken and was a great deal more convenient than having to find reasonable grounds for suspecting a named individual.[14] The disruption of anti-government activity was a useful end in itself, even if no indictment for seditious libel resulted. The Treasury Solicitor's private notes, which have survived, show that he advised specifically against naming Wilkes in the warrant.

Whether thanks to Wilkes' self-confidence or to hesitancy on the part of the Messengers, Wilkes was able, before being formally arrested, to

---

[14] It is now known that a general warrant in the same terms had been drawn up, though not issued, in November 1762 after publication of an earlier number of the *North Briton*.

go to Balfe's printshop, destroy the manuscript of no. 45 and take no. 46 off the press. He then accompanied the messengers, in a sedan chair, the few yards to Lord Halifax's house, where he refused to answer any questions. Meanwhile his lawyers were applying to the Chief Justice of the Court of Common Pleas, Sir Charles Pratt (later Lord Camden), for a writ of habeas corpus requiring the Messengers who had arrested him to justify his detention. The application was granted, but because Wilkes was by then in the hands of the Secretaries of State a new writ was needed, and while it was awaited Halifax had Wilkes's house ransacked.

A fresh writ of habeas corpus eventually secured Wilkes' production before the judges at Westminster Hall. With a sympathetic audience packed into the court, Wilkes took the opportunity to make a rousing speech on his own behalf before his counsel, Serjeant Glynn, was able to get a word in edgewise. Unlike Wilkes, who had taken the point that general warrants were illegal the moment he was arrested, Glynn did not at this stage raise the issue. But he succeeded in his submission that it required a breach of the peace to defeat an MP's immunity for things done outside the House, and the court agreed that there was no breach of the peace here.

While the Law Officers debated whether to take the case against Wilkes to the King's Bench, where they thought (mistakenly as it turned out) that Lord Mansfield might be better disposed towards the government than Pratt evidently was, Wilkes struck first. He issued civil proceedings against Halifax and his underlings for trespass and assault, starting a small avalanche of successful claims. In July 1763 – litigation moved at a decent pace in those days – William Huckle and thirteen other printers were awarded a total of £2,900 in damages for trespass, assault and false imprisonment. An attempt to set aside the £1,000 that the jury had awarded Huckle gave the Court of Common Pleas the opportunity, in refusing the application, to point out that the fact that the Messengers had treated the plaintiff "very civilly . . . with beefsteaks and beer" did not mitigate the gravity of the government's "exercising arbitrary power, violating Magna Carta, and attempting to destroy the liberty of the subject".[15]

In December 1763 Wilkes was awarded £1,000 against the under-Secretary of State Robert Wood for trespass to his house and papers.[16]

---

[15] *Huckle* v. *Money* (1763) 2 Wils. KB 205   [16] *Wilkes* v. *Wood* (1763) 2 Wils. KB 204

In separate proceedings in 1765 Dryden Leach recovered £400 against the King's Messengers who had mistakenly arrested him as the printer of issue no. 45. Burrow's report of *Leach's Case* has the shortest headnote in the entire body of law reports: "General warrants illegal".[17] One result of Leach's victory was that by 1769, when Wilkes' own action against Lord Halifax finally came to trial, the illegality of the general warrant was settled law and the only surprise – at least to Wilkes' supporters – was that the jury awarded him a mere £4,000 in damages.

Entick v. Carrington

The greatest and most enduring of the free-speech cases, because the most fully reasoned, was the case mounted on the back of the others by the Rev. John Entick against the four King's Messengers of whom Nathan Carrington happened to be the first-named. Entick had had nothing to do with the *North Briton*: he was the editor of an opposition paper named *The Monitor*.[18] His home had been raided the previous November under a warrant, likewise issued by Lord Halifax, authorising his arrest together with a search of his premises and seizure of any seditious matter found there. It was the early victories of Wilkes and others following the *North Briton* raid that prompted Entick to bring his own claim. Heard in 1765, it gave the Court of Common Pleas the opportunity which the chief justice had wanted to deliver a fully reasoned judgment on fundamental questions of personal liberty in the post-1689 state.

Although Entick himself had been arrested, he had been named in the warrant, and there was authority to support a defence that a secretary of state had power to commit (and hence to arrest) for sedition as well as for treason. Entick's counsel therefore stuck to the unresolved question of ministerial powers of search and seizure, limiting his claim to trespass to Entick's house and goods.

---

[17] *Leach* v. *Money* (1765) 3 Burr. 1742. In 2012 the New Zealand High Court reasserted the common law's objection to general warrants, holding the warrant used to raid the home of an internet maverick accused of breaching US copyrights to be void for generality: *Dotcom* v. *A-G* [2012] NZHC 1494, paras. 27–8 (Winkelmann J). The decision was overset on appeal by a majority of the NZ Supreme Court [2014] NZSC 199; but see the cogent dissent of Elias CJ.

[18] (1765) 19 St. Tr. 1035

Two defences were advanced: that a secretary of state had the status and powers of a justice of the peace, so that Carrington was entitled the protection given by the Constables Protection Act 1750[19] to persons executing a justice's warrant; alternatively that Lord Halifax had authority to issue a search warrant as a minister of the Crown and a privy counsellor. Although there was authority to support the first defence and a history of unchallenged ministerial practice to support the second, both defences failed.

Lord Camden's account of how the Royal Household's secretaries had come *de facto* to exercise large state powers is knowledgeable and important. So are his reasons for holding that a secretary of state as a privy counsellor possessed no power to authorise arrests (except collectively in council in cases of treason), whether as a conservator of the peace or as a minister of the Crown; and that long practice could not give colour of law to an illegal assumption of judicial power.

There was authority,[20] some of it deriving from the great chief justice of the post-1689 generation Sir John Holt, and there was good evidence of previously unchallenged practice, both of which pointed in the opposite direction and which the Court of Common Pleas could have adopted in order to validate Halifax's warrant. That they refused to do so, and that instead they reasoned to an opposite conclusion, has had implications of enduring constitutional importance. Taking a critical step in the developing separation of the state's powers, the court made it clear that it was the job of the justice system, not of politicians, to enforce the law: JPs, but not ministers, had the power to order search and arrest, and then only of named premises or persons.

There is an ongoing debate[21] about what *Entick* v. *Carrington* formally decided, both because the claim was purely in trespass to land and goods, and because Camden in his judgment seemingly took the court to be bound by the cases which had upheld ministerial powers of arrest.[22] If in reality he was deferring to these decisions, the rest of his judgment was obiter; but Holdsworth's view was that he was declining to follow them.[23] In this situation what matters is what history and law have made of

---

[19] 24 Geo. 2 c.44

[20] *R* v. *Kendall and Rowe* (1700) 1 Ld. Raym. 65; *R* v. *Derby* (1711) Fort. 140; *R* v. *Erbury* (1722) 8 Mod. 177

[21] See T. Hickman, 'Revisiting *Entick* v. *Carrington*' in A. Tomkins and P. Scott (eds.), Entick *v.* Carrington – *250 Years of the Rule of Law* (2015).

[22] "We are now bound by the case of *R* v. *Derby* and *R* v. *Earbury*".

[23] W. S. Holdsworth, *A History of English Law*, Vol. X (1938), p. 667

Camden's judgment, which for 250 years has been taken to establish that in the United Kingdom executive office[24] carries no judicial powers.

Freedom of expression

It was suggested earlier in this chapter that a prime effect of *Entick* v. *Carrington* and the *North Briton* cases was to inhibit the use of state power to suppress freedom of expression. While this can legitimately be perceived as a long-term outcome, it was certainly not an immediately perceptible effect in England, where prosecutions continued to be brought for seditious libel against anyone who publicly criticised government activity or policy.

One of these prosecutions was against John Horne Tooke, who in June 1775 had placed an advertisement in a number of newspapers (the printers of which were also prosecuted) appealing for funds for the dependants of "our beloved American fellow-subjects" who had been "murdered by the King's troops at or near Lexington and Concord". The chief justice of the King's Bench, Lord Mansfield (a former Attorney-General), who imposed heavy sentences on conviction and was a known hawk during the American War of Independence, became a hate-figure in the United States.[25] When Madison's Bill of Rights secured ratification in December 1791, the first amendment it made to the new constitution was to add:

> Congress shall make no law ... abridging the freedom of speech, or of the press.

Whether or not this provision was motivated by antipathy to the current use of criminal law in Britain, it was rapidly honoured in the breach, first by the enactment of the federal Sedition Act 1798 to suppress support for revolutionary France, then by states' use of the common law of seditious libel against dissidents.[26] It was not until the twentieth century[27] that the culture of liberality now associated with the First Amendment manifested itself, finally justifying Wilkes' boast:

---

[24] With the anomalous exception, until the Constitutional Reform Act 2005, of the office of Lord Chancellor. "The whole office of the Lord Chancellor is a heap of anomalies": W. Bagehot, *The English Constitution* (2nd edn, 1889) p. 225.

[25] See N. S. Poser, *Lord Mansfield: Justice in the Age of Reason* (2013), p. 312.

[26] R. Hargreaves, *The First Freedom: A History of Free Speech* (2002), pp. 183–94, p. 89

[27] *Schenk* v. *United States* 249 US 47 (1919); cf. *Abrams* v. *United States* 250 US 616 (1919)

The liberty of the press is the birthright of a Briton, and is justly esteemed
the firmest bulwark of the liberties of this country.[28]

Equality before the law

A third effect of the *North Briton* cases, albeit a negative one, has
continuing implications for the principle of equality before the law. Until
the Crown Proceedings Act 1947 the Crown, at least in England and
Wales, could not be sued in tort. But in none of the *North Briton* cases
did any defendant, from the Secretary of State to the King's Messengers,
attempt to shelter behind the Crown – that is, to submit that because the
monarch was beyond the reach of the law of trespass and assault, so were
his ministers. Lord Halifax dragged out Wilkes' lawsuit against him until
1769 by seeking to plead his status as a peer, but he did not attempt to
invoke his office as a minister of the Crown as a bar to the claim; and
when Wilkes' case reached the Court of Common Pleas, the new chief
justice, Lord Wilmot, told the jury:

> The law makes no difference between great and petty officers. Thank God,
> they are all amenable to justice, and the law will reach them if they step
> over the boundaries which the law has prescribed.[29]

The amenability of ministers of the Crown to legal process did not
become a discrete issue again until, in 1990, it was resurrected in the
case of *M* v. *Home Office*. In between, a striking opportunity had
occurred to take the point. In 1865 the governor of Jamaica, Edward
Eyre – the Queen's own representative in the colony, with plenary
legislative powers – put down a local rising with appalling brutality and
was sued in this country for some of the things he did in the course of it.
He pleaded in his defence an act of indemnity to which, as governor, he
had set his own hand in order to immunise himself from lawsuits or
prosecutions arising out of the revolt. But, although represented and
advised by a future Lord Chancellor, Hardinge Giffard QC (Lord Halsbury), Eyre never attempted to argue that as the Queen's alter ego he was
beyond the reach of the law.

It was not until the late twentieth century that this was attempted. By
then some of the lessons of the *North Briton* had faded in the bright light

---

[28] Hargreaves, *The First Freedom*, p. 89 – a claim which now sits under the long shadow of
the endemic misconduct which prompted the Leveson Inquiry.

[29] *Wilkes* v. *Lord Halifax* (1769) 19 St. Tr. 1406

of the expanding Victorian state and of Disraeli's near-deification of Victoria as Queen-Empress, giving rise to a largely unspoken belief, despite Dicey's famous assertion to the contrary, that not only the monarch but her ministers stood above the general law.

Ministers and the courts today

On 23 September 1990, a young Zairean teacher named Makunsa Mbala, who had been arrested and tortured for organising public protests against the regime of General Mobutu, sought asylum in the UK. The Home Office disbelieved him, but a report from the Medical Foundation for the Care of Victims of Torture confirmed the likelihood that his condition was the result of severe beatings. An emergency application for permission to bring a claim for judicial review against the Home Office was adjourned on the Home Secretary's undertaking that Mbala would not be removed from the UK in the meantime. Despite this, he was put on a plane for Kinshasa. The judge ordered his return but, in the erroneous belief that the order had been made without jurisdiction, the Home Secretary ignored it. Proceedings were accordingly issued to have the Home Secretary committed to prison or fined. In due course he was held, first by a majority of the Court of Appeal[30] and then by a unanimous House of Lords,[31] to have been guilty of contempt of court, though because he had acted on advice he was spared any penalty.[32]

Makunsa Mbala never got back to Britain, but he had changed our constitutional law and our legal history.[33] The law lords' confirmation that ministers of the Crown and their executive departments answer to the courts not as a matter of grace but as a matter of constitutional and legal obligation was described by Professor Wade[34] as the most important decision of our courts for over 200 years – in effect since *Entick* v. *Carrington*.

The full reasons for the decision were spelt out in the speech of Lord Woolf, himself a former standing counsel to the Crown; but one can

---

[30] [1992] QB 270   [31] [1994] 1 AC 377

[32] For a fuller account of this case see S. Sedley, *Ashes and Sparks* (2011), Ch. 28, "The Crown in its own Courts".

[33] Legal aid was granted to enable him to pursue his application and to resist the Home Secretary's appeal.

[34] H. W. R. Wade, case comment [1992] 108 LQR 173; "The Crown – old platitudes and new heresies", [1992] 142 NLJ 1275, suggesting that the claim to ministerial immunity from suit "would mean the end of the rule of law in its generally accepted sense".

settle for Lord Templeman's concurring speech in which he set out in brief terms the modern constitutional position and – in a sentence that echoes Lord Justice Diplock's judgment in *Ex parte Lain*[35] – pointed out that the Home Secretary's stance, were it correct, would reverse the result of the Civil War. There are no doubt people who would like to do this; but it would return us not to good King Charles's golden days – an imagined tranquil age of benign absolutism – but to a seething quarrel between monarch, ministers, Parliament and judges about where state power lay.

[35] See Introduction, p. 18 above.

4

Parchment in the fire: public law in the Interregnum

Official history has not been generous to the republicans who in the middle years of the seventeenth century defeated the king in a civil war and tried to construct a democracy without a hereditary upper chamber or a monarchy. Their legislation, which has been deleted from the statute book, reveals a series of endeavours to reform the law in ways which it has taken most of the intervening centuries to retrace. It included, in the Instrument of Government 1653, Britain's first and only written constitution, on which the framers of the Bill of Rights twenty-five years later perceptibly drew.

Doing history

If the history you were taught at school is anything like the history I was taught at school, your picture of the mid-seventeenth century probably goes something like this:

> In 1642, an army of republicans with cropped heads and round helmets, led by Oliver Cromwell, started a civil war which ended in 1649 with the defeat of the Cavaliers and the execution of King Charles I. The country was taken over by psalm-singing Puritans in tall hats and black cloaks, who closed the theatres, abolished Christmas and made everyone's life a misery until Charles II was restored to the throne in 1660. Not long afterwards, in 1689, the Glorious Revolution gave us a constitutional monarchy.

Or as Sellar and Yeatman immortally recounted it in *1066 and All That*:

> Charles I was a Cavalier King and therefore had a small pointed beard, long flowing curls, a large, flat, flowing hat and *gay attire.* The Round-heads, on the other hand, were clean-shaven and wore tall, conical hats, white ties and *sombre garments.* Under these circumstances a Civil War was inevitable.

When I read for the Bar in the early 1960s, the lecturer who taught legal history stopped when he reached 1649 and moved on directly to 1660 because, he explained, everything that had happened in between was a legal nullity. Using the same airbrush, the definitive edition of the *Statutes at Large*[1] stops abruptly with the Long Parliament's first year, 1640–1, and resumes on the next page with the first acts of the Restoration parliament in the year 1660, "the twelfth year of the reign of our most gracious sovereign lord Charles the Second".[2] In this way the eighteen years of the Civil War and the English Republic have been wiped from the pages of our legal history. They are referred to either as the Interregnum – the space between two reigns – or, in the sobriquet devised by the Victorian historian S. R. Gardiner, the Puritan Revolution.

The context

Charles I had ruled without a Parliament from 1629 until, in 1640, he was finally compelled to summon one. Although it became a conservative rump in its later years, the Long Parliament came in like a March wind: in its first year it halted government by prerogative power and abolished Star Chamber and the other prerogative courts;[3] it took away the criminal jurisdiction of the ecclesiastical courts;[4] it confined the issue of all new proceedings to the regular courts of law; and it reversed the infamous ship money judgment.[5] The vacancy in sovereign power brought about by the execution of the King in February 1649 was filled by legislation passed within weeks to abolish the monarchy and

---

[1] Ed. Danby Pickering (1763)

[2] It was not until 1911 that the Statute Law Committee completed the record by publishing the *Acts and Ordinances of the Interregnum*, ed. C. H. Firth and R. S. Rait (hereafter "Firth and Rait"). The term "act" is used for legislative measures of Parliament acting as sole sovereign authority between January 1649 and May 1660, following the Commons resolution of 4 January 1949 declaring "That whatsoever is enacted or declared for law by the Commons in Parliament assembled, hath the force of law ... although the consent and concurrence of the King or House of Peers be not had thereunto". The term "ordinance" is used for (a) the measures of the Long Parliament between 1642 and 1649, which passed the Lords but never received the royal assent, and (b) those measures of Oliver Cromwell as Lord Protector between 1653 and 1654 which did not subsequently receive Parliament's endorsement as required by the Instrument of Government.

[3] 16 Car.I, c.10. This act, however, was considered not to have abolished the Privy Council's appellate jurisdiction over the Channel Islands, a jurisdiction which grew after the Restoration to encompass the American and other colonies: see J. H. Smith, *Appeals to the Privy Council from the American Plantations* (1950).

[4] 16 Car.I, c.11   [5] 16 Car.I, c.14

the House of Lords[6] and to elevate the Speaker into the space formerly occupied by the Crown.

On 20 April 1653 Cromwell arrived at the House of Commons with a detachment of musketeers from his own regiment, cleared it of MPs and dissolved his own council of state. Two months later, in his capacity as Captain-General of the Army, he summoned a Parliament of members nominated by the congregational churches in each county.[7] But, far from sucking society into a religious vortex, the nominated Parliament which history has chosen to name after one of its more obscure Puritan members, Praisegod Barebones, set about initiating some serious reforms. To the chagrin of the established church and the legal profession the Barebones Parliament instituted civil marriage, revived the project of disestablishing the Church of England and set in earnest about reforming the law and the courts.

These were not Parliament's own ideas. They had all surfaced during the Civil War of the 1640s[8] when – as a Digger pamphlet put it – the old world was running up like parchment in the fire[9] and for a time, especially to the people at the bottom of society, everything seemed possible.

A Puritan revolution?

What did Puritanism have to do with any of this? In one sense almost everything, in a second sense almost nothing.

The sense in which the twelve years of the Commonwealth and the Protectorate can properly be called a Puritan revolution is the sense in which the historian Christopher Hill read Puritanism: as the amalgam of social, political and religious dissent which had challenged the established church and the monarchy since the later sixteenth century. Like many other factions – Quakers, Levellers, Ranters – the name Puritan was given to them by their opponents. "Rascal people," Bishop Sanderson remarked, "will call any man that beareth but the face of honesty a

---

[6] Firth and Rait, vol. I, p. 18 ("... the office of a King ... is unnecessary, burthensom and dangerous..."), p. 24 ("... finding by long experience, that the House of Lords is useless and dangerous to the People...").

[7] See S. R. Gardiner, *The Constitutional Documents of the Puritan Revolution, 1625–1660* (2nd edn, 1899), p. 405.

[8] See Donald Veall, *The Popular Movement for Law Reform, 1640–1660* (1970).

[9] John Taylor *et al.* (including Gerard Winstanley), *The True Levellers Standard Advanced* (1649). "In the beginning of time, the great Creator, Reason, made the earth to be a common treasury ...".

Puritan".[10] Francis Bacon considered that "the greatest part of the body of the subjects" were "honest religious men ... traduced by" the name Puritan.[11] The name had come by the time of the Civil War to include any opponent of the hierarchy and the Court. It is why Hill considered Puritan a valid portmanteau term for the very large body of citizens who wanted radical change in the state, in church policy, in religious practice and in private morality – the broad body of dissent which contemporaries also took the word to mean.[12] In this large and loose sense, the Civil War can be said to have ushered in a Puritan revolution.

Within the movement for change, however, though without any formal organisation, was a body of protestant sectarians, some of them the kind of zealot who, as Bishop Curle put it, loved God with all his soul and hated his neighbour with all his heart.[13] In this second and narrow sense, Puritanism was not central to the revolutionary events of the Interregnum; but, like other militant orthodoxies, it had an influence well beyond its immediate adherents. The New Model Army marched into battle singing psalms. Rather worse, the Long Parliament in May 1648 was induced to enact an ordinance making any denial of protestant religious orthodoxy – spelt out at great theological length – a capital felony without benefit of clergy.[14]

Censorship and cultural liberation

One result of the Long Parliament's abolition of Star Chamber was that licensing of the press broke down. Newspapers, which until then had

---

[10] R. Sanderson, *Sermons XXXV*, cit. Hill, *Society and Puritanism in Pre-Revolutionary England* (1964), p. 16.

[11] Bacon, *Works, XIV*, p. 449, cit. Hill, *Society and Puritanism*.

[12] See Hill, *Society and Puritanism*, Ch. 1 *passim*. Cf. the exchange about the meaning of Puritanism between Richard Hoggart, who had described *Lady Chatterley's Lover* in the witness box as "almost puritanical", and the prosecutor, Mervyn Griffith-Jones QC, who asked: "I must have lived my entire life under a misapprehension as to the meaning of the word 'puritanical'; will you help me?" "Yes," said Hoggart, ignoring the sarcasm, "many people do live their lives under a misapprehension of the meaning of the word 'puritanical'. This is the way in which language decays.... The word has been extended to mean somebody who is against anything pleasurable, particularly sex. The proper meaning ... is somebody who belongs to the tradition of British puritanism generally, and the distinguishing feature of that is an intense sense of responsibility for one's conscience. In this sense the book is puritanical."

[13] *Diary of John Manningham*, quoted by C. Hill, *Society and Puritanism*, p. 24.

[14] An Ordinance for the punishing of blasphemies and heresies, 2 May 1648: Firth and Rait, vol. I, p. 1133

been confined to foreign news, began reporting home affairs. As the Civil War broke out and ran its course, a flood of pamphlets, typeset in small printshops all over the country, came on to the streets, many of them selling well over a thousand copies an issue. The press controls which Parliament sought to reimpose in 1643 failed to work.

But once the monarchy had been displaced and Parliament was in sole command, the religious Puritan element found itself able to exert its influence on the law. In the Rump and Nominated Parliaments the godly succeeded in prohibiting the sale of goods on the Sabbath (a prohibition which lasted well into the twentieth century), in criminalising "dancing, profanely singing, drinking or tippling" on Sundays, in making adultery a capital felony and fornication a misdemeanour, and in setting a tariff of fines[15] for swearing and cursing. At the same time popular newspapers like the *Mercurius Democritus* continued to flourish.

It was in 1642 that the Long Parliament had first legislated to close the theatres. There is little doubt that this was principally the work of the Puritan element in the House of Commons, but Puritan in the broad political, not the narrow sectarian, sense. The theatre, in long decline from its Elizabethan and Jacobean heyday, was seen as one of the strongholds of royalism. But it has also been suggested[16] that the closure of the theatres had the effect of shutting down a forum for radical agitation, as the levelling movement gained support and cohesion within and beyond the New Model Army. The ban was enforced much more rigorously against the theatres than against other forms of popular entertainment. In October 1647 a new ordinance[17] authorised the sheriffs of London, Middlesex and Surrey to raid theatres and arrest anyone found acting in them; and the following February an ordinance[18] was made "for the utter suppression and abolishing of all stage-plays and interludes [with] the penalties to be inflicted on the actors and spectators . . . ". Seized box-office takings were to be distributed to the poor.

---

[15] The tariff was scrupulously egalitarian: a lord who swore was to be fined thirty shillings, a baronet or knight twenty shillings, a gentleman six shillings and eightpence, and a commoner three shillings and fourpence.

[16] M. Heinemann, *Puritanism and Theatre* (1980), Chs. 12, 13. Heinemann suggests that it was in the radical pamphlets of the Civil War that the English of the King James Bible (the only book, she points out, that many of the rank and file will have known) continued to thrive.

[17] Firth and Rait, vol. I, p. 1027   [18] Ibid., vol. I, p. 1070

After 1660, however, the popular playhouses were not refurbished or rebuilt. Attempts were made to revive popular drama; but the continental culture that returned with the court and the cavaliers demanded a different and more elaborate stage, and the patents granted in 1663 to Thomas Killigrew for Drury Lane and to Sir William Davenant[19] for Covent Garden stifled the renascent demotic theatre and exerted an influence on style and content which is with us to this day.

The bad times through which the English stage undoubtedly went in the mid-seventeenth century were thus the product of far more than the hostility of religious bigots. And there are many indicators that, in other spheres, cultural freedom flourished in these years. To take a single example, the Stationers' Company in 1650 licensed the publication by the bookseller and musicologist John Playford, who had his shop by the porch of the Temple Church,[20] of The English Dancing Master. The book, which went through numerous editions, growing to three volumes by the mid-nineteenth century, carried the tunes and the steps for a large number of traditional English dances, some of which would have been lost but for Playford's enterprise. What was particularly significant in 1650 was the book's title. Until the fall of the monarchy, every dancing master, and every fashionable dance, had been French. The recovery of English popular dance was as much a political as a cultural gesture and one which, judging by the number of editions through which the book rapidly ran,[21] found a ready uptake. It also appears to have encountered no obstacle from the Puritan lobby which we have learned to believe spent the 1650s stifling such pastimes; though Playford, himself a serious musicologist and historian, grumbled after the Restoration that "all solemn musick is much laid aside, being too heavy and dull for the light heels and brains of this nimble and wanton age".

The tale that the Puritans abolished Christmas probably originates with an ordinance passed in December 1644[22] to deal with the problem that the coming Christmas Day fell on the last Wednesday of the month, which was by tradition a religious fasting day. For this one year

---

[19] Even so, Davenant's Siege of Rhodes, generally reckoned to be the first English opera, was staged under the Protectorate in 1656.
[20] The rent was £2 a year.
[21] The second edition, in 1653, dropped the word 'English' from the title: the first edition had sufficiently made the point, and the book's success was already assured.
[22] Firth and Rait, vol. I, p. 580

Puritanism got its way: the fast was to take precedence over the feast. This was followed by Parliament's adoption in 1645 of a Directory of Public Worship which sought to eliminate all the principal religious festivals – Easter, Whitsun and Christmas – because of their pagan origins and Popish associations, in favour of a more sober calendar.[23] But the ordinances which sought to give legal effect to the Directory of Public Worship had the reverse effect, attested by a large and heated pamphlet literature, of driving the seasonal festivals out of the churches and into the secular world, where Christmas has remained to this day. Whatever else the Puritan sectaries achieved, they did not succeed in abolishing Christmas, though they may well have done a good deal of harm to popular support for the republic by trying to.[24]

Popular grievances

The English Civil War was not a war of the rich against the poor.

> "The establishment of parliamentary supremacy," wrote Christopher Hill, "[and] of the rule of law, no doubt mainly benefited the men of property. But on any showing the abolition of Star Chamber and High Commission and monopolies were to the advantage of the majority of Englishmen. And political ideas had outstripped constitutional achievement. The course of the Revolution itself led to the emergence of systematic democratic political theories, for the first time in modern history."[25]

The common lawyers in general supported Parliament, at least until it started undermining their lucrative privileges. At the outset of the Civil War the Inns of Court raised an élite troop, some of whose members went on to achieve high military rank, to serve as a lifeguard for

---

[23] In June 1647 an Ordinance for Abolishing of Festivals (Firth and Rait, vol. I, p. 954) sought to replace the three main church festivals with a holiday for students, servants and apprentices on the second Tuesday of every month. In subsequent years shops were allowed to open on Christmas Day (provoking riots in London and East Anglia), and Parliament sat. In Kent, official attempts to suppress Christmas in 1647 probably helped to consolidate support for the monarchy in the Second Civil War. John Lambert (see below) saw, too late, that the attempt to abolish traditional festivities had much to do with the eventual failure of the republican enterprise to retain popular support. Not for the last time, sectarianism had first infiltrated and then debilitated a popular movement.

[24] See Christopher Durston, "Lords of Misrule: the Puritan War on Christmas, 1642–1660", 35 (12) (1985) *History Today* 7. The antipathy is found at least as early as Stubbes' *Anatomie of Abuses* (1583). The Puritans had a point, for these were indeed pagan festivals.

[25] C. Hill, *Puritanism and Revolution* (1958), pp. 30–1

Cromwell, Fairfax and Monck.[26] Notwithstanding this, the stranglehold
of the legal profession on access to the courts, with their arcane script and
impenetrable jargon, most of it in Latin and law French, their colossal
fees, their interminable procedures and their devious practices, was one
of the major grievances of the radical pamphleteers of the 1640s. These
without any doubt were voicing the views of a large section of the
population, running from Puritan dissidents to Cromwell himself, and
including some of the more honest lawyers.

> "There is one general grievance in the nation," said Cromwell to Parliament
> in September 1656. "It is the law … There are wicked and abominable
> laws that will be in your power to alter. To hang a man for six-and-
> eightpence and I know not what … This is a thing God will reckon for."[27]

Discontent with lawyers and the law was profound and longstanding.[28]
One of the most penetrating of the radical commentators, John Warr,
wrote in 1649:

> When the poor and oppressed want right, they meet with law, which
> (as 'tis managed) is their greatest wrong … [T]he web of the law entan-
> gles the small flies and dismisseth the great …[29]
>
> "Why," asked Warr,[30] "are there so many delays, turnings and wind-
> ings in the law of England?
>
> Why is our law a meander of intricacies, where a man must have
> contrary winds before he can arrive at his desired port?
>
> Why are so many men destroyed for want of a formality and punctilio
> in the law? …
>
> Why do the issue of most lawsuits depend upon precedents rather than
> the rule, especially the rule of reason?
>
> Why are men's lives forfeited by the law on light and trivial grounds? …
>
> Why is the law still kept in an unknown tongue … ?
>
> Why are courts not rejourned into every county, that the people may
> have right at their own doors …?

---

[26] C. Firth and G. Davies, *Regimental History of Cromwell's Army* (1991), vol. I, p. 43

[27] W. C. Abbott, *Writings and Speeches of Oliver Cromwell* (1937), vol. IV, p. 274, quo.
Veall, *The Popular Movement for Law Reform*, p. 1. This is the version generally cited; but
C. L. Stainer's 1901 edition of Cromwell's speeches gives "sixpence, thirteen pence,
I know not what" – a phrase which makes more sense, because a value of twelve pence
was enough to make a theft a felony.

[28] See Barbara Shapiro, "Law Reform in Seventeenth Century England', 19(4) (1975) *Am. Jo.
of Legal History*, 280.

[29] John Warr, *The Corruption and Deficiency of the Laws of England* (June 1649), Ch. II,
reprinted in S. Sedley and L. Kaplan (eds.), *A Spark in the Ashes, the Pamphlets of John
Warr* (1992)

[30] Ibid., Ch. III

Warr's concluding hope "that the reformation of the times will be in the breasts of our reformers" proved not to be entirely vain.

Alongside radical writers like Warr, the more moderate reformers included the former Solicitor-General John Cooke, who had conducted the prosecution of Charles I with exemplary fairness. Cooke never sided with the radicals in calling for a legal system free of lawyers, but he shared their frustration at the cost and complexity of the system. Law reform, Cooke wrote, was the "one great thing that my honoured friends in the Army told me they fought for".[31] When Parliament in late 1649 appointed him Chief Justice of Munster he set about implementing his ideas. In a remarkable step, three full centuries ahead of its time, he empowered his judges to administer both law and equity.[32] Cromwell told Edmund Ludlow that Cooke, "by proceeding in a summary and expeditious way, determined more causes in a week than Westminster Hall in a year".[33] One consequence of this, Cooke said in his speech from the scaffold in 1660, was that he faced "more than ordinary persecution"[34] from the legal profession. It was not until 2012 that Gray's Inn, of which he was a member, finally commemorated him.[35]

Gaol for debt

The gaoling of debtors at the suit of their creditors, or – just as often – of people who claimed to be their creditors, was a running sore of Jacobean society. Since land could not be distrained on, the usefulness of gaol was to squeeze those who appeared to have some resources for cash as the price of liberty; those who were visibly penniless were mostly left alone. One of Cooke's chief proposals, reform of the law of debt, became a reality early in the life of the Commonwealth. Instead of sending hard-up debtors to sit indefinitely in prison, two acts passed in late 1649[36] allowed them, on proof that they were worth no more than £5 in addition to their

[31] Letter to the Lord Deputy (1655), cited by Veall, *The Popular Movement for Law Reform*, p. 73 n. 5.

[32] Veall, *The Popular Movement for Law Reform*, pp. 184–5

[33] E. Ludlow, *Memoirs* (1894), vol. I, p. 246, cited by Veall, *The Popular Movement for Law Reform*, p. 113, fn 1.

[34] See G. Robertson, *The Tyrannicide Brief* (2005), a political biography of Cooke.

[35] In 2012 Gray's Inn staged a play based on Geoffrey Robertson's biography of Cooke, and added to its collection of portraits those of Cooke and of John Bradshaw, the judge who presided at the King's trial.

[36] Firth and Rait, vol. II, pp. 240–1; 321–44

clothing, bedding and tools, to secure discharge from prison, though not from their indebtedness.

The first law commission

Before the conclusion of the Civil War, in 1646, Parliament had set up two committees to look into the procedures and costs of the chancery and common law courts. These had run into the sand. Then in January 1652 the Parliamentary Law Committee set up an advisory body of twenty-one members, none of them MPs, to advise on reform of the law. Its chairman was Sir Matthew Hale, a scholarly, religious and conservative lawyer who reached high judicial office after the Restoration. It was not the kind of body in which Lilburne or the Levellers would have reposed any trust. But the Hale Commission set about its work energetically. Between January and July 1652 it held seventy-one sittings. By appointing subcommittees it produced a set of sixteen bills, sufficiently comprehensive to become known as the System of the Law and covering criminal, matrimonial, probate and mercantile law, the procedures of the criminal, common law and chancery courts, the establishment of county courts, small claims courts and deeds registries, and – here the warning flares went up – the regulation of the legal profession.

This is how the historian of the seventeenth-century movement for law reform, Donald Veall, summarised the Hale Commission's agenda:

> [T]he lawyers were to be regulated and their fees controlled at rates lower than those prevailing at the time. No MP was to plead in court except when acting on behalf of the commonwealth. The courts were to be regulated; sale of office abolished; jurisdiction of courts redefined to avoid conflicts between the courts; county judicatures, small claims courts, and appeals courts set up; a poor persons' procedure introduced, and a property qualification laid down for jurors. Deeds registries were to be set up in every county; disposition of entailed property made easier; copyhold fines limited. The death penalty was to be modified, the *peine forte et dure* and benefit of clergy abolished, [and] criminal procedure improved by allowing the defence to call witnesses and have legal representation.[37]

---

[37] Veall, *The Popular Movement for Law Reform*, p. 120. Veall (pp. 93–4) pays particular tribute to William Sheppard, the author of (among many other books) *England's Balme* (1656), an elegant scheme for the codification and simplification of the law, anticipating the Code Napoléon.

The Nominated Parliament[38] summoned in July 1653, though dismissed by chroniclers as a body of "artificers, tradesmen and mechanics", was in fact a body of landowners and merchants, at least forty of them members of the Inns of Court. It set vigorously about enacting the Hale Commission's bills. In the five months of its life it passed twenty-six acts and set up its own committees on law reform and prisons, which sat daily and reported regularly to the whole House.

But Hale's programme was not to be realised in his lifetime or for generations after it. In August 1653 Parliament, encouraged by the commission's work, took on the biggest beast in the legal jungle: it voted unanimously to abolish the Court of Chancery with the freehold offices of its Six Clerks who monopolised access to the court, and directed the Parliamentary Law Committee to draft the necessary legislation. The bill ran into trouble, first with the moderates and then with the radicals, and was still being worked on by the Law Committee in December 1653 when a dissolution of Parliament was engineered, with the Speaker's connivance, by a group of conservative members. The dissolution, according to a contemporary chronicler, was greeted in the Temple with "great joy in making bonfires and drinking sack".[39]

It was the straw that broke the back of the republican enterprise – representative government shorn of Crown, aristocracy and the locust plague of lawyers. On 16 December 1653, four days after Parliament had dissolved itself, Cromwell was proclaimed Lord Protector, and a new chapter in the history of English republicanism began. The impetus for codification had gone, and in 1654 Hale was moved from his advisory post to become a judge of the Court of Common Pleas.

The Instrument of Government

The office of Lord Protector was brought into being by the country's first, and still its only, written constitution, the Instrument of Government. Far from being a blank cheque for dictatorship, the Instrument of Government was a republican constitution which not only reflected some

---

[38] The Nominated Parliament (the "Barebones Parliament") was intended to be an advisory body of individuals nominated by the Independent churches; but it assumed the role of a legislature: C. Hill, *The Century of Revolution, 1603–1714*, p. 135.

[39] Veall, *The Popular Movement for Law Reform*, p. 88, n. 1

of the democratic proposals advanced by the Army Council in 1647 and by the Levellers in their spell of influence from 1646 to 1649,[40] but in major respects anticipated the Bill of Rights of 1689, the compact between Parliament and Crown under which Britain has now been governed for more than three centuries.

The authorship of the Instrument is uncertain, but the principal hand in its composition and adoption was almost certainly that of John Lambert,[41] one of the organisers of the *coup* which shortly before had brought down the Barebones Parliament. It appears to have been Lambert who persuaded his colleagues that, while Parliament should retain the last word, a presidential office was now necessary for effective government. It went without saying that the first incumbent, for the remainder of his life, was to be Oliver Cromwell. But there is no evidence that Cromwell himself had any hand in composing the document. Hill describes the Instrument of Government as "the attempt of the more conservative Generals to find a modus vivendi between Army and electorate";[42] but its significance is considerably greater than this.

For the newly unified state and its colonies the Instrument began by providing

> That the supreme legislative authority ... shall be and reside in one person, and the people assembled in Parliament: the style of which person shall be the Lord Protector of the Commonwealth of England, Scotland and Ireland.

[40] For instance the Army's *Heads of Proposals* (August 1647) included biennial parliaments not subject to arbitrary prorogation, an equitable distribution of seats, free and open elections, freedom of speech in Parliament and parliamentary control of the armed forces. These demands, from which monarch and lords were conspicuously absent, were echoed in the successive versions of the *Agreement of the People* which followed. See Sedley, *Ashes and Sparks,* Ch. 8; A. Blick, *Beyond Magna Carta* (2015), Ch. 4.

[41] Lambert (1619–84) was a Cambridge graduate and a member of the Bar, whose support for the Parliamentary cause was political, not religious. He earned distinction, still in his twenties, as a courageous and resourceful cavalry commander and by 1647 was a major-general, ranking third after Cromwell and Fairfax. As the Rump Parliament sank, Lambert advised Cromwell to replace it with a legislative council of twelve men. In April 1653 a ten-member executive Council of State was appointed, but a 129-member legislative assembly was also summoned to meet in July. Lambert played little part in it: he was probably now preparing, with others, the Instrument of Government, which he produced in the Council Chamber in December 1653 and which was adopted after a few days' debate. Lambert travelled in the Protector's coach to the inaugural ceremony where he presented Cromwell with the sword of state.

[42] C. Hill, *The Century of Revolution, 1603–1714,* p. 135

The Protector, with the support of an advisory council, was to govern as chief magistrate[43] and administrator, and to be commander in chief of the armed forces. He was to fulfil all these roles as prescribed by the Instrument of Government. While they were roles which went well beyond those of any modern ceremonial presidency, they are quite closely paralleled by the modern presidency created by the constitution of the United States.[44]

So far, Parliament appeared to have no role. The Instrument allowed the Protector to legislate when Parliament was not sitting, provided his acts were then ratified by Parliament. Then came this:

> That the laws shall not be altered, suspended, abrogated or repealed, nor any new law made, nor any tax, charge or imposition laid upon the people, but by common consent in Parliament . . .[45]

Compare the Bill of Rights, enacted thirty-five years later:

> That the pretended power of suspending of laws . . . without consent of Parlyament is illegall.[46]
>
> That the pretended power of dispensing with laws or the execution of laws by regal authority . . . is illegall
>
> That levying money for or to the use of the Crowne by [pretence] of prerogative without grant of Parlyament . . . is illegal.

Next, the Instrument of Government provided for triennial parliaments. Again, compare the Bill of Rights:

> And that for redresse of all grievances and for the amending, strengthening and preserving of the laws Parlyaments ought to be held frequently.

The Instrument of Government went on to forbid the proroguing of any Parliament within its first five months without its consent. It made detailed provision for a more representative allocation of seats, but set

---

[43] This designation did not have its modern judicial meaning. It meant the head of state.

[44] This thesis is explored in A. Blick, *Beyond Magna Carta* (2015), Ch. 4, which contains a conspectus of the constitutional struggles of the seventeenth century.

[45] The article continued: "save only as is expressed in the thirtieth article". The thirtieth article, echoing the constitutional issue which had led to the Petition of Right in 1628, gave the Protector an emergency power to raise military and naval taxes until Parliament could assemble.

[46] Cf. the development in the United States of a presidential power of suspending congressional legislation, a monarchical procedure outlawed in this country both by the Instrument of Government and by its successor, the Bill of Rights. See M. Foley, *The Silence of Constitutions* (1989); Sedley, *Ashes and Sparks*, Ch. 7, p. 69.

a £200 property qualification for voting.[47] The Bill of Rights contains no such detail but provides delphically:

> That election of members of Parlyament ought to be free.

Both instruments excluded Catholics from office.[48] Neither lifted the disabilities on dissenters or Jews.[49]

It was thus the Instrument of Government which, thirty-five years before the Bill of Rights, established Parliament's constitutional supremacy.[50] The Instrument went on to provide that "the office of Lord Protector . . . shall be elective and not hereditary"[51] and to appoint Oliver Cromwell the first Lord Protector for life.[52] It also made Parliament responsible for electing the Chancellor (no longer a Lord Chancellor) and the chief justices of "both the benches".[53]

The matrix was thus neither monarchist nor Bonapartist. Although the elevation of Cromwell reflected his personal power and authority, the office of Lord Protector after his death was to stand open; and the Protector's powers were to be secondary to those of an elected parliament. The office was to be, in modern terms, the presidency of a republic, and none the less so because, by the time of Cromwell's death in 1658 and the brief installation of his son Richard in the Protector's seat, the republican experiment was in free-fall. The competent governance of the regions by Cromwell's major-generals could not disguise the fact that power now rested on the bayonets of a large and costly standing army and on the personal authority of Cromwell himself.

---

[47] Art. XVIII: cf. the forty shilling property qualification introduced by an act of 1430 (8 Hen. 6, c.7), which lasted, apart from the Protectorate, into the nineteenth century: see F. W. Maitland, *Constitutional History of England* (1889), p. 87.

[48] It was not until 1829 that the legal disabilities on Roman Catholics were repealed.

[49] The readmission of Jews to Britain under the Protectorate in 1656 (they had been expelled in 1290), although a historic event, was less an act of toleration than a commercial calculation, supported by the legal profession but opposed by the churches and the merchants, designed to draw Amsterdam's financial power away from the Catholic states of Europe. It was managed informally, without legislation, and was kept in being after the Restoration.

[50] The Instrument does not anticipate the Bill of Rights in one notable respect – the prohibition of "cruell and unusuall punishments" (art. X). This had, however, been prefigured by the *General Lawes and Liberties* of Massachusetts which in 1647 banned punishments which were "in-humane, barbarous or cruel".

[51] Art. XXXII   [52] Art. XXXIII

[53] Art. XXXIV. The two benches were now the Common Pleas and the Upper Bench.

Overview

The Instrument of Government was considerably more than a flash in the pan of constitutional reform. It formed part of a decade-long endeavour to reconstruct the state, including the courts and the law, on a scale of time and magnitude unmatched before or since.[54] Significant elements of the Leveller programme of 1647, *The Agreement of the People*, the first-ever modern political manifesto, are visible in it. True, most of what was accomplished at a constitutional level was frustrated by events – beginning with the effective repeal of the Instrument of Government by the *Humble Petition and Advice* of May 1657 and culminating in the humiliating offer to Cromwell of the crown – and reversed at the Restoration. But in the centuries which have followed, the changes first made or attempted in the years of the Commonwealth and the Protectorate have returned like a slow tide.[55]

Public administration

It was the Protectorate which saw the tentative origins of the modern civil service (and indeed of the concept of the state itself).[56]

> "For the last time in English history before the nineteenth century," wrote Hill, "local government was run from Whitehall."[57]

In place of the officers of state, who were literally the monarch's secretaries and had left London with the Court in 1642, administrations and committees were set up, often in the halls of the City corporations. Officials emerged like the treasurer of the navy, Sir Henry Vane, whose ethos of public service rather than private gain was carried on after the Restoration by administrators like Samuel Pepys.

---

[54] It was followed, in 1654, by an abortive Constitutional Bill, which sought to allocate greater authority to Parliament, and in the dying days of the Protectorate by Milton's *Readie and Easie Way to Establish a Free Commonwealth* (1660), proposing an elected Grand Council which would sit in perpetuity, vacancies being filled by further election.

[55] In what follows I have drawn extensively on Donald Veall, *The Popular Movement for Law Reform 1640–1660* (1970), and on two of Veall's secondary sources, G. B. Nourse, "Law Reform under the Commonwealth and Protectorate" (1959) 75 LQR 512, and R. Robinson, "Anticipations under the Commonwealth of Changes in the Law" (1869/70), reprinted in *Select Essays in Anglo-American Legal History* (1907–9), vol. I, p. 467.

[56] See Ch. 11; G. E. Aylmer, *The State's Servants: The Civil Service of the English Republic 1649–1660* (1973).

[57] Hill, *The Century of Revolution, 1603–1714*, p. 137

Moonlighting MPs

One thing which both the Instrument of Government and the Bill of Rights failed to tackle was the problem – still a problem today – of lawyer MPs who continue to practise law while in office. Both the Levellers[58] and the Hale Commission saw this not only as a fraud on the electorate but as a built-in obstacle to any radical legislative reform of the legal system.[59] As we shall see, they were proved right.

The use of English

One of the first reforms carried through by the Commonwealth was the enactment in 1650, in a statute less than a page long, of a ban on the use of any language but English in the conduct and recording of legal proceedings.[60] The unintelligible script used in court records was to be replaced by "an ordinary, usual and legible hand and character", on pain of a fine of "twenty pounds of lawful English money". Only the Admiralty court, which for intelligible reasons conducted its proceedings in Latin, was exempted. All other proceedings during the Commonwealth and Protectorate were accordingly conducted in English – a reform which was badly needed, which worked well, and which was promptly and pointlessly reversed at the Restoration.[61]

The courts

In 1649, in the wake of the abolition of both the monarchy and the House of Lords, six of the twelve judges of the Common Pleas and the Upper

---

[58] *The Agreement of the People* (1648; 1649)

[59] Veall, *The Popular Movement for Law Reform*, pp. 203–5, quotes an anonymous pamphleteer's comment on the still-used excuse that legal practice makes better parliamentarians: "The knowledge of the common law doth in no way conduce to the making of a statesman; it is a confined and topical kind of learning, calculated only for the meridian of Westminster Hall ... If you have many lawyers, they will never suffer any effectual law to pass ... because they get more by the corruption and delay of the law, than by the law itself."

[60] "An Act for turning the Books of the Law, and all process and Proceedings in Courts of Justice, into English" (22 November 1650), Firth and Rait, vol. II, pp. 455–6. A supplementary act of 9 April 1651 placed the duty of securing translations on named officers of state and took the precaution of preventing lawyers from taking objection to proceedings or laws on the ground of mistranslation (ibid. pp. 510–1).

[61] All laws of the Interregnum were treated without more as void. But 12 Car. II c.3, s.4, validated proceedings conducted or recorded in English between 1651 and 1660.

Bench (as the King's Bench had been renamed) resigned their offices. The remaining six made their continued tenure conditional on an undertaking that "the fundamental laws" would be maintained. The six vacancies were filled, and England and Wales retained an independent and competent judiciary through the years of the Commonwealth and the Protectorate. But the Commonwealth also considered it necessary to replicate the special court set up to try the King in 1649 with a succession of special courts to try its enemies, mostly recalcitrant royalists, dispensing, like Star Chamber, with privileges of rank and criminalising as treason any denunciation of the government as "tyrannical, usurped or unlawful".[62]

Judicial independence

The principle that judges are entitled to secure tenure of their office conditionally on good behaviour – that is to say, on continuing fitness for office – was first extracted by the Long Parliament in 1642 from Charles I, for whom dismissal at pleasure had been an attractive and useful expedient,[63] and confirmed by an ordinance of 1648.[64] From 1645 judicial appointments ceased to be profitable freeholds and began to be made by Parliament in place of the monarch. Fees, instead of being pocketed by judges and clerks, became payable into a public account. Fixed salaries – set at £1,000 a year by a Commons resolution of September 1645 – were introduced in order to place the judiciary beyond the reach of corruption.[65]

Inevitably the constituents of good and bad judicial behaviour were capable of being politicised. When Justices Newdigate and Thorpe were removed from the bench in 1655, Bulstrode Whitelocke accused Cromwell of dismissing them because their judgments had displeased him. But it can probably be said that judicial independence, though never entirely

---

[62] If special courts do not sound too good, one should perhaps not forget that in the interests of state security the United Kingdom has set up closed courts and has legislated to allow the ordinary courts to conceal the state's evidence from its antagonists: see Ch. 8. Justice and convenience, as Lord Atkin was to remark in the 1930s, are often not on speaking terms.

[63] S. R. Gardiner, *History of England 1603–1642*, cited by Veall, *The Popular Movement for Law Reform*, p. 199 n. 1

[64] Firth and Rait, vol. I, pp. 1226–7, appointing a number of judges to the bench "*quamdiu se bene gesserint*". Since 1700, see the Act of Settlement (now the Senior Courts Act 1981, s. 11(3)).

[65] Veall, *The Popular Movement for Law Reform*, pp. 197–8

secure, was no worse respected during the Commonwealth and Protectorate than in either the preceding or the succeeding Stuart reigns.

The Court of Chancery

One of Cromwell's first acts as Protector was to make an ordinance in
August 1654[66] to reform the Court of Chancery, taking on where the
Barebones Parliament had left off and adopting most of the Hale Commission's proposals. No hearing was to last longer than a day. The
freehold office of the Six Clerks was abolished. They were to be replaced
by three chief clerks, who were to administer the court's process and were
prohibited from "intermeddling in any Cause as Attorneys". A body of
not more than sixty licensed attorneys, drawn by the Master of the Rolls
from such of the existing clerks as were able and honest, were to have the
right of audience. They were to be paid the six clerks' former fee of 3s 4d
a term, and were forbidden to take anything more from their clients. It
was, in effect, a primitive legal aid system. The ordinance set out a
comprehensive table of fees and set time limits for pleadings.

Making it all happen was another matter. The Master of the Rolls,
William Lenthall, and the two Commissioners of the Great Seal refused
to implement the ordinance. Cromwell moved the two commissioners to
other offices; but Lenthall, having started by swearing that he would be
hanged at the Rolls Gate before he would implement the ordinance, had
second thoughts and came into line. Parliament confirmed the ordinance
in 1657,[67] but inertia supervened, and in 1658 it was allowed to lapse.

Public law

In 1641 the Commissioners of Sewers for Yorkshire decided that the entire
cost of repairing a section of the sea wall should be paid by the lessee of the
adjacent land, whose lease had almost expired, and that none of the cost
was to fall on the landlord. A challenge by way of certiorari[68] was met with
the objection that the commissioners were a court which was not subject
to judicial review. The King's Bench by a majority held that certiorari
lay to remove the commissioners' order into their court, with the result that

---

[66] Firth and Rait, vol. II, p. 949   [67] Firth and Rait, vol. II, p. 1140

[68] *Commins* v. *Massam* (1642), Controlment Roll 291, m.39, cited in E. G. Henderson,
   Foundations of English Administrative Law (1963) pp. 101–6. Cf. *Rooke's Case* (1598) 5
   Co. Rep. 99b

the new removal procedure quickly became popular: the Controlment Roll for 1649 alone contains fifteen examples of its use ... For the period 1642–1700 the reports contain over fifty cases and it is a fair inference that there were several hundred unreported ones.

Although much of the evolution of both certiorari and mandamus took place during the troubled years of the Civil War and the Interregnum, no one seems to have held it against them: their use and development continued unbroken after the Restoration ... perhaps because the bar had generally supported both the Long Parliament and the Restoration.[69]

The common law courts

The common law attorneys proved readier than the chancery lawyers to reform their procedures. At a general meeting in May 1651 they agreed on a series of measures for reducing delays. They also proposed – in an interesting anticipation of the Woolf reforms of the late twentieth century[70] – that every plaintiff at common law should be required to swear to the veracity of his claim. A few years later the Hale Commission proposed fixed lawyers' fees, to a maximum of £5 per case, to be repaid in full if the attorney failed to see the case through; an obligatory code of ethical conduct designed to save clients expense and courts time; and rights of audience for barristers as well as serjeants-at-law in the Common Pleas. But here too practice limped behind theory, and one barrister who took the new right of audience to be as good as law found himself thrown by the serjeants over the spiked rail which separated the inner from the outer bar in Westminster Hall.[71]

Even so, perhaps the most striking comment on the legal profession in the decade of the republic is that of the Victorian historian F. A. Inderwick. During those years, he wrote, counsel

> conducted their cases with independence and decorum ... [and with] an absence of those insults and brutalities which gained so unenviable a notoriety for some of the counsel of succeeding reigns.[72]

---

[69] Henderson, *Foundations of English Administrative Law*, p. 106

[70] Civil Procedure Rules 1998, Pt. 22. The object was to discourage collusive, speculative and dishonest lawsuits.

[71] Veall, *The Popular Movement for Law Reform*, p. 188, n. 1

[72] F. A. Inderwick, *The Interregnum* (1891). The few law reports which span the Common-wealth and Protectorate (principally Hardres' Exchequer reports, Style's King's Bench/Upper Bench reports, and Nelson's chancery reports) show no obvious change in the

Criminal procedure

The Conservative historian and jurist Sir James Stephen[73] noted a
marked upturn between 1640 and 1660 in the standard of conduct of
criminal trials. The right, on which the Levellers insisted, to confront the
prosecution's witnesses and not to be compelled to incriminate oneself
became recognised in legal practice. The assembly of a jury to try
individuals according to their "common fame" in the locality gave way
to what is today recognised as proof by due process. Defendants, contrary
to previous practice, were now permitted both to cross-examine witnesses and to call witnesses of their own. The use of paid informers was
stopped.

The special courts mentioned earlier, though without doubt designed
to prevent unwanted acquittals, conducted their proceedings in public
before a panel of thirty or forty members presided over by a judge. At the
Restoration the worst thing the Earl of Clarendon could find to say about
them was that they had failed to observe "distinction of quality" and had
"made the greatest lord and the meanest peasant undergo the same
judicatory and form of trial". That, some might have said, was what the
Civil War was fought for. In fact the radical John Lilburne had refused to
sit on the special court that tried Charles I because he considered that the
King ought to be facing an ordinary court of criminal jurisdiction.

The ecclesiastical courts

One of the first measures of the Long Parliament, anticipating even the
outbreak of the Civil War, was the abolition in 1641 of the criminal
jurisdiction of the ecclesiastical courts. Five years later the statute abolishing the episcopacy remitted all offences within the episcopal jurisdiction to the courts of common law. Sin and crime, as Veall remarked,[74]
had become distinct. One historic effect of this restriction of the spiritual
courts to spiritual matters, together with the abolition of the prerogative
courts, was that the use of torture and the inquisitorial use of the *ex
officio* oath ceased, since the common law courts did not countenance
these methods. Another was that a temporal court composed of twenty

---

kinds of issue and the kinds of litigant coming before those courts, or in the outcomes.
The state litigated after 1653 in the name of the Protector or the Attorney-General.

[73] J. F. Stephen, *History of the Criminal Law of England* (1883), vol. I, pp. 357–68
[74] *The Popular Movement for Law Reform*, p. 139

judges, among them Matthew Hale, was set up in 1653 to exercise the jurisdiction formerly exercised by the consistory and prerogative courts over wills, tithes, divorce and marriage.

Crime and sin

On the moral front Puritan zealotry was able in some degree to get its way. The Assembly of Divines, which in 1643 had complained to the House of Commons that there was no longer any way of punishing sexual offences, finally succeeded in 1650 in getting Parliament to criminalise at a single blow incest, adultery and fornication, making the first two capital felonies without benefit of clergy. The combination of jury trial with procedural safeguards – in particular the ban on the use of paid informers – seems, however, to have kept the number of convictions for moral offences low.[75]

Civil marriage

More radically, an ordinance of 1653[76] provided for the institution of civil marriage, of which notice could be given either in church or in the marketplace. Solemnisation was to be before a justice of the peace. The same measure instituted the public registration of births (rather than baptisms), marriages and burials. These reforms may well have been driven by Puritan antagonism to the established church, but they constituted an innovative series of steps towards separation of church and state.

Registration of land

Legislation was introduced in 1656 to set up the first local civil claims courts, county offices empowered to grant probate of wills (a function which had already been taken away from the ecclesiastical courts), and registries of title to land. But the bill was obstructed and finally talked out by the lawyers.

A very wide band of opinion nevertheless supported the establishment of a public registry of deeds, of interests in land, or of both. Radical

---

[75] Ibid., p. 141

[76] Firth and Rait, vol. II, pp. 715–18. Following the Restoration, by 12 Car. II c.33, civil marriages solemnised before JPs were ratified.

reformers had also proposed the abolition of all forms of tenure other than fee simple, and the conversion of all copyhold – repeatedly described as a badge of servility – to freehold. Bills were introduced between 1650 and 1653 to set up local land registries, but all of them foundered on practical difficulties.

The post

There was still more. Although the Crown had for many years held – and rented out – a monopoly of the carriage of mails, it was the Protectorate which in 1654 legislated for the first universal postal service, licensing a named individual, John Manley, to exercise the state's monopoly on strict terms: he was to pay £10,000 a year for the privilege; he was to carry mails to every corner of the country and abroad at fixed rates; and his riders were to have fresh horses at every post.[77] It was an early private finance initiative, arguably a much better one than some of its modern successors; and by an act of 1657 the monopoly it created was transmuted into the first General Post Office, under the control of a public servant, the Postmaster General.[78]

The turn of the tide

History has been kind to the revanchism of the Restoration. The so-called Act of Oblivion[79] excluded forty-nine named republicans from its general amnesty and required them to be tried for treason.[80] Many of those named managed to flee, but the able and honourable commander of the Leveller cavalry regiments, Adrian Scroope, and John Cooke, the former Solicitor-General and Chief Justice of Munster, along with seven others, were put to death by public hanging, drawing and quartering. By order of the two Houses of Parliament, six of the principal republican enactments[81] were burned by the public hangman, and a search was

---

[77] An Ordinance touching the Office of Postage of Letters, Inland and Foreign (2 September 1654), Firth and Rait, vol. II, p. 1007.

[78] An act for settling the Postage (9 June 1657), Firth and Rait, vol. II, p. 1110.

[79] 12 Car.2, c.11   [80] Ibid., s. 34

[81] Viz. the Solemn League and Covenant, 1643; the act of 1649 setting up a court to try the King; the act which declared England a commonwealth; the act "for subscribing the Engagement"; the act annulling the title of the monarch; and the act "for securing the Lord Protector's person".

ordered to be made in the law courts for "the traitorous writing called the Instrument of Government".[82]

The restored regime reversed the legal reforms of the republican years by the simple expedient – visible to this day in the printed volumes of English statute law – of treating all the acts and ordinances of the republic as void. Some of their provisions were temporarily re-enacted – the general post office set up by the Protectorate in 1654 had to be re-established – but the ordinance protecting the judges from political interference fell without a sound at the Restoration. It was not until the passage of the Act of Settlement 1700 that judicial office again became constitutionally secure.

English was not restored as the language of the law until 1731. The first registry of deeds was finally opened in 1703, but a national land register had to wait until 1875, and it was only in the late twentieth century that it became publicly accessible. Civil marriage did not return until 1836. Equity and law were in theory fused by the Judicature Acts 1873–5, though the liaison of the two systems is to this day regarded in parts of the profession as a shotgun marriage. The predatory Six Clerks returned to the court of chancery at the Restoration and were not done away with until 1842.[83]

The right to defence counsel and witnesses was reintroduced in treason trials in 1697 and in felony in the first part of the eighteenth century. In 1772 *peine forte et dure* – the pressing to death of prisoners who refused to plead – was abolished for the second time. Local small claims courts – county courts – were re-established in 1846, and the following year the Court of Common Pleas finally opened its bar to all barristers.

Even though within six years of the Restoration the Earl of Clarendon was put in charge of a committee designed to resume where the Hale Commission had left off, to this day codification of the law, except in a few limited areas, remains a pipe-dream. It was not until 1965, three hundred and thirteen years after Matthew Hale and his colleagues first set about the methodical reform of the law, that a standing law commission was finally established.[84] As to what one pamphleteer called the "juggling tricks and devices" of the law,[85] there were still

---

[82] For an account of the survival of the texts of laws made between 1642 and 1660, see Firth and Rait, vol. III, Introduction, passim.

[83] Court of Chancery Act, 1842, s. 1. Their office was on the site where the Law Society's building now stands.

[84] Law Commissions Act 1965

[85] J. Frese, *Every Man's Right*, 15 June 1646, quo. Veall, *The Popular Movement for Law Reform* p. 202

enough of them at the end of the twentieth century to call for Lord Woolf's clean-up of the rule book.[86]

If the endeavour to reform access to justice in the twelve years of the English republic was largely frustrated by the legal profession, that will not have surprised Matthew Hale or John Cooke. But it will have angered those radicals and visionaries who, in the brief window of time between the Putney debates in the winter of 1647 and the Burford mutiny in the summer of 1649, had hoped that, from a world turned upside down, a decent, rational and honest society was going to emerge.

> "The minds of men," wrote John Warr, "are the great wheels of things. Thence come changes and alterations in the world. Teeming freedom exerts and puts forth itself. The unjust world would suppress its appearance. Many fall in this conflict, but freedom will at last prevail and give law to all things."[87]

---

[86] Civil Procedure Rules 1998, made under the Civil Procedure Act 1997.

[87] J. Warr, "The Corruption and Deficiency of the Laws of England" (1649) in Sedley and Kaplan (eds.), *A Spark in the Ashes*, p. 92. "Exerts" = thrusts out.

5

The future of public law

This chapter reflects on some of the demands and strictures placed on modern public law. It then looks at two areas of potential development: the control of policy and the growth of a new paradigm of constitutionalism.

The Judge Over Your Shoulder

In his speech at the annual dinner of the Administrative Law Bar Association in 1987, the guest of honour, Sir John Donaldson MR, read out, to gales of laughter, the final checklist in a newly produced handbook for civil servants on how to avoid judicial review, entitled *The Judge Over Your Shoulder*. Before signing off a decision, the handbook advised, civil servants would do well to ask themselves such questions as:

- Are you exercising the power for the purpose for which it was given?
- Are you acting for the right reasons?
- Have you made up your mind in advance ...?
- Do you propose to act in a way which a court may regard as ... so unreasonable that it is likely to find against you?[1]

Nobody had told the Master of the Rolls that the author of the handbook, the principal assistant Treasury Solicitor, Robert Ricks, was sitting a few feet away from him. Ricks took the laughter in good part; but a quarter of a century later, it may be his successors who are going to get the last

---

[1] *The Judge Over Your Shoulder* (1st edn, March 1987) § 26. The author told me in 1989 that the handbook was the product of a working party set up to disseminate knowledge about judicial review and was not, as I suspected it might be, the aftermath of an abortive ministerial plan to abolish judicial review. He assured me that the title was not intended to suggest Big Brother in ermine but to echo Jessie Matthews' song "Over My Shoulder Goes One Care" – though the image of a civil servant tossing a judge over his shoulder was hardly more respectful.

laugh. The self-confidence with which the legal profession entered the
1990s, reflected both in the anxious tone of the civil service's handbook
and in the amusement it generated among administrative lawyers, are no
longer part of the landscape.

In the intervening years *The Judge Over Your Shoulder* has run
through a series of editions, each considerably longer than the last. It
now has to take in human rights, devolution and a growing range of EU
law. But it remains laudably focused: its purpose, says the preface,

> is not "How to survive judicial review" but rather to inform and improve
> the quality of administrative decision-making.[2]

Nobody could quarrel with that. If the long-term effect of judicial review
has been a general improvement in the standard of governmental
decision-making, it will have achieved its principal purpose. But it is
doubtful whether this has happened. What seems to many public law
practitioners to have happened instead is twofold. First, there has been a
development of defensive decision-making. Secondly, the executive and
its ministerial heads have been thinking about how to roll back the whole
judicial review process.

Defensive decision-making

The first of these reactions, defensive decision-making, is something for
which public law has to accept much of the responsibility. Administrators tend to respond to the fear of legal challenge not, as most
lawyers would, by keeping the explanation of a decision and the reasons
for it to a minimum, but by doing the opposite: covering every possible
angle and eventuality, sometimes even by cutting and pasting ready-
made paragraphs from a departmental template. This is particularly
characteristic of Home Office practice in immigration and asylum
cases, where decisions are made under unremitting pressure of time
and an ever-present threat of legal challenge. It has led to the adoption
of undisclosed departmental policies, which in turn have invited further
legal challenge when they have come to light.[3] Courts and tribunals
have sought to avoid excessive legalism in scrutinising such decisions,

---

[2] *The Judge Over Your Shoulder* (4th edn, 2006). The handbook had by this time become
known by its acronym, JOYS.
[3] See below, n. 18.

but when human safety and possibly human life depend on these, there is a limit to what can be decently overlooked.

The empire strikes back

The second and much more radical reaction needs first to be seen in historical perspective. The reawakening of public law in the later twentieth century has been controversial. Criticism has come not simply from ministers, starting with Michael Howard who, as Conservative Home Secretary from 1993 to 1997, broke constitutional propriety by publicly attacking named judges whose decisions he objected to,[4] and whose example was followed by a succession of Labour Home Secretaries; it had been coming for years before this from the opposite end of the political spectrum, most notably from the formidable John Griffith.[5]

The Politics of the Judiciary

John Griffith was a democratic socialist for whom (as for many since) the achievements of the post-war Labour government in nationalising the mines, docks and railways and instituting a national health service were a high point of history. The accomplishment of the Attlee government's radical socio-economic programme had been largely due to the almost uncontested power of its mandarin-led civil service and to the continuing abstention of the judges from interference with the business of government.[6] Griffith accordingly viewed the revival of public law from the 1970s as a dangerous development,[7] motivated – and in this he had the concurrence of his philosophical opponent Sir William Wade – by a judicial determination that such events should not be allowed to recur without searching judicial scrutiny.

Griffith came at the issue obliquely through the successive editions of his book, *The Politics of the Judiciary*. The title referred, he would explain with his tongue not very far from his cheek, not to the judges' own political views, which of course were non-existent, but (as he put it in the

---

[4] For a narrative account see Joshua Rozenberg, *Trial of Strength* (1997).
[5] 1918–2010; professor of public law, London School of Economics.   [6] See Ch. 1.
[7] See his articles "The Common Law and the Political Constitution" (2001) 117 LQR 42, criticising the present writer's views, and "The Brave New World of Sir John Laws" (2000) 63 MLR 159.

first edition[8]) to "the relationship between the judiciary and politics". The book, like much of Griffith's work, is a detailed study of the interpenetration of adjudication, legislation and administration. In the course of successive editions, however, it became apparent that Griffith was being led by his own radicalism to applaud, or at least not to criticise, a number of decisions in which a now self-confident judiciary was standing up to authoritarian acts of a Conservative government. By the time of his fifth edition, in 1997, he was not only applauding the departure of the courts from Denning's earlier refusal to countenance prisoners' rights[9] but was criticising them for not being interventionist enough on such issues as race discrimination.[10]

It there is a moral it is that, while what matters to the wider world is what judges do, what matters to judges is why they do it.

The way we live now

Faced with the modern development of public law, there has been a distinct and calculated shift within government away from prior attention to legality and towards a "see you in court" culture. Lord Woolf, who from 1974 to 1979 had been the government's standing counsel, said in 1985:

> It used to be the case that, if the legality of a course of action was in doubt, it was not adopted. Now it appears . . . anything is permissible unless and until it is stopped by the courts.[11]

But ministers have one resource which the judges do not possess: the power to secure primary legislation by which the courts will be bound. The executive's domination of Parliament in this respect has for a long time been ruefully acknowledged:

> "Parliamentary sovereignty," wrote the political scientist and MP Tony Wright, "provides a cloak of legitimacy for executive and party dominance."[12]

---

[8] *The Politics of the Judiciary* (1st edn, 1977), p. 15. Griffith was certainly not, as a review alleged in the *Times Literary Supplement*, "aligned with the Baader-Meinhof gang in believing that every criminal trial is categorically unjust".

[9] *The Politics of the Judiciary* (5th edn, 1997), pp. 171ff.   [10] Ibid., pp. 175ff

[11] Sir Harry Woolf, Second Street Lecture, [1986] PL 220, 221–2. The *Pergau Dam* case, which is discussed in Ch. 12, is a striking illustration of what Woolf was describing.

[12] Tony Wright, *Citizens and Subjects* (1993), p. 6

Lord Radcliffe in his 1951 Reith Lectures put it even more sharply: by the party political system, he said,

> "carried to its logical conclusion, Parliament is turned into the instrument of power instead of being its holder."[13]

The dominant party's grip on the legislative process is consolidated by the largely illusory procedure for private members' bills. Unless these measures secure government support, they can be simply talked out by government supporters or killed by a solitary objection – something that in the past has been done repeatedly, and with malign consequences, by a single member[14] with an obsessive hostility to regulation of any kind.

Within these wheels are more wheels. For much of the twentieth century the central cogwheel of executive and party was Cabinet; but Cabinet itself has increasingly been marginalised over recent decades by a presidential mode of government in which prime ministers gather power to themselves and exercise it not through ministers but through advisers and spokespersons. The political veteran Roy Hattersley remarked in 1998:

> Cabinet government has been dying for forty years in this country. I'm not sure if it's quite dead yet, but Tony [Blair] has given it a lethal injection.[15]

Yet the historic compromise of the end of the seventeenth century, giving Parliament the last word on what the law is to be, still holds. Its counterpart, which is no less important, has been that it is for the judges to determine what the law is, whether by interpreting and applying acts of Parliament and delegated legislation, or by deploying and developing the common law. No Parliament sought to reverse *Entick* v. *Carrington*,[16] which stifled the claim of ministers to judicial power, or *Anisminic*,[17] which opened the workings of public administration to unforeseen legal scrutiny.

Things to come

Against this background let me pick out two processes which may acquire greater importance in public law in the coming years. One is

---

[13] C. Radcliffe, *The Problem of Power* (1951, edn 1958), p. 59   [14] Eric Forth MP, d. 2006
[15] Quoted by Peter Hennessy, "Re-engineering the State in Flight: A Year in the Life of the British Constitution", a Lloyds TSB Forum lecture, April 1998.
[16] See Ch. 3.   [17] [1969] 2 AC 147; see Ch. 1.

the interpenetration of policy and law; the second is what could be called the reconstitution of the constitution.

Prosecution policies

I will say something later in this book[18] about the development of the law of legitimate expectation as a response to the use of policy to affect or determine entitlements. The reason why it is likely to matter even more in the future is that policy is used increasingly to do things that legislation cannot or prefers not to do.

One of many instances is the use made by successive Directors of Public Prosecutions of policies for the use of prosecutorial discretions in relation to crimes which are ethically and morally sensitive. The issues this process raises cannot be stowed away in a locker marked "Criminal Law". Not only is the DPP a public official whose powers and discretions are matters of public law; any submission in a court of criminal jurisdiction that a particular prosecution, by departing from a published policy, is an abuse of the court's process will at heart be a submission of public law, because it relates not to guilt or innocence but to the propriety of the state's conduct.

Since 2010 the DPP has developed and published policies for deciding whether or not to prosecute in – so far – six classes of case:

- assisted suicide,[19]
- journalistic sources,[20]
- sexual abuse of children,[21]
- sexual transmission of disease,[22]
- social media,[23] and
- concurrent jurisdiction.[24]

The last of these is largely technical, but you can readily see from the description of the remainder that they concern some of the most fraught issues in contemporary society. These are issues which it would not only be highly problematical to legislate for with hard-edged definitions of

---

[18] See Ch. 7; see also "Policy and Law", in M. Andenas and D. Fairgrieve (eds.), *Judicial Review in International Perspective* (2000), vol. II, p. 259, reprinted in S. Sedley, *Ashes and Sparks* (2011), Ch. 26.

[19] *Policy for Prosecutors in Respect of Cases of Encouraging or Assisting Suicide,* Director of Public Prosecutions, 25 February 2010; supplemented 16 October 2014

[20] 13 September 2012   [21] 17 October 2013   [22] n.d.   [23] 20 June 2013

[24] 25 October 2012

criminality and exemptions from it,[25] but which parliamentarians, aware that they are issues which earn few votes and can lose a great many, would rather not have to confront.

What has happened in relation to assisting or encouraging suicide exemplifies all these elements. The DPP's policy came into existence not spontaneously or as a form of surrogate legislation but because the House of Lords' judicial committee in 2009, in attempting to decide Debbie Purdy's case without themselves legislating, called upon the DPP to state publicly when he would and would not initiate a prosecution for assisting a suicide. The first such policy to be promulgated, it became a trailblazer for what is now an established practice.

Mrs Purdy was dying of progressive multiple sclerosis. She had an entirely rational wish to end her life before it became unbearable, but to do so she would need her husband's help. Whether he helped her to die here or abroad, he would be open to prosecution for assisting her to commit suicide, a crime created to replace murder in the second degree when suicide itself was decriminalised.[26] The law lords, recognising that they could not simply forbid prosecution, accepted Mrs Purdy's case that the DPP was under a public law duty to promulgate a policy stating in principle when he would and would not give his consent to a prosecution.[27] This the then DPP, Keir Starmer QC, did after conducting an extensive series of consultations with different interest groups. The resultant policy inevitably attracted criticism, both from those who believe that any acceleration of the process of dying is unethical and should be unlawful, and from those who cannot understand why the people best equipped to assist a dignified and painless end, medical practitioners, are the most likely to be prosecuted under the policy. But the policy meets the essential purpose of letting people know where they stand.

Among a number of legal issues thrown up both by the assisted suicide policy and by its companions, one can pick out at least these. First, each of the policies is bound, indeed intended, to have effects on individuals' rights, liabilities and expectations. It must therefore be open to challenge if it is thought to be contrary to law. Because each policy is configured to such hard law as there is in its field of operation, any challenge for

---

[25] See Lord Hope at § 26 in *R (Purdy) v. DPP* [2009] UKHL 45.

[26] Suicide Act 1961, ss. 1, 2

[27] One of the House's reasons, § 47, was that published policies such as the *Code for Crown Prosecutors* amounted to law for the purposes of Article 8(2) of the ECHR.

simple illegality is improbable; but there is a constitutional question. Article I of the Bill of Rights 1689 declares

> That the pretended power of suspending of laws or the execution of laws
> by regall authority without consent of Parlyament is illegall.

Is a policy of non-prosecution in an entire class of cases, as distinct from an individual decision not to prosecute, a "pretended power of suspending the execution of laws"?[28]

Secondly, and more pragmatically, what is to happen when a prosecution is brought in any of the fields now covered by a published prosecution policy, and the accused asserts that he or she is within the class which the DPP has undertaken not to prosecute – for example because he or she has acted out of compassion in assisting a spouse's suicide? When, in such a case, an application is made to the trial judge to dismiss or stay the proceedings for abuse of process, can the DPP properly submit that it is only a policy and creates no legal rights? It is hard to imagine that she[29] would wish to: it would appear mean-spirited and duplicitous. Much more probably, the DPP would explain why, in her judgment, the case does not meet the non-prosecution criteria in the policy – for example because she considers that the accused acted out of frustration rather than compassion – but would accept that, if the judge found this not to be so, the prosecution should be stayed. Such a course would be honourable, but it would open Pandora's box. If, for example, the answer depended on an appraisal of the evidence, either the judge would have to form a view of the facts, which is not ordinarily the judicial role in a jury trial; or the accused would have to take the evidence at its highest against him or her.

Either way, the judge will in substance be treating the policy as if it were law. And what if the judge rules that the prosecution can proceed? The defence will have no legal entitlement to rely on the DPP's policy before the jury, but prosecuting counsel may well be entitled – may even feel duty bound – to invite the jury to acquit if in their view the facts come within the DPP's non-prosecution criteria, even though the elements of the crime are all established. For the trial judge in turn this will

---

[28] A related issue arose under the Market Abuse Directive: could domestic legislation (the Financial Services and Markets Act 2000) authorise the Financial Services Authority to grant dispensations from liability for certain forms of market behaviour? See also the account in Ch. 6 of the Revenue's practice of granting extra-statutory tax concessions.

[29] The DPP at the time of writing is Alison Saunders.

pose a serious dilemma: to direct the jury to acquit if they find that the case falls within the policy exemption, and thereby effectively to turn policy into law, or to direct the jury to ignore what counsel on both sides are inviting them to do, namely apply the DPP's policy.

If public law has eventually to choose between accommodating policies of this kind and rolling them back, it is going to have to take some hard policy decisions of its own.

The reconstitution of the constitution

There has been growing unease among the higher judiciary at evidence that both ministers and Parliament itself are prepared to manipulate or even abandon constitutional norms for short-term ends. The era when a permanent secretary could simply tell his minister that such a thing was not possible has gone with the erosion of the civil service's security of tenure and the populating of Whitehall with ministers' own political advisers.

Constitutional manipulation

In 1996 an MP, Neil Hamilton, sued Mohammed al Fayed and *The Guardian* newspaper for alleging that he had been taking payments for asking questions in the House. His action had to be stayed because it was going to require the use of parliamentary records, violating article IX of the Bill of Rights, which forbids the calling in question of Parliament's proceedings in a court of law. To help Hamilton out of this corner, the government secured the inclusion of a clause in a defamation bill then going through the Lords, amending the Bill of Rights so as to permit an individual MP to waive article IX for his or her own purposes.[30] The amendment thus treats the privilege created by article IX not as a constitutional protection of Parliament itself but as a personal benefit for individual members, to be used or discarded as they choose. In spite of the clear advice of a parliamentary committee that the provision should be repealed, it is still on the statute book,[31] giving support to the view that

---

[30] Defamation Act 1996, s. 13. In the event the libel jury found against Hamilton.
[31] See A. W. Bradley [2000] PL 556; A. W. Bradley and K. D. Ewing, *Constitutional and Administrative Law* (15th edn, 2010), p. 216.

parliamentarians may have less regard for constitutional propriety than for their own private interests. If so, who is to protect the constitution against Parliamentary subversion?

Constitutional statutes

In the so-called *Metric Martyrs* case,[32] Lord Justice Laws said:

> In the present state of its maturity the common law has come to recognise that there exist rights which should properly be classified as constitutional or fundamental ... The special status of constitutional statutes follows the special status of constitutional rights. Examples are the Magna Carta, the Bill of Rights 1689, the Act of Union, the Reform Acts which distributed and enlarged the franchise, the Human Rights Act, the Scotland Act 1998 and the Government of Wales Act 1998. The European Communities Act clearly belongs in this family ...
>
> Ordinary statutes may be impliedly repealed. Constitutional statutes may not ...
>
> This development of the common law regarding constitutional rights, and as I would say constitutional statutes, is highly beneficial. It gives us most of the benefits of a written constitution, in which fundamental rights are accorded special respect. But it preserves the sovereignty of the legislature and the flexibility of our uncodified constitution. It accepts the relation between legislative supremacy and fundamental rights is not fixed or brittle: rather the courts (in interpreting statutes, and now, applying the HRA) will pay more or less deference to the legislature, or other public decision-maker, according to the subject in hand.

This passage provoked a good deal of academic interest and some sharp criticism,[33] because it departed from the traditional viewpoint that all statutes are equal, albeit that later ones may have to be given precedence over earlier ones with which they are inconsistent. But its practical relevance to modern constitutional law became apparent only with the decision of the Supreme Court in the HS2 litigation.[34]

---

[32] *Thoburn* v. *Sunderland City Council* [2002] EWHC 195 (Admin), [62–3]; the tag was an inflated journalistic description of a contest about the legality of regulations substituting metric for imperial measure in retail businesses.

[33] A. Perrau-Saussine [2002] CLJ 528; G. Marshall (2002) 118 LQR 493; D. Campbell and J. Young [2002] PL 399

[34] *R (on the application of HS2 Action Alliance Limited)* v. *The Secretary of State for Transport and another* [2014] UKSC 3

The HS2 case

The case, which concerned the validity of legislation designed to pave the way for the construction of a new high-speed rail link between London and the West Midlands, raised the question whether the intended use of the parliamentary procedure for hybrid bills was compatible with EU law. To the court's evident surprise no party, including the Secretary of State for Transport, drew attention to the bar contained in article IX of the Bill of Rights on questioning parliament's proceedings in a court of law. The Supreme Court concluded in the event that there was no requirement of EU law that member states' courts should scrutinise national legislative processes for compliance with EU requirements;[35] but it is the court's reasons for reaching this conclusion that contain what may be the seeds of future growth.

Lord Reed put it this way:

> The separation of powers is a fundamental aspect of most if not all of the constitutions of the member states . . .
>
> There is . . . much to be said for the view, advanced by the German Federal Constitutional Court . . . that as part of a co-operative relationship, a decision of the Court of Justice should not be read by a national court in a way that places in question the identity of the national constitutional order.[36]

Building on this, Lord Neuberger and Lord Mance in a joint concurring judgment said:

> The United Kingdom has no written constitution, but we have a number of constitutional instruments . . . The common law itself also recognises certain principles as fundamental to the rule of law . . . [T]here may be fundamental principles, whether contained in other constitutional instruments or recognised at common law, of which Parliament when it enacted the European Communities Act 1972 did not either contemplate or authorise the abrogation.
>
> . . . Important insights into potential issues in this area are to be found in their penetrating discussion by Laws LJ in the Divisional Court in

---

[35] Cf. R (Jackson) v. Attorney-General [2005] UKHL 56, discussed in Ch. 7, where the law lords adjudicated without objection on the detail of the Parliament Act procedures by which the Hunting Act 2004 had been passed.

[36] Ibid. [110]–[111]. The German text, as set out by Lord Reed, reads: "Im Sinne eines kooperativen Miteinanders zwischen dem Bundesverfassungsgericht und dem Europäischen Gerichtshof ... darf dieser Entscheidung keine Lesart unterlegt werden, nach der diese offensichtlich als Ultra-vires-Akt zu beurteilen wäre oder Schutz und Durchsetzung der mitgliedstaatlichen Grundrechte in einer Weise gefährdete ..., dass dies die Identität der durch das Grundgesetz errichteten Verfassungsordnung in Frage stellte" (Judgment of 24 April 2013, 1 BvR 1215/07, para. 91)

Thoburn v. *Sunderland City Council* . . . although the focus there was the possibility of conflict between an earlier "constitutional" and later "ordinary" statute, rather than, as here, between two constitutional instruments, which raises yet further considerations.[37]

It will not have been by chance that the Supreme Court drew on the jurisprudence of the German Constitutional Court in support of Laws' construct. Of all the European supreme courts, it is the Bundesverfassungsgericht which has been firmest in its insistence that the incorporation of EU law is a domestic act, done within the powers created by the country's Basic Law – in effect its constitution – and continuing to be subject to it. By endorsing the judgment in *Thoburn*, the Supreme Court has begun to set constitutional adjudication on a course which, while accepting that procedurally all laws are equal, recognises that some are constitutionally more equal than others.

Where next?

It is now well over a century since Dicey asserted that the English (he eschewed "British") constitution was in all its essentials judge-made. If he was mistaken then – and he was[38] – he would be doubly mistaken now, for the statutory component of the constitution today is massive. But the rule of law, a constitutional principle now enshrined in statute,[39] by articulating the twin sovereignties of legislature and judicature affords the courts a statutory vantage point. From it they can, for example, examine the constitutionality of a legislative usurpation of the judicial function.[40]

The jurisprudential impulse towards constitutionalism may at one level be a response to a growing sense, now publicly shared by a number of senior judges, that the UK's political and legal sovereignty has been compromised by or surrendered to supra-national courts and institutions.[41]

---

[37] Ibid., [207]–[208]   [38] See Ch. 14.

[39] Constitutional Reform Act 2005, s. 1: "This Act does not adversely affect . . . the existing constitutional principle of the rule of law . . .".

[40] E.g. Asylum and Immigration (Treatment of Claimants) Act 2004, s. 8: see Ch. 7

[41] Lord Hoffmann, "The Continuing Importance of the Protection of Fundamental Human Rights at Common Law", ALBA lecture, 23 October 2014; Lord Justice Laws, "The Common Law and Europe", Hamlyn Lectures, 2013; Lord Sumption, "The Limits of Law", Kuala Lumpur, 20 November 2013; Lord Judge, "Constitutional Change: Unfinished Business", UCL, 4 December 2013. The political rhetoric tends to locate these threats in Brussels, Luxembourg and Strasbourg, but a greater threat to national sovereignty probably lies in the mooted Transatlantic Trade and Investment Partnership.

But it also reflects a sense that constitutionalism itself may need to be defended against the demands of political expediency, whether these come from Whitehall or from Westminster. What ought to distinguish the emerging constitutional jurisprudence from the surrounding political clamour is the premise that statute and common law contain principles of equal fundamentality which together make up the UK's constitution.[42]

This in turn begins to answer some of the radical questions opened up by the House of Lords in 2005 in *Jackson*, in particular Lord Steyn's question whether, if Parliament were to set about disrupting fundamental constitutional standards or processes, its sovereignty – "a principle", said Lord Steyn, "established on a different hypothesis of constitutionalism" – might have to be "qualified" by the courts. The possibility of the courts reacting negatively to unconstitutional acts of the legislature is not new: a number of judges have contemplated it in recent years,[43] as Coke and other judges did four centuries before them.[44] What may be developing in this situation is a constitutional model in which the respective sovereignties of Parliament and the courts, rather than assuming an ultimate deference of the latter to the former, interact (as common law, prerogative and statute did four centuries ago) in generating a constitutional morality built on the rule of law and adapted to its time.

---

[42] See further Ch. 7, "Can Parliament Break the Law?"   [43] See Ch. 7, n. 4.
[44] See Ch. 7.

PART II

Themes

6

The royal prerogative

The claims of the Tudor and Stuart monarchs to unrestricted state power were repudiated by judges who held that the Crown had only those prerogatives which the law accorded it. The residue of authority which this has afforded the Crown and its ministers has nevertheless remained a controversial source of state power.

The throne and the lions

If anyone imagines that judges overreaching themselves and interfering in politics is a complaint confined to modern judicial review, they need look no further than Bacon's essay "Of Judicature", published in 1625.

> "Let judges also remember," Bacon wrote, "that Solomon's throne was supported by lions on both sides: let them be lions, but yet lions under the throne; being circumspect that they do not check or oppose any points of sovereignty."[1]

Much of the history considered in this book begins in Bacon's working lifetime, between his call to the Bar by Gray's Inn in 1582 and his disgrace and demotion from the chancellorship in the early 1620s. It is a history which not only explains why Bacon wrote what he did about the proper place of the judiciary but also helps to explain why critiques

---

[1] F. Bacon, *Essaies* (1625 edn). The essay did not feature in the original edition published in 1597. It first appeared in the 1612 edition, but it did not include this celebrated passage. It may well have been his differences with Coke which led Bacon to introduce it into the final version. Bacon was careful in his metaphor to distinguish Solomon's throne, protected by twenty six lions in columns to either side and down its steps (1 Kings 10), from the throne of England, constructed in 1297 and used in every coronation since the enthronement of Edward II in 1308. The four gilded lions known to Bacon, which formed its feet and thus sat under the throne, had been added to it in the sixteenth century. They were replaced in 1727 by the four lions which are there today: see the front cover.

continue to be directed at what is conventionally dubbed judicial activism.[2]

Public law, as Bacon pointed out, has a proper sphere of operation which does not include the business of government. What Bacon was also taking care to point out, however, was that the state itself must operate within the law: that was the principle which the judicial lions were there to guard, and it is why he went on to say:

> Let not judges also be so ignorant of their own right as to think there is not left them, as a principal part of their own office, a wise use and application of laws.

The location of the borderline between public law and public administration is still disputed, but Bacon's admonition is striking evidence that it had already become controversial by the end of the sixteenth century. Monarchs such as Elizabeth I or James I, ruling by divine right, ought to have been able to dictate both law and justice at will: yet by the first decade of the seventeenth century their judges, Coke prominent among them but by no means on his own, had established an autonomy for the common law which survives to this day and which is one of the shaping forces of the constitution.

Sir Edward Coke

The *Case of Prohibitions* arose out of a dispute which was brought before the King in person by the Archbishop of Canterbury, who asserted that scripture gave James power to decide it. Coke, with the backing of all English judges, held otherwise. This is how he reported his own decision:

> "A controversy of land between parties was heard by the King, and sentence given, which was repealed for this, that it did belong to the common law: then the King said, that he thought the law was founded upon reason. And that he and others had reason, as well as the Judges: to which it was answered by me," – wrote Coke – "that true it was, that God had endowed his Majesty with excellent science, and great endowments of nature; but his Majesty was not learned in the laws of his realm of England, and causes which concern the life, or inheritance, or goods, or fortunes of his subjects, are not to be decided by natural reason but by the artificial reason and judgment of law, which law is an act which requires long study and experience, before that a man can attain to the cognizance of it: that the law was the golden metwand and measure to try the causes

---

[2] The word has no jurisprudential meaning. A judge is either active or asleep.

of the subjects; and which protected His Majesty in safety and peace: with which the King was greatly offended, and said, that he should then be under the law, which was treason to affirm, as he said; to which I said, that Bracton saith, *quod Rex non debet esse sub homine, sed sub Deo et lege.*"[3]

A contemporary record describes the resulting confrontation in which, as Plucknett put it, the King lost his dignity and Coke lost his nerve:

> his Majestie . . . looking and speaking fiercely with bended fist offering to strike him, which the Lord Coke perceiving, fell flatt on all fower.[4]

Bacon would have enjoyed the symbolism of the judicial lion being ordered back under the throne. So would Dr Cowell, the Oxford professor of civil law, who in 1607[5] wrote: "I have heard some to be of opinion that the laws be above the King", but asserted unequivocally that the King "is above the law by his absolute power; he may alter or suspend any particular law that seemeth hurtful to the publick estate." But history was on Coke's side.

Monopolies

One of the Tudor monarchy's most profitable sidelines was the grant of monopolies – an exercise of the prerogative in its Blackstonian sense of power to do things that no individual could. Monopolies were, however, a serious handicap on trade: they stifled competition and inflated prices. When Parliament set about legislating to constrain their use, Elizabeth backed down. In November 1601 she issued a proclamation[6] withdrawing a considerable number of them on the ground that they had been abused, and allowing anyone who had been harmed by such abuse to "take their ordinary remedy by her Highness' laws of this realm".

One of the grants she withdrew was a monopoly of the making and importation of playing cards, which she had issued to Edward Darcy, a groom of the privy chamber, in return for a fee of 100 marks a year. Earlier in 1601 Darcy had brought a lawsuit against a haberdasher named

---

[3] *Prohibitions del Roy* (1607) 12 Co. Rep. 63. The Latin words mean "for the King must not be beneath men, but beneath God and the law".

[4] Quo. T. Plucknett, *A Concise History of the Common Law* (4th edn, 1948), p. 49 n. 1

[5] *The Interpreter*, Cowell's law dictionary; quo. C. D. Bowen, *The Lion and the Throne: The Life and Times of Sir Edward Coke* (1990), p. 255

[6] *Tudor Royal Proclamations*, vol. III, #812, "Reforming Patent Abuses", Westminster, 28 November 1601

Allein who had infringed his monopoly.[7] Sir Edward Coke A-G, Darcy's counsel in what has become known as the *Case of Monopolies*, accepted that the courts had control of the grant of monopolies but defended this one on the ground that the Queen was entitled to restrict the availability of playing cards for reasons of public morality. Chief Justice Popham, speaking for the full court, held that all monopoly was contrary to common law because it restricted employment and for that reason lay beyond the prerogative power:

> The Queen could not suppress the making of cards within the realm, no more than the making of dice, bowls, balls, hawks' hoods, bells, lures, dog-couples and other the like, which are works of labour and art, although they serve for pleasure, recreation and pastime, and cannot be suppressed but by Parliament . . .

Popham's court gave a second reason which is of interest because it prefigures the House of Lords' decision in *Padfield's Case*[8] that administrative action may not run counter to the policy and objects of the enabling statute. The preamble of Darcy's grant recited that the Queen's purpose in making it was to advance the public good; but since all it had done was fill Darcy's pocket, said Popham, "the Queen was deceived in her grant" – that is to say the monopoly had failed in its purpose.

Popham cited in support of his court's decision a fourteenth-century statute which had annulled the King's grant of a monopoly of importing sweet wines into London: once again the Commons and the judges were closing the trap on the monarch's prerogatives. But the monarchy could still bite back. The following year, 1602, the Queen's Privy Council ordered some traders (who may have included Allein) to be gaoled for infringing Darcy's monopoly, probably on the ground – which would have represented a defiance of Popham's decision that the grant was void – that at the time of infringement the royal grant had not yet been revoked.

The last word went to Coke. By the time he published his report of the *Case of Monopolies*, James I was on the throne and had published a book in which he declared all monopolies to be unlawful, "and therefore," Coke announced, "expressly commands that no suitor presume to move him to grant any of them".

This, however, concerned domestic monopolies: the courts were astute to see the link between job creation at home (which meant suppressing

---

[7] *The Case of Monopolies, Darcy* v. *Allein* 11 Co. Rep. 84
[8] *Padfield* v. *Minister of Agriculture* [1968] AC 997

domestic monopolies)[9] and the exclusion or restriction of foreign imports (which meant upholding external ones). There was thus every reason to preserve the monopolies of the eleven international trading companies, among them the Merchant Adventurers and the East India Company, which by 1600 had been granted exclusive licences by royal charter.[10]

The judges and the prerogative

All of this helps to explain why Coke, in his time, did not stand alone. Modern work on the prerogative writ of habeas corpus has shown how, towards the end of Elizabeth's reign and into the reign of James I, at least three of the senior judges had made it their business to establish judicial oversight of local courts, bodies and functionaries which took it on themselves to deprive individuals of their liberty. The first was Sir John Popham, Chief Justice of the King's Bench from 1592 until his death in 1607.[11] The second was Sir Thomas Fleming, who succeeded him. Coke, who succeeded Fleming in 1613 but was ousted three years later, was the third. Of these chief justices, Paul Halliday says:

> Coke is by far the best known of these three today.[12] But his two prede-
> cessors in King's Bench did more to transform habeas corpus from an
> instrument for moving around bodies as part of routine court business
> into an instrument for controlling other jurisdictions. They did this by
> capturing the king's prerogative for their own, then defending this capture
> with procedural innovations.[13]

Prerogative and law

This is the situation in which the lions begin to emerge from beneath the throne and the royal prerogative begins to be drawn into the portals of

---

[9] A body of case law held that the holders of chartered or *de facto* monopolies such as toll bridges and wharfs could only charge reasonable fees: see P. Craig, "Constitutions, Property and Regulation" [1991] PL 538. Until the early nineteenth century the courts also penalised market manipulation: see S. Sedley *Freedom, Law and Justice* (1999), pp. 35–6. Unreasonable covenants in restraint of trade continue to be justiciable.

[10] C. Arnold-Baker, *Companion to British History*, "Chartered Companies'"

[11] It was Popham who had decided the *Case of Monopolies* against Coke's arguments.

[12] Principally, however, through his tenure from 1606 of the office of Chief Justice of the Court of Common Pleas.

[13] Paul D. Halliday, *Habeas Corpus, from England to Empire* (2010), p. 22

the common law.[14] In the *Case of Proclamations*,[15] in 1611, Coke articulated what had become and still is the foundational principle of a constitutional monarchy:

> The King hath no prerogative but what the law of the land allows him.

I say "had become" because as early as the thirteenth century Bracton had written: "The king ought not to be subject to men but to God and the law, for law makes a king". Two centuries later Sir John Fortescue in his treatise *In Praise of the Laws of England*[16] had asserted that the King in his political capacity had no power either to alter the law or to administer it: his two bodies, the body natural and the body politic, were wholly distinct.

In today's very different political context, what Coke derived from longstanding principle remains the law:

> It is for the courts to inquire whether a particular prerogative power exists or not, and, if it does exist, into its extent.[17] Over the centuries the scope of the royal prerogative has been steadily eroded, and it cannot today be enlarged …[18] When the existence or effect of the royal prerogative is in question the courts must conduct an historical inquiry to ascertain whether there is any precedent for the exercise of the power in the given circumstances. "If it is law, it will be found in our books. If it is not to be found there, it is not law."[19]

The prerogative strikes back

By the beginning of the seventeenth century the judges were in consequence not simply corralling the royal prerogative. As Halliday suggests, they were themselves exercising it. Chief Justice Fleming made it quite clear that the writs of habeas corpus, prohibition, certiorari and mandamus – the prerogative writs or orders as they continued to be called until

---

[14] As to the prerogative court of Star Chamber, which survived until 1641, see Ch. 9.

[15] (1611) 12 Co.Rep.74; applied in *Pankina* v. *Home Secretary* [2010] EWCA Civ 719; [2012] UKSC 33 affirmed on appeal on other grounds.

[16] *De Laudibus Legum Angliae*, first printed 1537 but written for Edward, Prince of Wales (1453–71), Ch. IX, Ch. VIII (Amos ed. pp. 26,22).

[17] *CCSU* v. *Minister for the Civil Service* [1985] AC 374, 398E

[18] *BBC* v. *Johns* [1965] Ch. 32, 79

[19] Per Lord Bingham, *R (Bancoult)* v. *Secretary of State for Foreign and Commonwealth Affairs* [2008] UKHL 61, [69] citing Lord Camden, *Entick* v. *Carrington* (1765) 19 St. Tr. 1030, 1066.

the late twentieth century – were issued in the exercise by the judges of the monarch's own powers:

> "This court," he said, "is the jurisdiction of the Queen herself. It is so high that in its presence all other jurisdictions cease."[20]

James I, who was not an ignorant man[21] and had been accustomed as James VI of Scotland to something approaching complete deference from his judges,[22] denounced Coke's stricture on the monarch's personal use of the prerogative power as treason. But he could no more adjudicate without his judges than he could raise money without Parliament. Sometimes James got his way, as he did in 1606, when an acquiescent Court of Exchequer allowed him, in defiance of a statute of 1372 forbidding the Crown to raise taxes without Parliament's consent, to levy a duty on the import of currants on the pretext that he was merely regulating trade[23] – a form of reasoning still familiar in the twenty-first century. His successor, Charles I, similarly persuaded a majority of the court of Exchequer Chamber[24] in 1637 to endorse his demand, famously opposed by John Hampden and others, for ship money to equip a navy. It is not without interest that Chief Justice Finch, in upholding the Crown's claim, held that "acts of parliament to take away [the] royal power in defence of the kingdom are void"; for here was Coke's notion of limited parliamentary power[25] being used not to mark out the fief of the common law but to preserve the fief of the prerogative. For a short time the jurisprudential pendulum was swinging back towards monarchical power. But the Long

---

[20] Lincoln's Inn MSS, Misc. 492 f.27v., cited by Halliday, *Habeas Corpus*, p. 75

[21] His published political works alone (1616 edn) ran to 265 pages, though his pamphlet against tobacco showed rather more foresight than his *Trew Law of Free Monarchies* ("which forme of government, as resembling the Divinitie, approacheth nearest to perfection ...").

[22] But not total deference, it seems. In 1599, before he ascended the throne of England, James had apparently been defied by the Court of Session in a lawsuit brought by Robert Bruce against Lord Hamilton. According to an eyewitness account sent to Sir Robert Cecil, the court found for Bruce in the face of James' intercession on behalf of Hamilton, holding that they did justice not according to the King's command but as their consciences led them. See Claire Palley, *The United Kingdom and Human Rights* (1991), p. 20, esp. n. 15.

[23] *The Case of Impositions (Bate's Case)* (1606) 2 St. Tr. 371: "The revenue of the Crown is the very essential part of the Crown, and he who rendeth that from the King pulleth also his Crown from his head ..."

[24] *The Case of Ship Money (R v. Hampden)* (1637) 3 St. Tr. 825

[25] See *Dr Bonham's Case* (1608/1610) 8 Co. Rep. 113b, discussed in Ch. 7, "The Supremacy of Parliament and the Abuse of Power".

Parliament in 1640, in the run-up to the Civil War, reversed the decision and reasserted parliamentary control over taxation.[26]

Dispensing with law

Following the Restoration, the courts attempted to restrict the royal power to dispense at will with legislation;[27] but James II, with the eventual acquiescence of his judges,[28] disapplied Parliament's laws for his own religious purposes until the Bill of Rights of 1689 put an end to the practice and restored a restriction on monarchical power which was already, in principle, centuries old.

We have learned to think that parliamentary control over taxation has consequently never since 1689 been contested. Yet in modern times the Crown, in its executive role as tax collector, has purported to waive Parliament's laws by letting defaulters off the tax they owed. Until the discontinuance of the practice was announced in 2014, the Inland Revenue annually published a volume unblushingly entitled "Extra-Statutory Concessions", setting out the situations in which it intended not to enforce the law laid down by Parliament.[29] Until 2008, when some of the exemptions were put on a somewhat exiguous statutory footing and others discontinued, this was done in the exercise by ministers and civil servants of a power which can only have been the royal prerogative.[30] Nobody appeared to be unduly troubled by the fact that the Bill of Rights three centuries earlier had abolished the Crown's dispensing power.[31]

Thus, somewhat contrary to Tennyson's vision of the grand sweep of English history, freedom over these centuries has not simply broadened down from precedent to precedent. The acquiescence of many of the judges

---

[26] The story is taken up in Ch. 4, on the Interregnum, and Ch. 3, on the Hanoverian confrontation.

[27] *Thomas* v. *Sorrell* (1674) Vaughan 330   [28] *Godden* v. *Hales* (1686) 11 St. Tr. 1165

[29] "An Extra-Statutory Concession is a relaxation which gives taxpayers a reduction in tax liability to which they would not be entitled under the strict letter of the law": HMRC Guide to ESCs, 6 April 2013. See *R (Wilkinson)* v. *IRC* [2005] 1 WLR 1718, esp. §§ 20 ff; J. Freedman and J. Vella, "Revenue Guidance: The Limits of Discretion and Legitimate Expectations" (2012) 128 LQR 192.

[30] The process, which had been announced in Parliament, was known as "offering Hansard" to tax defaulters. Cf. the discussion (below) of the supposed "third source" of governmental power. See, however, Ch. 5 in relation to the discretion of the DPP not to prosecute.

[31] Bill of Rights 1688, art. II: "That the pretended power of dispensing with laws or the execution of laws by regall authoritie . . . is illegall."

in the despotism of the later Stuarts led the historian George Trevelyan to treat Bacon's metaphor of lions under the throne as an image of servility rather than of vigilance.[32] And it is the very ambiguity of the image – the king of beasts in a submissive posture – which characterises both the history of public law and the controversy which continues to surround it.

Nevertheless, the fact that it was not until 1700, when the Act of Settlement was passed, that the judges of the higher courts were made secure against dismissal at the will of the Crown makes striking the principled stand that some of them took, in the period following the Restoration, against regal autocracy. When James II set about packing the court that was to decide *Godden* v. *Hales*,[33] the case on the legality of his use of the dispensing power to allow Roman Catholics to hold military commissions, he told the Chief Justice of the Common Pleas, Sir Thomas Jones, that he must either give up his opinion or his place.

> "For my place," said Jones, "I care little. I am old and worn out in the service of the Crown. But I am mortified to find that Your Majesty thinks me capable of giving a judgment which none but an ignorant or a dishonest man could give ... Your majesty may find twelve judges of your mind, but hardly twelve lawyers."[34]

The long revolution

The history of public law thus offers a qualification to the conventional wisdom that it was in 1689, by what Trevelyan called "this beneficent Revolution", that "the liberty of the subject and the power of Parliament were finally secured against the power of the Crown". The principles of a constitutional monarchy had been laid down long before 1689. They had been fought over in a civil war which ousted a monarch who would not accept constitutional restrictions on his power. They had been flouted by the monarchs who returned after the failure of the Commonwealth and the collapse of the Protectorate. But, although consolidated in the Bill of Rights 1689,[35] they have continued to be fought over, for the royal

---

[32] G. M. Trevelyan, *England under the Stuarts* (1904), Folio ed., p. 359

[33] (1686) 11 St. Tr. 1165

[34] Macaulay, *The History of England from the Accession of James II* (1914 edn), vol. II, p. 735 (quo. Bradley [2008] PL 471). Macaulay may have been guessing what Jones would have liked to say.

[35] Part of the Bill of Rights replicated the Instrument of Government 1653, by which the Protectorate was instituted: see Ch. 4.

prerogative has not withered away in the four centuries since Coke's time. Notwithstanding Lord Bingham's stricture, it has changed in form, in content, and above all in its relationship with the law; but it remains the element in which central government lives and moves and has its being.

The Privy Council

Perhaps the most remarkable survivor of the centuries of constitutional conflict and vicissitude has been the Privy Council. All the great departments of state – the Treasury, the Home Office, the Foreign and Commonwealth Office – and many of the powerful government commissions and boards to which major executive functions were assigned in the course of the eighteenth and nineteenth centuries were emanations of the Crown: no Parliament ever legislated to bring them into being. But while these departments and bodies have no lawmaking powers that have not been granted by Parliament or which can therefore escape the oversight of the courts, the Privy Council, whose powers derive in part from statute and in part from the royal prerogative, continues to be used by governments as a means of introducing laws without scrutiny or vote.[36]

One of the signal achievements of the common law during the twentieth century, however, was the affirmation of the power of the ordinary courts to supervise the legality of prerogative acts of the Crown, whether in relation to the disbursement of *ex gratia* payments,[37] the recognition of civil service unions,[38] the liability of ministers for contempt of court[39] or the making of Orders in Council for the governance of colonies.[40] But while it is known[41] that in 2002, 372 Orders in Council were made under

---

[36] See Patrick O'Connor QC, *The Constitutional Role of the Privy Council and the Prerogative* (2009). Separately, and by statute (the Judicial Committee Act 1833), its judicial committee, composed of senior UK and Commonwealth judges, still functions as the final court of appeal for a small number of former colonies.

[37] *R v. Criminal Injuries Compensation Board, ex p Lain* [1967] 2 QB 864

[38] *CCSU v. Minister for the Civil Service* [1985] AC 374

[39] *M v. Home Office* [1994] AC 377

[40] *R (Bancoult) v. Foreign and Commonwealth Secretary (No.2)* [2007] EWCA Civ 498; [2008] UKHL 61. The Court of Appeal in paras. 44–7 questions whether any of the high prerogative functions are today beyond the reach of public law.

[41] From a parliamentary answer: see O'Connor, *The Constitutional Role of the Privy Council and the Prerogative*, p. 8.

statutory powers as against 154 in the exercise of the prerogative, both classes are constitutionally problematical.

For example, the entire Scottish independence plebiscite in 2014 depended upon a single Privy Council measure. Using a power of amendment given to the Privy Council by the Scotland Act 1998, an Order in Council[42] was made, removing an independence referendum from the scheduled list of reserved (i.e. undevolved) matters. No legislation was passed to give effect to a Yes vote. Instead, by undertaking to respect the result, the leaders of the three main parties, without the authority of Parliament, endorsed a plebiscite on the possible break-up of the United Kingdom in which the majority of the UK's population had had no vote. It will never be known whether, had the Yes side won in Scotland, the Westminster Parliament would have proceeded without more to repeal the Union with Scotland Act 1706.

To take a rather different example, power to legislate by Order in Council was granted to the Privy Council by the United Nations Act 1946, in order to implement UN decisions. The provision appeared, and was almost certainly intended, to cater simply for administrative measures. When the power was used in 2006 to enact an extra-judicial confiscation regime for use on terrorism suspects, the question arose whether, without explicit power to do so, a statutory Order in Council could take away the right of access to the courts. The Supreme Court held that it could not lawfully be done.[43]

Thus at least Orders in Council purporting to be made under statutory powers can be measured by the courts against those powers and struck down if they are non-compliant. Those made under non-statutory prerogative powers, which include the entire governance of Britain's remaining colonial territories, are subject to no such legislative control.[44] This was how Jack Straw, as Foreign and Commonwealth Secretary, was able, without the knowledge of Parliament and without any consultation with those affected, to take away the right of the exiled Chagos islanders to return to their home. Although the House of Lords, in a much-criticised

---

[42] 2013 no. 242

[43] *A, K et al.* v. *HM Treasury* [2008] EWHC 869 (Collins J); sub nom. *Ahmed* v. *HM Treasury* [2008] EWCA Civ 1187 (CA); [2010] UKSC 2.

[44] "The royal prerogative to legislate by order in council is indeed an anachronistic survival" (Lord Bingham in *R (Bancoult)* v. *Secretary of State for Foreign and Commonwealth Affairs (No. 2)* [2006] EWHC 1038 (Admin); [2007] EWCA Civ 498; [2008] UKHL 61, [69]). Prerogative orders in council are assimilated to primary legislation for the purposes of the Human Rights Act 1998: see s. 21(1).

majority decision, held this ministerial use of the royal prerogative to have been lawful on the facts of the case, the courts at every level[45] accepted that the prerogative power to make orders in council is today justiciable for abuse of power.[46] Judicial review in this area, however, is a longstop. At departmental level, a Secretary of State can put a draft Order in Council before the Queen for signature without either the public or Parliament knowing about it until it is signed and sealed.

At a political level, the Privy Council today deliberates and legislates as an outgrowth of Cabinet. This is accomplished by excluding from its discussions all privy counsellors except those who are currently cabinet ministers, on the ground that it is only on the advice of her government that the Queen may act. The Privy Council's deliberations – most of them on deeply unexciting questions like the closure of burial grounds, but some on such important issues as the royal charter in support of press regulation – are accordingly conducted principally by inter-departmental memorandum; actual meetings are extremely rare. More significantly, there is no participation at any stage by privy counsellors from the opposition or by the large number of non-political privy counsellors who might well have useful contributions to make.

It is possible to regard the continued existence of such a narrowly constituted body, empowered to make legally binding enactments behind closed doors without public notice or debate, as an affront to the rule of law. But the Privy Council is by no means the only manifestation of the prerogative power of the Crown in the functioning of modern government, and the availability of judicial review to keep it within the law continues to matter.

A "third source" of power?

Are there nevertheless what Bacon called "points of sovereignty" beyond the reach of the law? Were the Queen's privy counsellors entitled, as the lawyer John Hawarde alleged in 1597,[47]

---

[45] R (Bancoult) v. Secretary of State for Foreign and Commonwealth Affairs (No.2) [2006] EWHC 1038 (Admin); [2007] EWCA Civ 498; [2008] UKHL 61.

[46] See also R v. Lords of the Privy Council, ex p Vijayatunga [1988] QB 322 where the jurisdiction of the High Court was invoked without contest to decide the propriety of the procedure adopted by an ad hoc committee of the Privy Council acting on behalf of a royal university visitor.

[47] John Hawarde, Les Reportes del Cases in Camera Stellata, 1593–1609, pp. 78–9, cited in James S. Hart, The Rule of Law 1603–1660 (2003), p. 6

to attribute to their councils and orders the vigour, force and power of a firm law, and of higher virtue and force, jurisdiction and pre-eminence, than any positive law, whether it be the common law or statute law?

There is a doctrinal dispute about what the royal prerogative is. Is it purely the great functions of state which no private individual could perform – making war or peace, conferring honours, entering into treaties, appointing ministers, summoning or proroguing Parliament, pardoning crimes: what one can call the high prerogative?[48] Or is it what can be called the broad prerogative: everything the state does which has no articulated authority in statute law or prerogative power but is ancillary to its express powers – formation of contracts, employment of staff, procurement of supplies, holding and disposal of land and so forth?[49] The difference has come to matter in recent years because of a debate among public lawyers about a "third source" of state power[50] which is said to originate neither in statute nor in the prerogative but in a previously unrecognised form of authority which places the state on a par with the private individual[51] and allows it to do anything that the law does not explicitly forbid.

While the ebb and flow of recent authority and commentary on the theory may be an unusual instance of legal history in the making, the theory itself is arguably a jurisprudential version of the emperor's new clothes.

The Ram doctrine

In 1945 Sir Granville Ram, the senior parliamentary drafter, explained in a memorandum that, unlike a statutory corporation – for example a local authority – which is axiomatically limited to the powers given to it by law, a minister

---

[48] This meaning is the one attributed to Blackstone by Sir William Wade: see Wade and Forsyth, *Administrative Law* (10th edn, 2009), p. 182. But Blackstone was clear that even the high prerogative was created and bounded by law: "the prerogative of the Crown extends not to do any injury: it is created for the benefit of the people, and therefore cannot be exerted to their prejudice" (Bl. Comm., I, 232, 239).

[49] And the provision by the Home Secretary of baton rounds and CS gas to local police forces as part of the Crown's peacekeeping function: *R v. Home Secretary, ex p Northumbria Police Authority* [1989] QB 26; cf. critique by A. W. Bradley [1988] PL 297.

[50] See B. V. Harris [1992] LQR 626; [2007] LQR 225; [2010] LQR 373.

[51] Cf. s. 1(1) of the Localism Act 2011: "A local authority has power to do anything that individuals generally may do." At the time of writing no decided case has explored the true reach of this provision. See further Ch. 11, "The Local State".

may, as an agent of the Crown, exercise any powers which the Crown has power to exercise, except so far as he is precluded from doing so by statute.[52]

The memorandum may not, in its time, have been mistaken in its suggestion that the only constraints on the use of prerogative power were statutory. Today, as the Attorney-General in 2013 told the House of Lords' Constitution Committee, the power "is circumscribed by public law; by propriety; by human rights".[53] But Ram's essential point, which is all that will have properly concerned him as senior parliamentary drafter, was perfectly correct: ministers have implied power to do what is reasonably ancillary to their role without any need for Parliament to spell out their authority to do it.[54] This, however, is not what was made of his memorandum in Whitehall: it was recycled, in the words of the Treasury's submission to the Constitution Committee, as a proposition that "ministers can do anything a natural person can do, unless limited by legislation".[55]

It would have been reasonable to expect that this hangover from the years of Whitehall supremacism was laid to rest by the response of the Constitution Committee:

> The Ram memorandum is not a source of law and ... not an accurate reflection of the law today . . .. The description of the common law powers of the Crown encapsulated by the phrase "the Ram doctrine" is inaccurate and should no longer be used.[56]

---

[52] Although widely used (and misused) in Whitehall, Ram's memorandum was not published until 2003, when it was extracted by persistent parliamentary questions put by Lord Lester QC.

[53] Report of the House of Lords Select Committee on the Constitution, "The Pre-emption of Parliament" (2013) §58. The A-G's inclusion of human rights as a non-statutory constraint was correct: see Ch. 11.

[54] A doctrine well established in company law (*Colman* v. *Eastern Counties Railway Co.* (1846) 10 Beav. 1), and in contract law (*The Moorcock* (1889) 14 PD 64), and known to public law: see *R* v. *Glamorganshire Inhabitants* (1700) 1 Ld. Raym. 580, holding the upkeep of ancillary weirs to be part of the statutory power to maintain a bridge; see also *Town Investments* v. *DoE* [1978] AC 359. Hence, for Ram's purposes, there was no need for empowering legislation to include comprehensive lists of ancillary powers. The same has always been true of local authority powers, although the ambit of these was first confirmed and then enlarged by statute: see below.

[55] Report on "The Pre-emption of Parliament", 2013, § 55

[56] Report on "The Pre-emption of Parliament", 2013, §§ 52, 54, 60. Lord Brown of Eaton-under-Heywood told the Committee in evidence that in the course of his five years as Treasury Devil from 1979 to 1984 he had never heard of the Ram doctrine. During my time at the Bar, in the course of which I argued cases against every Treasury Devil from

In the intervening years, however, the suppositious Ram doctrine has made an inroad into the rule of law which it may take more than a parliamentary report to correct.

In 2000 a challenge came before the Court of Appeal to the maintenance by the Department of Health of a list of persons who ought not to work with children.[57] There was no statutory authority to maintain such a list, but the Department relied on its inherent powers to authorise what it was doing. The court might have found the maintenance of the list to be ancillary to the Department's statutory functions, but that is not what it did. Without explicit reference to Ram, Hale LJ, giving the single reasoned judgment, adopted a passage from Halsbury's *Laws of England*:

> At common law the Crown, as a corporation possessing legal personality, has the capacities of a natural person and thus the same liberties as the individual.[58]

This passage, taken from a footnote in Halsbury's *Laws* which cited no authority, was something of a trap.[59] That a corporation, including the Crown, may have the capacities, and even the liberties, of a natural person does not mean that it has their powers. The Crown and the individual share the capacity to dispense their money or property stupidly, maliciously or capriciously; but where the individual is also legally free to do so, the Crown is not. The reason is constitutionally fundamental: the Crown's powers exist not for its own benefit but for the public good.[60]

Nigel Bridge to John Laws, I never heard the Ram doctrine mentioned, much less relied on. But Sir Philip Sales (Treasury Devil 1997–2008), in October 2013 told an Oxford seminar that on his appointment he had been inducted into the doctrine, and that it "has always been followed and applied within central government" (P. Sales, "Crown Powers, the Royal Prerogative and Fundamental Rights", unpubd., n. 49).

[57] *R v. Secretary of State for Health, ex p C* [2000] FLR 627 (Lord Woolf MR, Hale LJ and Lord Mustill [who had retired as a law lord in 1997 and is misnamed in the report as Mustill LJ]).

[58] Halsbury's *Laws of England* (4th edn) vol. 8(2) "Constitutional Law and Human Rights", § 101 (*cap.* "Fundamental Rights and Freedoms of the Individual"), n. 6. The footnote cited no authority but referred back to § 6 of the same volume, a paragraph on the principle of legality in constitutional law which began: "The Crown is a corporation sole or aggregate and so has general legal capacity ..." None of this supports the use made of it by the court and, in reliance on the court, by commentators.

[59] Possibly for this reason, it does not appear in the 5th (2014) edition.

[60] See fn. 46 above. This, in fact, appeared to have been acknowledged by the Court of Appeal, for Hale LJ added that the power to maintain the contentious list had to be exercised fairly and reasonably. But this does not tell us what the powers actually are.

Thus the case for a third source of public power appears flawed at base.[61] But when, some years after the decision on the maintenance of a list of people unsuited to work with children, a related issue came before a differently constituted Court of Appeal,[62] the court considered itself bound by *Ex parte C* to validate measures taken by the Secretary of State to implement legislation which had not yet been passed – a step therefore not logically capable of being ancillary to any positive law.

In this way constitutional solecism can filter into public law and become embedded there, at least until a higher authority intervenes;[63] for although, as the Constitution Committee noted,

> The true extent of the common law powers of the Crown may be definitively determined only by the courts,

there is little evidence[64] that any notice is being taken in Whitehall, or by counsel representing the executive, of what the Committee said next:

---

[61] The 5th (2014) edition of Halsbury's *Laws*, vol. 20, "Constitutional and Administrative Law", makes no reference at all to *Ex parte C*. Nor does A. W. Bradley and K. D. Ewing, *Constitutional and Administrative Law* (16th edn, 2014). The High Court of Australia has rejected the third source theory: *Williams v. Commonwealth* [2012] HCA 23.

[62] *R (Shrewsbury and Atcham BC)* v. *Secretary of State for Local Government* [2008] EWCA Civ 148, (Carnwath LJ) and (Richards LJ). Uniquely among English courts, the civil division of the Court of Appeal is bound by its own previous decisions. Halsbury's *Laws* (5th edn, 2014), vol. 20, § 601, n. 9, treats the *Shrewsbury* decision simply as an illustration of the proposition that "the promotion of new policies through legislation is a necessary and incidental part of the ordinary business of central government". But Carnwath LJ (§ 44–8) set out a cogent case for doubting whether *Ex parte C* had been correctly decided. The judgment of Richards LJ (§§ 72–4), who had decided *Ex parte C* at first instance and who continued to favour its reasoning, is less convincing. The third member of the court, Waller LJ, took neither side.

[63] In *R (New London College)* v. *Home Secretary* [2013] UKSC 51, the issue was broached (§ 28, cf. § 34) but did not have to be resolved. The remark at § 28 ("the Crown possesses some general administrative powers to carry on the ordinary business of government which are not exercises of the royal prerogative and do not require statutory authority") does not necessarily support a third source of power rather than the concept of implied ancillary powers familiar from contract as well as public law: cf. ibid. ". . . the statutory power of the Secretary of State to administer the system of immigration control must necessarily extend to a range of ancillary and incidental administrative powers not expressly spelt out in the Act . . ." It appears from the judgments, however, that Treasury counsel had been attempting to rely on the "third source" of power as a surrogate for the Ram doctrine. Government lawyers now speak of the Crown having "common law powers" distinct from both statutory and prerogative powers, but these must by definition be dependent on the courts.

[64] In response to an enquiry, the Treasury Solicitor in June 2014 wrote that the training of all government lawyers now "makes explicit reference to the Committee's report and its

[T]he constrained nature of the Crown's common law powers is seldom made clear in Government documents. We note in particular that the Cabinet Manual describes the power of a minister to exercise "any of the legal powers of an individual",[65] but makes no reference to the fact that, whereas private individuals are free to exercise their powers irrationally (for example), ministers are not. We recommend that, where Government publications refer to the Crown's common law powers, it is made clear that these powers are limited by the restraints of public law and constitutional principle.[66]

It is of course important that, whatever the constitutional source of an executive power, its exercise is acknowledged to be constrained by ordinary principles of public law. But this leaves open the question of the existence and ambit of the power itself. If the claimed power is statutory, the statute book will define it; if prerogative, the common law will say whether it exists and how far it reaches; but if it is neither, who is to say what the power is and what its limits are, even if it is exercised with complete procedural propriety? The third source of executive power is at base a theory of government outside the law, and it would be better not to find government seeking juridical endorsement of it.

Power beyond law?

This said, the sovereignty which Bacon regarded as a reservoir of unreviewable monarchical power was not necessarily at odds with the royal prerogative which Coke held to be defined by the common law: both agreed that beyond the perimeter of the law the monarch possessed prerogative powers which the courts could not touch. The prerogatives of mercy and pardon would at the time have been in both men's minds.[67]

---

comments on the 'Ram doctrine' (we tend to avoid using that label now)". But cf. the previous footnote.

[65] *Cabinet Manual*, 2011, § 3.31   [66] "The pre-emption of Parliament" § 65

[67] The prerogative of pardon was a valuable instrument in seventeenth-century endeavours to control piracy: a number of prolific buccaneers were induced to give up piracy by the grant of free pardons: see Adrian Tinniswood, *Pirates of Barbary* (2011), Ch. 5. In the years of the Black Act and the game laws the prerogative of mercy was a significant means of social control, allowing condemned prisoners to escape the gallows by the grant of royal clemency, exercised by the Home Secretary. Before 1717, when transportation was made available as a lawful sentence, reprieve was frequently granted by use of the prerogative on condition that the prisoner agreed to be transported. In recent years the prerogative of pardon has become a means of rewarding prison informers for giving (frequently mendacious) testimony against other prisoners: see P. Foot, *Murder at the Farm* (2nd edn, 1993), pp. 271–2. In the US it has become a presidential power used to

But how much of the prerogative remains unreviewable by the courts in the twenty-first century?

It was in relation to the initial Criminal Injuries Compensation Scheme, set up by a White Paper in 1964[68] without any statutory authority, that the amenability of the prerogative to judicial review came directly in issue. In 1967 the government, faced with a challenge by a policeman's widow to a refusal of compensation, went confidently into the Divisional Court to argue that the administration of the scheme was beyond the reach of the courts. To its surprise, it lost.[69] In a farsighted judgment which recognised the historic character of the issue, Lord Justice Diplock held that the last prize of the English Civil War, the royal prerogative, which ministers had jealously guarded as their final reserve of arbitrary power, was today subject to the supervisory jurisdiction of the courts – not in order to substitute the judges' own decisions but in order to ensure that, in exercising the prerogative power to distribute bounty, the Home Office behaved fairly and followed the rules which it itself had published.[70]

> "It may be a novel development in constitutional practice," said Diplock, "to govern by public statement of intention made by the executive government instead of by legislation. This is no more, however, than a reversion to the ancient practice of government by royal proclamation, although it is now subject to the limitations imposed on that practice by the development of constitutional law in the seventeenth century."[71]

Although *Ex parte Lain* is still rarely given the accolade it deserves, its importance was recognised by Lord Scarman two decades later in the *CCSU* case,[72] where the reviewability of the prerogative – in the form of governmental action taken without statutory underpinning, in that case

---

pay political debts or to secure political advantages: see Tom Bingham, *Lives of the Law* (2011), Ch. 15. The law has, however, forbidden the Crown to exercise these prerogatives so as to defeat private law rights.

[68] Cmnd. 2323

[69] *R v. Criminal Injuries Compensation Board, ex p Lain* [1967] 2 QB 864

[70] Today this would be recognised as a class of legitimate expectation.

[71] *R v. Criminal Injuries Compensation Board, ex p Lain* [1967] 2 QB 886. Today the White Paper which set up the Criminal Injuries Compensation Scheme would be recognised without difficulty as a policy for the disbursement of public funds, and the courts would require government to give effect to the legitimate expectations it created unless for some acceptable reason it was necessary to depart from the scheme.

[72] *Council of Civil Service Unions v. Minister for the Civil Service* [1985] AC 374

the employment of staff – was confirmed. Lord Scarman picked up the importance of *Ex parte Lain*, matching it with the *Case of Proclamations*.

But the *CCSU* case did not determine how far judicial review of the high prerogative could now reach. It may be that some things in the governance of the state are by nature non-justiciable, but what they are is by no means as apparent today as it was when the *CCSU* case was decided. Lord Roskill's tabulation in the *CCSU* case of prerogative functions which were probably unreviewable[73] – the prerogative of mercy, the grant of honours, the defence of the realm, the making of treaties and of Orders in Council, the appointment of ministers, the dissolution of Parliament and so forth – invites the question whether experience might require us to think again about them. What if honours were to be granted in return for payment? What if a war of aggression were to be launched in breach of international law? What if a prerogative Order in Council were to be made for an ulterior purpose or a corrupt motive? Would the courts be forbidden by constitutional principle to intervene; or might constitutional principle, on the contrary, require them to do so?[74]

Envoi

A state in which the executive possesses powers of governance beyond the reach of legality is a state in which the rule of law is deficient. In the wake of a civil war and a *coup d'état* which halted the use of the royal prerogative to make or waive law, the eighteenth-century metamorphosis of regal power into ministerial authority[75] altered the form but not the substance of the dichotomy of law and government. Ministers, albeit appointed since the days of the Hanoverians on the advice of an elected prime minister, are not themselves elected to office, and the authority they deploy is not that of the legislature but that of the monarch. Hence the significance of the constraint placed by the common law courts in *Entick* v. *Carrington* on the power of the King's ministers to issue search-and-arrest warrants against

---

[73] At 418

[74] In *R (Bancoult)* v. *Secretary of State for Foreign and Commonwealth Affairs (No.2)* [2006] EWHC 1038 (Admin); [2007] EWCA Civ 498; [2008] UKHL 61, the justiciability for abuse of power of Orders in Council made by the Queen for the governance of colonies in the exercise of the high prerogative was accepted both by the majority of the House of Lords which found against the Chagos Islanders and by the minority which, together with two unanimous courts below, would have found for them.

[75] See Ch. 3.

the government's critics, and of the assertion in the *CCSU* case of the judicial power of review of prerogative acts. If it is the law of the land which still, to use Coke's verb, allows the Crown's ministers to deploy both high and broad prerogative powers, then the courts have a continuing obligation to ensure that these powers are exercised within the law.

7

The sovereignty of Parliament and the abuse of power

One of the future possibilities touched on in Chapter 5 was the development of a constitutionalism premised on the rule of law rather than solely
on Parliamentary supremacy. This chapter looks at how, historically, this
dualism has been managed, and at judicial control of abuses of power.
A note is appended to it on the origin of the expression *"ultra vires"*.

Dr Bonham and the College of Physicians

Dr Bonham, a Cambridge-trained physician, set up a medical practice in
London without the licence of the Royal College of Physicians. The
college had him arrested and thrown into the Fleet prison. When he
sued them for false imprisonment, the college censors pleaded their
statute of incorporation, which empowered them to imprison or fine
anyone who broke their regulations.

Although it was not necessary to his court's decision in favour of Bonham,
Coke fastened on the impropriety of allowing a regulatory body to appropriate a share of the fines it imposed. Such a provision made every disciplinary cause the College's own and the College the judge of it. Coke's judgment
in *Bonham's Case*[1] denounces the impropriety of any such arrangement:
it was an abuse of power, said Coke, and any fines should go to the Crown.

Parliament's powers

Had it stopped there, the case would still be important. Parliament today
would never, one hopes, allow a statutory regulator to finance itself out of
the fines it levied.[2] But it was because, in *Bonham's Case,* Parliament had

---

[1] (1608/1610) 8 Co. Rep. 114a; approved *City of London* v. *Wood* [1701] 12 Mod. 6699
(Holt CJ)

[2] In his *Inquiry into the Culture, Practices and Ethics of the Press*, HC 780 (November 2012)
Lord Justice Leveson, possibly overlooking the principle of *Bonham's Case*, advised that a

done just this that Coke confronted what is still a critical question in Britain: can even a sovereign Parliament legislate in violation of fundamental or natural law? Can it abuse its powers?

> "In many cases," said Coke,[3] "the common law will control acts of parliament, and sometimes adjudge them to be utterly void: for when an act of parliament is against common right and reason, or repugnant, or impossible to be performed, the common law will control it, and adjudge such act to be void."

Coke was not alone: Chief Justice Hobart was shortly afterwards to hold:

> Even an Act of Parliament made against natural equity, as to make a man judge in his own case, is void in itself . . .[4]

This is both the issue on which Thomas More had gone to the scaffold in 1535 and an issue on which modern judges have continued to express concern.[5] Can Parliament, as Burleigh asserted in the sixteenth century and as Dicey reasserted in the nineteenth, do anything it chooses except (as Dicey suggested, for probably malicious reasons deriving from his opposition to votes for women) make a woman a man[6] – or, as Thomas More debated with his interrogator Richard Rich, abolish God?

Thomas More's nemesis

More's fatal dialogue in the Tower with the solicitor-general Richard Rich has been rendered iconic by Robert Bolt's drama *A Man for All Seasons*. Although no contemporary record suggests that the dialogue formed part of the evidence at his trial, it was set out in the grand jury's indictment and is recorded both in a surviving manuscript note and in More's own correspondence with his daughter Margaret.[7] Urged by Rich to accept the Act making Henry supreme spiritual head of the church in

---

new regulatory body should be empowered to "establish a ringfenced enforcement fund, into which receipts from fines could be paid, for the purpose of funding investigations" (part K.7, § 4.39; summarised at L.39).

[3] At 118a   [4] *Day* v. *Savadge* (1614) Hobart 85

[5] See *Taylor* v. *NZ Poultry Board* [1984] 1 NZLR 394,398 (Lord Cooke); [1995] PL 57, 69 (Lord Woolf); *R* v. *Jackson* [2005] UKHL 56 [102] (Lord Steyn; ibid. Lord Hope and Lady Hale). See also Holt CJ, *City of London* v. *Wood* (1702) 12 Mod. 669, 687; Lord Neuberger, 2014 Conkerton Lecture ("judges cannot decide that a statute is invalid on the ground that it infringes the UK constitution – save possibly in exceptional circumstances.").

[6] Dicey was wrong about this too: see the Gender Recognition Act 2004.

[7] See H. A. Kelly *et al.* (eds.),*Thomas More's Trial by Jury* (2011).

England, More had replied "Your conscience will save you, and my conscience will save me". Rich then asked More directly whether, if Parliament were to make Rich king, it would be treason to deny his kingship. More replied that denial would be treason, since it would lie in his power to accept it. But if, More then asked in response, Parliament were to enact that God should not be God, would resistance be treason? Rich, accepting that "it is impossible to bring it about that God be not God", responded with the real question: why should More not accept that the King had been lawfully constituted supreme head on earth of the English church? The cases are not alike, More replied, because a subject can consent to Parliament's making of a King, but not to its making of a primate. In other words, the conferment of supreme spiritual authority lay beyond the powers of a temporal legislature. In the twenty-first century this remains the source of the schism between the Vatican and the Church of England.

What limits?

The life-and-death debate between Richard Rich and Thomas More crystallised what is still the issue of the limits of parliamentary sovereignty. By the 1530s it was accepted that the monarch could legislate only with the advice and consent of Parliament, as Henry VIII repeatedly did to secure his marital and political ends. By the 1640s it had also been established that he could adjudicate only through independent courts.[8] Thus two of the main elements of the constitutional monarchy which had come into being by the end of the seventeenth century were present before the civil war of 1642–9 broke the Crown's resistance to Parliament's powers. But Parliament's now unquestioned supremacy, confirmed by the Bill of Rights, posed again the question whether there was anything it could not decide to do.

The judges have never, so far, invalidated a statute enacted by Parliament, though it appears that in the case against the Hunting Act 2004 they were prepared on procedural grounds to consider doing so.[9] But Coke's lesser proposition, that the common law will "control" unreasonable legislation, has been vindicated repeatedly as the courts have

---

[8] As a principle, this had been established by the first decade of the century, but it was only with the abolition of the prerogative court of Star Chamber in 1641 that it became fully effective.

[9] See Ch. 5.

grappled with opaque, contradictory or unjust legislation, reading it down or supplementing it as necessary.

Where the shortcoming has been inadvertent, this is unproblematical. When Parliament in 1875 passed an act authorising public authorities which supplied water to lay pipes,[10] it was left to the courts to point out that without first laying pipes they couldn't supply water, and to adjust the legislation accordingly. But the courts have also felt able, indeed obliged, to read down legislation which has threatened to interfere with judicial independence or to permit administrative injustice – in other words, which has tended to disrupt the rule of law, for example by allowing people to be penalised without being heard.[11] These are the points at which we have come closest to the situation envisaged by Coke and others of Parliament acting in a manner which might be classed as unconstitutional. But unconstitutionality is itself a moving target.

Cases in point

Section 8 of the Asylum and Immigration (Treatment of Claimants) Act 2004 purports to dictate to immigration judges, who are judicial office-holders, what facts they are to find in particular situations. The section lays down that the credibility of asylum-seekers shall be treated as damaged – for example in recounting the torture they have been subjected to – if, among other things, they have entered or tried to enter using a false passport. Since there is often no other way of escaping from a brutal regime, one effect of this provision, if taken literally, would be to compel judges to deny asylum to genuine applicants.

The enactment was a salvo in David Blunkett's war with the judges during his tenure of office as Home Secretary: he had boasted to the press that he was going to tie their hands. When section 8 finally came before the Court of Appeal, however, counsel for the Home Secretary did not attempt to support its ostensible meaning. Both sides adopted the ministerial explanation which had been given to the Lords, that the clause would "not force a deciding authority to give undue weight to any of the factors it lists". With this assistance the court decided that the words requiring judges to treat the listed acts as damaging the claimant's credibility were to be read as if they said "potentially damaging the claimant's credibility". They did so on the ground that it was to be

---

[10] Public Health Act 1875, s. 54; *Jones* v. *Conway etc Water Supply Board* [1893] 2 Ch. 603
[11] See Ch. 8.

assumed that Parliament did not intend to interfere with judicial independence.[12] The Home Secretary may have intended exactly this; but ministers are not Parliament. As the Attorney-General reminded the House of Lords in *Pepper* v. *Hart*,[13] ministers address Parliament not to explain but to persuade. The intent of a statute comes not from them but from its words in their constitutional setting.

This is not the only instance of the legislature trenching upon the judicial function. In 1990 Parliament enacted a provision to the effect that, where a departmental social security decision had been overset for error of law, subsequent decisions were to continue to be made on the same erroneous basis as before.[14] The executive, by contrast, cannot do such things: in Australia and New Zealand in the course of the twentieth century challenges were raised to the establishment by the Crown of inquiries which threatened to trespass on the adjudicative role of the courts, and in at least one case the Crown was held to have acted in contempt of court by doing so.[15]

Constitutionality

So the first question is still whether, in spite of its ostensible omnipotence, Parliament is legally capable of abusing its constitutional power. The second is whether, even if it is, the courts can do anything about it. The answer to the first question has surely to be yes: prolonging its own life indefinitely would be one example; authorising slavery or torture would be another. The Diceyan answer to the second question must be that the courts could do nothing about it – supremacy

---

[12] *JT (Cameroon)* v. *Home Secretary* [2008] EWCA Civ 878. When the legislation was first promoted it also contained a clause which would have taken away all appeal against asylum and immigration adjudications, and all judicial review of them. Lawyers of distinction argued that if this were to become law it would be unconstitutional and legally void. It will never be known whether they were right, because ministers withdrew the clause. It had fulfilled the function of a lightning conductor, enabling the comparably objectionable clause 8 to become law almost unnoticed.

[13] [1993] AC 593, 607, where Sir Nicholas Lyell QC, A-G, advances a clear account of the separation of the judicial, legislative and executive powers of the state.

[14] Social Security Act 1975, s. 104(7) and (8) as amended by the Social Security Act 1990, Sch. 6, para. 7(1); *Bate* v. *Chief Adjudication Officer* [1996] 1 WLR 814 (HL, reversing a powerful judgment of the Court of Appeal, transcript CSA.94.1565, unrep.).

[15] *Cock* v. *Attorney-General of New Zealand* (1909) 28 NZLR 405; see also *Clough* v. *Leahy* (1904) CLR 156, *McGuinness* v. *Attorney-General of Victoria* (1940) 63 CLR 73, *Victoria* v. *Australian Building Federation* (1982) 152 CLR 25, esp. [26].

means what it says. Others may want to wait and see. Lord Steyn in the case on the Hunting Act[16] took the opportunity to ask whether Dicey's model of unquestioned parliamentary supremacy was "out of place in the modern United Kingdom". In fact Dicey himself abandoned his supremacist position when Parliament began to consider granting home rule to Ireland: he joined Carson and other Unionists in contending that this was something Parliament lacked authority to do.[17]

When the Countryside Alliance challenged the validity of the Hunting Act[18] essentially on the ground that the Parliament Act 1949, which had been used to get the legislation through, was itself invalid, the Attorney-General did not argue that the submission was barred by article IX of the Bill of Rights, which forbids any questioning in the courts of Parliament's proceedings. His reticence may have been tactical, but it respected the logic that if the courts are to defer to an act of Parliament, they must be entitled first to decide whether the document before them is in truth such an act; and for that purpose they may be required to consider what limits there are to Parliament's own powers. If that is right, it opens a door in the wall of Parliamentary supremacy which appeared to have been closed for good when in 1974 the House of Lords held that the courts had no jurisdiction to consider a claim that a private Act of Parliament had been procured by fraud.[19] Indeed it is probable that the very fact that the law lords adjudicated on the validity of the Hunting Act establishes their jurisdiction to do so, since jurisdiction cannot be created either by silence or by consent.

Natural law

The Levellers in the Civil War saw this issue coming in the first days of parliamentary supremacy: Parliament, they argued, was no more than the delegate of the people, and since natural law denied the people the power to tyrannise over others,[20] Parliament was under the same constraint:

---

[16] R (Jackson) v. Attorney-General [2005] UKHL 56   [17] See Ch. 14, n. 3.
[18] R (Jackson) v. Attorney-General [2005] UKHL 56
[19] Pickin v. British Railways Board [1974] AC 765
[20] P. Chakravarty, Like Parchment in the Fire (2006), Ch. 2 "Natural Law as a Radical Weapon: John Warr, the Levellers and John Locke". See also Introduction, n. 17, for Ireton's shrewd argument in the Putney debates that looking backward to pre-Norman law was a dead end, and that the Levellers' true resort had to be to natural law.

We could not confer a power that was not in ourselves.[21]

The Levellers' *Agreement of the People*, the first-ever modern political programme, in 1648 sought to lay down:

> That no representative shall in any wise render up, or give, or take away any of the foundations of common right, liberty or safety . . .[22]

The silent step which was accomplished in the Hunting Act case by simple reticence may not be a recognition of such radical limitations on the legislative power; but it is not unrelated, at least in kind, to the larger stride taken by the US Supreme Court in *Marbury* v. *Madison*[23] when it established the reviewability of congressional legislation for unconstitutionality. The UK's courts in fact did something analogous, albeit with Parliamentary authority, when in 1991 they decided[24] that part of Parliament's merchant shipping legislation was void for inconsistency with the European Communities Act. But the larger question is whether the rule of law makes the courts custodians of fundamental standards which they are required to uphold even if Parliament says otherwise.

Lord Bingham was prepared to describe parliamentary supremacy and the rule of law as "not entirely harmonious bedfellows", but he refused to go the distance that other senior judges had gone in contemplating the possibility that the courts might refuse to recognise unconstitutional acts of Parliament.[25] He limited himself to the hope that such a confrontation would never occur. Our courts, however, have been prepared to find that in other countries it has already happened. In 1976 Lord Simon of Glaisdale, in a case in which the House of Lords had to deal with the consequences in this country of an anti-Semitic law adopted by Nazi Germany, said:

> To my mind a law of this sort constitutes so grave an infringement of human rights that the courts of this country ought to refuse to recognise it as a law at all.[26]

Can we be completely confident that it could never happen here?

---

[21] *The Remonstrance of Many Thousand Citizens* (1646)   [22] See Ch. 4.
[23] 1 Cranch 137 (1803)
[24] *R* v. *Secretary of State for Transport, ex p Factortame (No 2)* [1991] 1 AC 603
[25] T. Bingham, *The Rule of Law* (2010), p. 167, citing with approval "[S]overeignty is incompatible, both internationally and internally, with another concept . . . which today is widely regarded as a paramount value: the rule of law" (F. Jacobs, *The Sovereignty of Law: the European Way* [the 2006 Hamlyn Lectures] (2007), p. 5).
[26] *Oppenheimer* v. *Cattermole* [1976] AC 249, 277–8

Can Parliament break the law?

And how historically secure is the concept of parliamentary omnipotence? Sir Frederick Pollock wrote in 1923:

> The omnipotence of Parliament was not the orthodox theory of English law, if orthodox at all, even in Holt's time. It was first formally adopted, and then not without lip-service to natural law, in Blackstone's *Commentaries* ... Down to the [Glorious] Revolution the common legal opinion was that statutes might be void as "contrary to common right" – an insular version ... of generally received natural law.[27]

In his seminal 1974 Hamlyn Lectures,[28] Sir Leslie Scarman, building on this, argued that the nineteenth-century view that individual rights were secure only against the executive was fallacious. He pointed not only to *Bonham's Case* but to *Foster's Case*,[29] in which Coke had asserted that the words of an act of Parliament

> shall not bind the King's Bench because the pleas there are *coram ipso rege*.[30]

Scarman went on to quote the speech in which Oliver Cromwell had urged:

> In every government there must be somewhat fundamental, somewhat like a Magna Charter, which should be standing, be unalterable ... That Parliaments should not make themselves perpetual is fundamental. Of what assurance is law to prevent so great an evil, if it lie in the same legislature to unlaw it again?[31]

Cromwell was not only, as Ferdinand Mount suggests,[32] "trying to crystallise the correct relationship between the legislature and the judiciary as they had been before the Stuart perversions and presumptions"; he was adopting the Levellers' claim that Parliament itself, as the delegate of the people, was limited by natural law in what it could do.[33]

---

[27] F. Pollock, "A Plea for Historical Interpretation", (1923) 39 LQR 163, 165

[28] L. Scarman, *English Law: The New Dimension* (1974)   [29] 11 Co. Rep. 1222

[30] At 1234; *coram ipso rege* = before the King himself. See also the citation in Ch. 6, 'The Prerogative Strikes Back', of the *Ship Money Case* in which Finch CJ denied that Parliament had any power to interfere with the royal prerogative.

[31] *Oliver Cromwell's Letters and Speeches*, ed. Carlyle, Part VIII, ¶ III

[32] F. Mount, *The British Constitution Now: Recovery or Decline* (1993), pp. 22–3

[33] See further on this issue Ch. 5.

Elections

The dichotomy of common law and parliamentary privilege has in the past been a source of conflict and rancour. The most persistent issue over which it repeatedly surfaced was the validity of elections. A handy way for the party in power to weaken the opposition in the eighteenth century was to secure a resolution that one of its members had been invalidly elected. It was less welcome when the courts held an MP of the majority party to have been invalidly elected, as happened in the great election case of *Ashby v. White*[34] in 1701, when Sir John Holt, the Chief Justice of the King's Bench, awarded damages to a voter who had been unlawfully kept out of the polls by the Mayor of Aylesbury. He dealt with the argument that this would open the floodgates to endless litigation with the remark

> If wrongs will be multiplied, remedies must be multiplied.

The House of Commons refused to accept this decision, and that in *Paty's Case*[35] which followed it, for reasons which were not entirely unrespectable. Appeal lay by way of writ of error from the King's Bench to the House of Lords, a hereditary chamber (apart from the senior bishops of the established church) in which any member could sit and vote on judicial appeals. This is what had in fact happened in *Ashby v. White*, and the Commons were legitimately concerned that by this means the Upper House was able to interfere directly in the functioning of the Lower House. It is said that the Speaker, fearing this, had sent his retinue to the King's Bench to tell Holt that if he did not stop hearing the case he would be in contempt of Parliament, and that Holt had told the retinue that unless they departed at once they would be gaoled for contempt of court "had you the whole House of Commons in your belly".[36]

When in 1770 Parliament passed Grenville's Act, taking the time-wasting process of deciding the validity of elections away from the House

---

[34] (1703) 2 Ld. Raym. 938   [35] (1704) 2 Ld. Raym. 1105

[36] The anecdote appears in the first edition of the DNB, where it is described as "mythical". It does not appear in the entry (by Paul Halliday) in the second, online, edition. Conceivably it was a variant of the better-authenticated story that Holt had stood up to the House of Lords in quashing a murder indictment against Charles Knollys on the ground that Knollys was entitled to be named as Earl of Banbury, a claim which the Lords had already rejected. Holt refused to justify his decision to the House: "I gave my judgment according to my conscience" (12 St. Tr. 1179).

and putting it in the hands of a committee, it was accompanied by a farcical procedure by which an initial committee of fifty-one was reduced to thirteen by each party in turn striking off a member – who would invariably be the most able of the other side's remaining members. The process became known, accurately, as knocking the brains out of the committee. It was not until 1868 that this pantomime was abandoned and election petitions handed over to the courts.

Parliamentary privilege

Underlying the manoeuvring and rancour, however, was something of enduring constitutional importance: the principle that while it was for Parliament alone to decide whether its privileges had been breached, it was for the common law to determine what its privileges were. Because of the Commons' sensitivity to the risk of illicit interference, increased perhaps by its collective memory of the struggles of the seventeenth century, it was not until the nineteenth century that this division of powers was accepted.[37] This is the allocation of functions which in recent times made it the business of the courts and not of the House to decide whether MPs' claims for unwarranted parliamentary expenses came within the protection of article IX of the Bill of Rights, blocking any prosecution.[38] Those MPs and peers who got their fingers burned in the scandal might have looked enviously back to the eighteenth century, when landowning MPs regularly used parliamentary privilege to arraign poachers for contempt of Parliament rather than let them be prosecuted before a local jury, or to evade legal process issued by their creditors: indeed, major debtors occasionally got themselves elected to Parliament for this purpose.[39]

Coke and Holt

I have travelled some distance from the big issue raised by Coke in *Bonham's Case*. Lord Ellesmere[40] in his *Observations* on Coke's reports criticised Coke severely for having "[struck] in sunder the bars of the

---

[37] Holdsworth, vol. X, p 539; *Burdett* v. *Abbott* (1811) 1 East 1.

[38] The public derision with which this legal defence was greeted in the press came close to contempt of court.

[39] It is probable that it was his status as an MP that kept Disraeli out of prison for debt.

[40] Lord Chancellor from 1603 to 1617.

College", frustrating its royal patent and the legislation confirming it, and "blowing them both away as vain, and of no value". However bold Coke had been, such a diatribe was unmerited. The last word, historically speaking, can go to Chief Justice Holt, who, admitting that "an act of Parliament can do no wrong, though it may do several things that look pretty odd", described as "far from any extravagancy" Coke's suggestion that not even Parliament could make a body judge in its own cause.[41] If, as both Coke and Holt thought, the supremacy of Parliament is not absolute, this is still a space to be watched.[42] Even on Dicey's submissive premise, the courts have strong obligations of vigilance.

Power and policy

Another and bigger space exists in the constitution, the space occupied not by law but by discretion. Government at all levels possesses extensive discretionary powers which it needs if it is to function at all. Modern judicial review has made it all but impossible to exercise such discretions in a vacuum: to do so leads swiftly either to arbitrariness as between one citizen and another, or to rigidity, which by vouchsafing the same outcome to everyone negates the point of having a discretion. This is the administrator's bed of Procrustes: somehow every choice must be both consistent with the choices made in other cases and appropriate to the case in hand.[43]

The solution in most cases is to adopt a policy. Policy has virtues of flexibility which rules lack and virtues of consistency which discretion lacks.[44] The courts have correspondingly recognised the legitimacy of policy as a guide to the exercise of discretion.[45] The other great advantage of policy is that it can be readily changed.

> "The liberty to make such changes," said Lord Diplock,[46] "is something that is inherent in our constitutional form of government. When a change in administrative policy takes place and is communicated in a

---

[41] *City of London* v. *Wood*, 12 Mod. 669

[42] See F. Maitland, *Constitutional History of England* (1909), p. 301.

[43] A model of adaptable policy implementation can be seen in the account of the DPP's reasoning in the case of Daniel James, *R (Purdy)* v. *DPP* [2009] UKHL 45, [49]–[51].

[44] *R* v. *Dept of Education, ex p Begbie* [2000] 1 WLR 1115, 1132

[45] *R* v. *Port of London Authority, ex p Kynoch* [1919] 1 KB 176; *British Oxygen* v. *Board of Trade* [1971] AC 610.

[46] *Hughes* v. *DHSS* [1985] AC 776, 788

> departmental circular ... any reasonable expectations that may have been
> aroused ... by any previous circular are destroyed ...

Policy is a slippery word. Its original meaning was pejorative: it meant
deceit and scheming. You find it used in this sense in the hymn of which
one verse begins:

> Perish policy and cunning, perish all that fears the light.[47]

Policy in the political sense differs not only from this but from policy in its
legal sense. In its political sense it connotes typically a set of governmental
objectives which generally have no basis in law, which are regularly
modified or abandoned, and which except in the rarest cases are beyond
the cognisance of the courts. What public law is concerned with is policy of
a different and more focused kind, by which the exercise of administrative
power is guided. The two classes are not entirely sealed off: major policy
documents such as the immigration rules, although designed to secure
consistency in the exercise of the prerogative power to control entry to the
United Kingdom, for obvious reasons have a macro-political input. But
most administrative policies are just that: they pursue neither ideological
nor electoral nor public relations ends but efficient and, with luck, judge-
proof administrative decisions.

The common law

The common law has had to start almost from scratch in responding
to these developments.[48] It has done it by recognising the imperman-
ence of policy but holding government, on grounds of good public
administration, to lawful policies on which it is unfair to renege, at
least without some form of cushioning. The growth of the law of
legitimate expectation, first, from the 1970s, in relation to procedural
guarantees, then, from the 1990s, in relation to substantive advantages,
has been public law's response.[49] Something analogous has been the case

---

[47] "Trust in God and Do the Right", Norman Macleod, 1857

[48] A variant of them is the practice, first developed in the field of town and country
planning, of requiring statutory decision-makers to have regard to published ministerial
policy or guidance. The legality of such guidance may itself be contested: see *Gudanavi-
ciene* v. *Lord Chancellor* [2014] EWHC 1840 (Admin), holding the Lord Chancellor's
statutory guidance on exceptional grants of legal aid to be unlawful.

[49] For a helpful account, see A. W. Bradley and K. D. Ewing, *Constitutional and Administrative Law* (16th edn, 2014), pp. 650–4.

in relation to the law governing public consultation, where the ancient right to be heard has been developed by the courts to fit modern governmental practice, extending it from the individual to the public at large and spreading it from consultations which are required by law to all public involvement in decision-making.[50]

Legitimate expectation

It was judicial recognition of the need for public law to stay abreast of developments in the mode of government, particularly the use of discretionary powers to modify rights and expectations, that in the course of the later twentieth century generated and moulded the doctrine of enforceable legitimate expectations. The concept, as a legal expression, originates in a decision of Lord Denning MR, *Schmidt* v. *Home Secretary*,[51] refusing to intervene in an immigration decision but – as often happens – indicating what might have produced a different outcome:

> some right or interest, or, I would add, some legitimate expectation, of which it would not be fair to deprive him without hearing what he has to say.

Within a few years a series of cases had located and enforced such expectations in a variety of situations.[52] In enforcing expectations of being heard before a decision was taken about some discretionary benefit, the courts were building on centuries of case-law establishing a right to be heard before some legal benefit was taken away.[53] In parallel they were establishing new legal principles of good administration: that where some detriment was in prospect, even if it did not invade a legal right, it could not be introduced arbitrarily. Arbitrariness itself was in due course broken down into two classes: failure to listen to those potentially affected before changing a policy,[54] and changing or departing from policy without proper regard to the impact on those affected.[55]

---

[50] *R (Moseley)* v. *LB Haringey* [2014] UKSC 56   [51] [1969] 2 Ch. 149, 170

[52] See De Smith, *Judicial Review* (6th edn, 2007), paras. 12–003 to 12–009.   [53] See Ch. 8.

[54] E.g. *R* v. *Liverpool Corporation, ex p Liverpool Taxi Fleet Operators' Association* [1972] 2 QB 299 (procedural expectations)

[55] *R* v. *North and East Devon HA, ex p Coughlan* [2001] QB 213 (substantive expectations)

Policy and publicity

It should not be supposed that all policies are public documents. Apart from the fact that some policies are little more than office cultures, and others orally transmitted, there was a long and unfortunate history in the Home Office of operating policies of which the public was unaware. One such policy was the internal document known as DP/2/93, and its successor DP/1/96, dealing with the discretion to grant leave to remain to illegal entrants who had settled and started families here. For some years during the 1990s it was operated without anybody outside the Home Office knowing what it said. Then a copy was produced before an adjudicator. From there it began to circulate in increasingly faint photocopies, and to be produced in High Court proceedings, where counsel for the Home Secretary, on instructions, neither objected to its production nor denied that it had a bearing. Eventually it was published.

We are now, it is to be hoped, past this point: immigration policy documents governing the exercise of the Home Secretary's prerogative and statutory powers, some of them more complex than the enabling legislation, are all now accessible on the web. Or almost all. It emerged in 2008 that the Home Office had for two years been operating an unpublished policy of automatically detaining foreign nationals facing deportation, in breach not only of the law (which permitted, though it did not mandate, their release) but of a published policy which made it look as if the law was being complied with.[56] The situation which was revealed in court, described by the judge as "in some respects unedifying and in other respects disquieting", looked like a reversion to the Machiavellian meaning of the word "policy".

Ultra vires acts and abuses of power

The development of the law of legitimate expectation has done much to conclude the argument about the moral and jurisprudential foundations of judicial review. In the course of the nineteenth century lawyers adopted the notion of a trust acting beyond its powers – *ultra vires* – and applied it to government.[57] For local government this worked, since local authorities, like private corporations, owed their existence to statute. But for central government it never made complete sense, since many of its powers were

---

[56] R *(Abdi and others)* v. *Home Secretary* [2008] EWHC 3166 (Admin) (Davis J)
[57] See the postscript to this chapter.

derived from the royal prerogative[58] and others were implicit in sometimes unspecific statutory delegations of power. Once it became established that discretion might lawfully be constrained by policy, but that if policy was changed it must not be changed so as to rob individuals of legitimately held expectations, it became fanciful to argue that such constraints derived from an unwritten rulebook. What the enforceability of legitimate expectations exemplifies is the opposition of the common law to the abuse of power – in this instance the power of government to change policy. So, too, when Coke fulminated at the statutory monopoly which made the College of Physicians judge in its own cause and the beneficiary of the fines it imposed, he was striving to correct an abuse of power irrespective of the fact that the abuse emanated from Parliament.

Postscript

The origin of "*ultra vires*"

The axiom that an order made without lawful power is void goes back a full four centuries. It has been suggested[59] that the characterisation of such orders by the Latin phrase "*ultra vires*" ("beyond the powers") originated in company law in the mid-nineteenth century and then leapt the gap to public law But it seems more probable that it entered the vocabulary of English law, both company and public law, through the usage of Scottish advocates who came to London to conduct appeals before the House of Lords.

The phrase first appears in the nominate English reports in 1813. In *Montgomery* v. *Charteris* (1813)[60] it was used by counsel in attacking the validity of a disposition of property in Scottish litigation about the Queensberry leases ("the said tack should be set aside as *ultra vires* of the grantor"). In the same year, in *Sharp* v. *Bury* (1813),[61] it was used by English counsel in a claim on a promissory note. It recurs in the pleaded cases in three Scottish civil appeals to the House of Lords in the 1830s: *Ewen* v. *Bannerman* (1830),[62] *McLellan* v. *Macleod* (1830)[63] and *Baillie* v. *Edinburgh Oil Co* (1835).[64]

---

[58] See Ch. 6.
[59] E.g. S. Sedley, *Freedom, Law and Justice (the Hamlyn Lectures)* (1998), pp. 26–7.
[60] (1813) 2 Dow. 90   [61] (1813) 1 Dow. 223   [62] (1830) 2 Dow. & Cl. 74
[63] (1830) 2 Dow. & Cl. 121   [64] (1835) 3 Cl. & F. 639

It is not until the 1840s that the phrase *"ultra vires"* enters the judicial lexicon. The first reported judicial use of it seems to have been in a startling remark by Lord Campbell, giving judgment in the House of Lords in *Ferguson v. Earl of Kinnoul* (1842),[65] about "the act of the 10th of Anne, chap. 12, which we must consider binding, although it has been said to be *ultra vires* of the British Parliament". Here was *"ultra vires"* in an undoubted public law context.[66]

It was used again in public law litigation by the Court of Exchequer in *Clarence Railway Co. v. Great North of England etc. Railway Co.* (1845).[67] On a special case stated by the Vice-Chancellor in a dispute about the right of one railway company to construct a bridge across another's line, Pollock CB held in the leading judgment that the county surveyor's award, "inasmuch as that award directed the bridge to be made partly upon the land of the Clarence company, which was not authorised by Act of Parliament, ... was an award *ultra vires*, not within the powers of the Act, and therefore no award at all."

By contrast, the expression is not used in the leading case on company powers, *Colman v. Eastern Counties Railway Co* (1846),[68] even though the case has been cited ever since as the source of the *ultra vires* doctrine in company law.

---

[65] (1842) 9 Cl.& F. 251, 311

[66] The case is interesting for another reason: it held that an action lay for damages for nonfeasance of a mandatory statutory duty.

[67] (1845) 13 M.& W. 706   [68] (1846) 10 Beav. 1

8

The right to be heard

If there are any self-evident truths in public law, one of them is the obligation of every decision-maker to learn both sides of a controversy before coming to a conclusion about it. Centuries of case-law say so; yet the twenty-first century has seen the principle steadily eroded. Are even the most basic principles artefacts of time and place?

"Everyone who decides anything"

Lord Loreburn, born Robert Reid in 1846, became a Liberal MP and in due course Attorney-General. A former supporter of the Boer cause, he became Lord Chancellor just before the great Liberal landslide of 1906, and in that capacity regularly presided in the Appellate Committee of the House of Lords. It was there that he delivered what Professor Wade later christened "Lord Loreburn's epitome" of the right to be heard:

> ... the Board of Education will have to ascertain the law and also to ascertain the facts. I need not add that in doing either they must act in good faith and listen fairly to both sides, for that is a duty lying upon everyone who decides anything. But I do not think they are bound to treat such a question as though it were a trial. ... They can obtain information in any way they think best, always giving a fair opportunity to those who are parties in the controversy for correcting or contradicting anything prejudicial to their view.[1]

Time and place

When it came to the legal status of women, the liberal Lord Loreburn was a dinosaur. In 1918 he moved the unsuccessful amendment which sought to remove from the Representation of the People Bill the section which was to give votes to women, making a speech of historic bigotry in the

---

[1] *Board of Education v. Rice* [1911] AC 179

process. Nine years earlier, sitting judicially, he had held the legal disabilities of women to be so self-evident that

> [i]t is incomprehensible ... that anyone acquainted with our laws or the
> methods by which they are ascertained can think, if indeed anyone does
> think, there is room for argument on such a point.[2]

As Lord Sankey was to remark when, two decades later, the Privy Council
on an appeal from Canada finally broke the bar on women holding
public office,

> Customs are apt to develop into traditions which are stronger than law.[3]

Was Loreburn's epitome of due process no more than such a tradition, as
contingent in time and place as his misogyny? Half a century earlier, the
Court of Common Pleas had held, that if the Metropolis Management Act
1855 said nothing about giving a houseowner a hearing before deciding
whether to pull down his property, it was not to be assumed that this was
because Parliament intended none. On the contrary, it was the task of the
court to fill the space left by Parliament with "the justice of the common law".[4]

This was the common sense which Lord Loreburn was articulating in
Rice. There followed a half-century of distinction-making and logic-
chopping about the differences between administrative and quasi-judicial
proceedings until in 1962[5] Lord Reid took a grip on the issue, expanding the
concept of a judicial decision to include every kind of decision with
a potentially adverse effect on someone's rights or interests, and restoring
the jurisprudence which demanded due process in all such decisions.

Fairness in private law

The authorities Reid relied on were not confined to public law:
there was parallel – in fact antecedent – private law jurisprudence
vouchsafing a fair hearing by voluntary associations such as trade
unions, using the mechanism of implied contractual terms to import
the "justice of the common law".[6]

---

[2] *Nairn v. St Andrews and Edinburgh University Courts* (1909) SC (HL) 10
[3] *Edwards v. Attorney-General for Canada* [1930] AC 124
[4] *Cooper v. Wandsworth Board of Works* (1863) 14 CB (NS) 180, per Byles J: see Ch. 2,
  "Back to the Future".
[5] *Ridge v. Baldwin* [1964] AC 40, the case of the chief constable of Brighton who had been
  dismissed without a hearing by the local watch committee. See also Ch. 1.
[6] See *Radford v. NATSOPA* [1972] ICR 486 and the cases cited in it.

In 1971 the law lords, again with Reid in the chair, set about importing the right to be heard into contractual employment, starting with employment in the nature of an office.[7] This innovative incremental extension of the common law was adopted and subsumed by legislation when the Industrial Relations Act 1971 introduced a new right not to be unfairly dismissed, carrying with it an entitlement for employees to be heard if dismissal was in prospect. The shift from contract to status in employment represented a rapprochement of private and public law which has not always been fully appreciated. It meant among other things that

[a] clause ... for automatic forfeiture of membership without the necessity for any charge or hearing ... would ... be ultra vires and void.[8]

The spread of due process

Since then, the obligation of public administrators to listen and think before they decide has ramified into a series of derivative doctrines. One is the doctrine of legitimate procedural expectation – that it may be a remediable abuse of power to renege on a public undertaking to listen to those affected before taking a decision.[9] Another is the body of common law which today governs public consultation: here, although there is generally no particular individual whose rights are at risk, the common law now requires intelligible proposals to be published at a formative stage and the responses to be properly considered.[10] A third is the group of cases which have extended the rule against ostensible bias to administrative decision-makers.[11] A fourth is the right to call witnesses if they have something relevant and admissible to say.[12] A fifth is the right in a variety of proceedings to have someone to speak for you.[13]

---

[7] *Malloch v. Aberdeen Corporation* [1971] 1 WLR 1578; *Stevenson v. United Road Transport Union* [1977] ICR 893.

[8] *Radford v. NATSOPA* [1972] ICR 484, 496 (Plowman J)

[9] *Ng Yuen Shiu* [1983] 2 AC 629   [10] *R (Moseley) v. LB Haringey* [2014] UKSC 56

[11] See W. Wade and C. Forsyth, *Administrative Law* (10th edn, 2009), pp. 389–92.

[12] *Leech v. Deputy Governor, HMP Parkhurst; Prevot v. Deputy Governor, HMP Long Lartin* [1988] AC 533; see Introduction, p. 16.

[13] *R v. Home Secretary, ex p Tarrant* [1985] QB 251; *R (AS) v. Gt Yarmouth Youth Court* [2011] EWHC 2059 (Admin).

The origins

First, however, it is useful to look at the lineage of cases which have ingrained this notion of fairness in the common law. It is a notion which is both subjective, in that it recognises the insult to human dignity of being condemned unheard, and objective, in that it recognises the near-impossibility of reaching a defensible conclusion on an issue without having heard both sides. The modern judges who restored the right to be heard and gave it a new breadth looked for the most part no further back than *Dr Bentley's Case* in the 1720s. But in this field, as in others, the story starts with Edward Coke.

Bagg's Case

By 1615 Coke, against his will, was Chief Justice of the less powerful though more prestigious court of King's Bench. Before the court came James Bagg, a burgess of the City of Plymouth who had been removed from office by the mayor and aldermen for inciting taverners not to pay the local duty on the wines they sold. The council had clearly had enough of Mr Bagg; but their return to the prerogative writ issued by the court gave no indication that they had given him any kind of hearing before deciding to remove him from office.

> [A]lthough they have lawful authority ... to remove anyone from the freedom, and that they have just cause to remove him; yet [if] it appears by the return that they have proceeded against him without hearing him answer to what was objected, or that he was not reasonably warned, such removal is void ... and ... is against justice and right.[14]

Coke's insistence on the fundamentality of hearing both sides did not come out of the blue. You can find it in Aeschylus's *Eumenides*, in Seneca's *Medea*[15] and in Bacon's attack on the Spanish Inquisition:

> ... the rule *audi alteram partem* is not of the formality, but the essence of justice: which is therefore figured with both eyes closed but both ears open: because she should hear both sides but respect neither.[16]

---

[14] *Bagg's Case* (1616) 11 Co. Rep. 93
[15] See Eric Metcalfe, *Secret Evidence* (Justice, 2009), para. 2.
[16] Bacon, *A Report on the Spanish grievances*, quo Metcalfe, *Secret Evidence*, para. 31

The right to know

Coke's holding in *Bagg's Case* has two intertwined strands. One is the obligation to listen. The other, which is equally important, is the obligation to give reasonable warning – in other words, to give fair notice of what is to be alleged. This was at a time when in criminal process there was no right even to see the indictment, so that the first the accused knew of the counts on which they might well be about to be hanged was when they were arraigned before the jury; a time – which lasted until the end of the nineteenth century – when defendants, even when they had heard the case against them, were unable to go into the witness box to answer it on oath; and a time when the role of the criminal jury was still largely its mediaeval role, which was less to appraise the evidence than to bring its collective knowledge of local rumour and reputation to bear on the accused. Coke had good reason to know this: as Attorney-General he had had Sir Walter Raleigh convicted on the basis of an accusation extracted by torture from Lord Cobham, despite Raleigh's pointed submission to the court:

> Good my Lords, let my accuser come face to face and be deposed [i.e. testify]. Were the case but for a small copyhold [i.e. a civil claim], you would have witnesses or good proof to lead the jury to a verdict; and I am here for my life.[17]

Dr Bentley's Case

It was not until the lawyers, William Garrow prominent among them, elbowed their way into the criminal trial process towards the end of the eighteenth century that some of the rules of fair play which we have come to regard as fundamental began to be recognised and implemented. By insisting in the early seventeenth century on a fundamental right to be heard in affairs governed by public law, Coke was moving well ahead of the still primitive processes of the criminal law.

The high point came just over a century later when the hierarchy of Cambridge University was confronted and defeated by the irascible Dr Richard Bentley, Master of Trinity College at the age of thirty eight and Regius Professor of Divinity by the time his row with the university erupted in litigation in the 1720s. He had allegedly told the messenger

---

[17] Jardine, (1832) 1 Criminal Trials, 389, 427, quo Metcalfe, *Secret Evidence*, para. 39

who summoned him to appear before the Vice-Chancellor that the Vice-Chancellor was behaving stupidly ("*stulte egit*") and, without being given any notice of the charge, was deprived of his degrees as a punishment for contempt.

The court of King's Bench was unanimous in holding the decision to be void for unfairness. Justice Fortescue's judgment is celebrated both for its learning and for its appeal to natural law as a source of indefeasible rights:

> The laws of God and man both give the party an opportunity to make his defence, if he has any ... [E]ven God himself did not pass sentence upon Adam before he was called upon to make his defence. Adam (says God) where art thou? Hast thou not eaten of the tree whereof I commanded thee that thou shouldst not eat? And the same question was put to Eve also.[18]

The right to an advocate

A right to be heard does not necessarily include an automatic right to an advocate. When the Kray brothers' enforcer, Frankie Fraser, was charged with prison mutiny, Lord Denning in the Court of Appeal would not countenance an order requiring the prison's board of visitors to hear counsel on his behalf. Prisoners, he held, enjoyed no such right.[19] But a decade later, in the Queen's Bench, a subtler argument succeeded: boards of visitors might have no uniform obligation to admit legal representatives, but they had a discretionary power to do so, and – as with most discretions – situations would arise in which the discretion could only lawfully be exercised in one way. A charge of prison mutiny, the court held, was such a situation.[20]

The turn of the tide

So far we seem to have been contemplating the kind of onward march of progress that Tennyson was contemplating when he described England as a land "where freedom slowly broadens down from precedent to

---

[18] *R v. University of Cambridge* (1723) 1 Str. 557. God, of course, already knew the answer. Bentley was satirised by Pope in the *Dunciad*: "Where Bentley late tempestuous wont to sport / In troubled waters, but now sleeps in Port".

[19] *Fraser* v. *Mudge* [1975] 1 WLR 1132

[20] *R v. Home Secretary, ex p Tarrant* [1985] QB 251

precedent". But while the tide of due process may have been steadily rising since the seventeenth century, a powerful undertow has begun running seawards, carrying some of the gains with it.

The starting point of this development lies in what Lord Denning pointed out in *Kanda's Case* in 1962:

> If the right to be heard is to be a real right which is worth anything, it must carry with it a right in the accused man to know the case which is made against him.[21]

Or as Canada's Chief Justice McLachlin put it:

> How can one meet a case one does not know?[22]

But what if the inculpating evidence is so sensitive that to disclose it would jeopardise national security? Historically and jurisprudentially there was a short answer to this: if the state cannot produce its evidence in open court, it cannot proceed at all. This remains the common law's default position. But the pressure of international and domestic terrorism, and of the threat or fear of it, have driven first Parliament and then the courts into sporadic retreat from one of the common law's most fundamental values.

The first turning of the tide predated 9/11 by several years. It was located in the always difficult field of immigration and deportation – difficult because admission to and removal from this country has always been at base a matter of executive discretion. Although increasingly governed by statute, until the introduction of a judicialised system of appeals it did not lend itself readily to the common law principles I have been discussing.[23] The appeal system initiated in 1973, however, excluded deportations on national security grounds. These went before a Home Office advisory panel which would allow prospective deportees to give and call evidence but was forbidden to let them know the evidence against them. The first and best-known casualty was the American journalist Mark Hosenball, whose challenge in 1977 to the still unexplained decision to deport him failed in the Court of Appeal. Lord

---

[21] *Kanda v. Government of Malaya* [1962] AC 322, 367; repeatedly endorsed: see Justice, *Secret Evidence*, n. 30.

[22] *Charkaoui v. Canada* [2007] 1 SCR 350, para. 64

[23] One reason is that immigration and asylum issues are rarely truly adversarial; they more usually involve probing the veracity of claims.

Denning, accepting that the rules of natural justice had been violated, held nevertheless that

> ... our history shows that, when the state itself is endangered, our cherished freedoms may have to take second place. Even natural justice itself may suffer a setback.[24]

Denning's appeal to history – he must have been thinking of *Liversidge* v. *Anderson*, decided during World War II[25] – was unfortunate, for that contentious decision was shortly to be held by the House of Lords to have been "expediently, and at that time perhaps excusably, wrong".[26] He went on in the same passage to demonstrate blithely the effect of hearing only one side of a case:

> "The rules of natural justice," he said, "have to be modified in regard to foreigners here who prove themselves unwelcome and ought to be deported."

Special advocates

But in 1996 the United Kingdom suffered a serious defeat in the European Court of Human Rights. It was held in *Chahal* v. *UK*[27] that in national security cases the deportation system lacked the judicial oversight required by article 5(4) of the European Convention wherever someone was deprived of their liberty, because the courts could not or would not consider the evidence for themselves. Very shortly afterwards the European Court of Justice came to a similar decision about the deportation or exclusion of two EU nationals on security grounds.[28] The result was the Special Immigration Appeals Commission Act 1997 which created a closed tribunal – SIAC – for immigration cases

---

[24] *R* v. *Home Secretary, ex p Hosenball* [1977] 3 All ER 452, 455

[25] [1942] AC 206. He may also have been thinking of his own wartime role as legal adviser to a regional commissioner, using the power of detention without trial under Order 18B. "We detained people, without trial, on suspicion that they were a danger ... Although there was no case against [one Yorkshire parson], no case at all, I detained him under '18B' ... This power was discretionary. It could not be questioned in the courts. It was so held by the House of Lords in *Liversidge* v. *Anderson*. But Lord Atkin gave a famous dissent – after my own heart ...." : A. Denning, *The Family Story* (1981), p. 130. Comment is superfluous.

[26] *R* v. *IRC ex p Rossminster Ltd* [1980] AC 952, 1011   [27] (1996) 23 EHRR 413

[28] *R* v. *Home Secretary ex p Shigara and Radiom* [1997] 1 ECR I-3343

with a security dimension, and introduced into it the "special advocate" in substitution for the right to be heard.

How this came about, and how it has since grown and spread, is an illustration of the capacity of the common law to adapt to new situations, if not always in a principled fashion.

Since the abolition of the prerogative court of Star Chamber on the eve of the English Civil War, the openness of justice has been accepted as an integral part of the due process of law. There are a dozen good reasons for this, but perhaps the most important is that it offers a constant check on judicial conduct. When in 1913 the House of Lords was asked to endorse a general power to close courts to the public, Lord Shaw responded that to turn the constitutional right to open justice into a judicial discretion would be "to shift the foundations of freedom from the rock to the sand".[29] He quoted Jeremy Bentham:

> Publicity is the very soul of justice.

Yet it is a necessary consequence of any procedure which denies one party sight or knowledge of the other party's case that the court itself must be closed so that the information does not leak out.

SIAC was the first tribunal in this country to be equipped with special advocates. These are experienced and security-cleared counsel who can test the closed material in the deportee's interests – but not on his behalf, since without knowing what the material is the deportee can give the advocate no instructions about it, whether by way of denial, admission or explanation.

Justice's report on the use of secret evidence[30] suggests, moreover, that the entire system has been built on air. The European Court of Human Rights in the *Chahal* case was led to believe that Canada had developed the kind of system I have just described. In fact it was not until 2002 that Canada legislated for closed hearings on security-sensitive immigration cases, and the legislation was struck down by the Supreme Court for incompatibility with the Charter right to a fair trial. However, on the basis of the court's suggestion that special advocates might fill the gap, preferably with a fuller role than in the UK model, the Canadian parliament in 2008 legislated to authorise a more sensitive version of the special advocate system. Meanwhile, in the belief that there already

---

[29] *Scott v. Scott* [1913] AC 417   [30] Para. 85; Part V *passim*

existed a Canadian system of special advocates approved by the European Court of Human Rights, the UK had introduced its own system.

Secret courts

By 2009, Justice was able to count fourteen statutes passed since 1997 authorising the use of secret evidence in tribunals covering issues as diverse as employment and planning. The same period, however, saw the historic decision of the House of Lords, chaired by Lord Bingham, in what has become known as the *Belmarsh Case*,[31] that the use of the immigration system to bring about indefinite detention of foreign security suspects without trial was unlawful. Government's response was to secure the swift passing of the Prevention of Terrorism Act 2005, creating a new system of indefinite, if partial, house arrest in the form of control orders. The system was made subject to judicial surveillance, but again with provision for secret evidence able to be tested only by a special advocate. The European Court of Human Rights accepted that full disclosure might not be demanded in cases involving national security. But this left open the question whether a withholding of the entirety of the evidence, if security was considered to demand this, would amount to a denial of the right to a fair hearing guaranteed by article 6 of the Convention.

When the issue came before our courts, the case for the government was that if its evidence was so strong that there could be no answer to it, there would be no unfairness in withholding the whole of it from the suspect. I disagreed:

> [I]t is ... seductively easy to conclude that there can be no answer to a case of which you have only heard one side.... [Y]ou cannot be sure of anything until all the evidence has been heard, and ... even then you may be wrong. It may be, for these reasons, that the answer to [the] question – what difference might disclosure have made? – is that you can never know.[32]

The Supreme Court too was not prepared to countenance a complete withholding of the evidence from the suspect.[33]

---

[31] *A v. Home Secretary* [2004] UKHL 56

[32] *AF (No 3) v. Home Secretary* [2008] EWCA Civ 1148, dissenting.

[33] [2009] UKHL 28 following the decision of the ECtHR in *A v. UK* [2009] ECHR 301 on control orders. See also *Kadi v. Commission* [2010] ECR-II in relation to freezing orders.

Closed materials

But the story was far from over. Following the government's settlement of the *Binyam Mohamed* case,[34] giving as its reason the impossibility of contesting it without opening up matters of national security, Parliament legislated[35] to allow ministers to certify evidence in any civil proceedings as requiring a closed material procedure which will enable it to be admitted but will keep it from the eyes of the other party, the media and the world. In this way the executive has been made to a significant extent judge in its own cause: subject to limited judicial oversight, it will be able to decide what evidence should be immunised from revelation, challenge or explanation, save to the restricted extent that a special advocate can perform this task.

The courts

The courts have not simply acquiesced. They have told government, so far as lay within their jurisdiction, when it has gone too far in denying a fair hearing to security suspects. They have set their face against the use of evidence which may have been obtained by torture.[36] They have refused to introduce closed material procedures into claims against the state for damages.[37] They have struck down as an abuse of power departmental orders freezing the entirety of a suspect's assets, making him effectively a prisoner of the state, on the basis of a listing made by a Security Council committee which held no hearing and was subject to no appeal.[38] They have granted a writ of habeas corpus requiring the Foreign Secretary to use whatever means are at his disposal to retrieve from US custody in Bagram air-base a Pakistani national handed over to US forces in Iraq seven years earlier by British forces.[39] They cannot be

---

[34] *R (Mohamed)* v. *Secretary of State for Foreign and Commonwealth Affairs* [2008] EWHC 2048 (Admin); *R (Mohamed)* v. *Secretary of State for Foreign and Commonwealth Affairs (No 2)* [2010] EWCA Civ 65 and 158: "a moment . . . [when] the English courts opened a window into the workings of the Intelligence Services and shone a light on their murky relationship with the CIA" (T. Hickman, "Turning Out the Lights?", *UK Const. L. Blog* 11 June 2013).

[35] Justice and Security Act 2013. See generally L. Lazarus *et al.*, (eds.) *Reasoning Rights: Comparative Judicial Engagement* (2014), Part III, "National Security and Human Rights".

[36] *A (FC)* v. *Home Secretary* [2005] UKHL 71

[37] *Al Rawi* v. *Security Service* [2011] UKSC 34   [38] [2010] UKSC 2, esp para. 45

[39] *Rahmatullah* v. *Foreign Secretary and Defence Secretary* [2011] EWCA Civ 1540

accused of the kind of passivity of which the law lords were guilty seventy years ago in *Liversidge* v. *Anderson*. But despite all this the courts have slowly retreated as the culture of secrecy has spread from statute to common law.

The common law

The retreat begins harmlessly enough in 2000 when the Court of Appeal, finding there was no provision in the statute for handling on appeal closed material used before SIAC, held itself to have inherent power to appoint a special advocate to protect the individual's interests.[40] In the event the special advocate did not need to be called on. But in 2002 a much larger step was taken. A notorious prisoner, Harry Roberts, who in 1966 had murdered three police officers, had become eligible for parole. The Home Office opposed his move to open prison and asked the Parole Board to hear some of its evidence without disclosing it to Roberts. The Parole Board took the view that, although it had no statutory authority to withhold disclosure, it had inherent power to restrict sight of this evidence to a special advocate without telling Roberts and his lawyers even the gist of it. The House of Lords, on a judicial review application, by a majority upheld this view.[41] They accepted that the use of a special advocate did not necessarily mean that the eventual proceedings would meet the Convention's requirement of a fair trial. But, in the face of powerful dissents from Lord Bingham and Lord Steyn, Lord Woolf, speaking for the majority, held that the special advocate procedure could be used compatibly with that requirement, and that the Parole Board was entitled to adopt it despite the absence of any statutory authority.

The *Roberts* case involved facts and allegations which are unlikely to be repeated. But a second area in which anonymous evidence has now been sanctioned is the making of ASBOs – anti-social behaviour orders. This is a difficult area: few witnesses are likely to come forward and give evidence face to face with a local hooligan, but allowing their statements to be anonymously read in court as evidence opens up equal and opposite possibilities of error and abuse. Justice estimates that thousands of ASBOs have been made in this way by local magistrates. In many of them it is likely that the common law's default position, which the House

---

[40] *Home Secretary* v. *Rehman* [2000] 3 All ER 778
[41] *Roberts* v. *Parole Board* [2005] UKHL 45

of Lords affirmed in *Roberts* – that if the entire case against the accused needs to be concealed, the trial cannot proceed – has been ignored.

Until it was put on a statutory footing in 2008, closed evidence had begun to be used on a similarly pragmatic basis in asset-freezing cases; and Justice lists other areas of adjudication – mental health review tribunals, immigration tribunals, employment tribunals – into which non-disclosure of one side's evidence to the other party has begun to creep. Lord Shaw, once again, in *Scott* v. *Scott*:[42]

> There is no greater danger of usurpation than that which proceeds little by little, under cover of rules of procedure, and at the instance of the judges themselves.

In every instance the change has been made on what appear to be good grounds and for limited purposes. But the undertow may be becoming stronger than the tide; the exception may become the norm; and the lion beneath the throne may find itself able to do little more than growl.

---

[42] at 477

9

The separation of powers

**Montesquieu's remark that without separation of the state's powers there
would be an end of everything was always an overstatement, but it contained an important truth. This chapter suggests that the separation of
powers in the British state, while it has long and deep historical roots, has
never been a fixed set of relationships and may today be under critical stress.**

What is it?

Everybody knows that the separation of powers is a good thing. It is less
easy to say how it came to be this way. In 1748, when Montesquieu[1]
commended England as a model of the separation of powers in a
democracy, judges still sat in Cabinet and the final court of appeal was
the upper chamber of the legislature. But the myth took hold, as myths
do. Within fifty years it had become solid doctrine in the French and
American revolutions: unless the state's principal powers were in separate hands, there would be (in Montesquieu's phrase) an end of
everything.

First, what does the separation of powers mean? In its platonic form it
means that the legislative, executive and judicial functions of the state are
carried out independently of one another. Plainly this is unreal: the
judiciary has to be appointed and paid by a body other than itself; the
law it interprets and applies has to be made in substantial part by a
legislature; the legislature is largely dependent for its own functioning on
the executive and its political heads – ministers who are almost invariably
parliamentarians; the executive requires a parliamentary mandate for
much of what it does; and the courts have to be able to say whether the
executive is acting within its mandate.[2]

---

[1] *De l'Esprit des Lois* (1748; English edn, Dublin, 1751)

[2] This web of crossovers is explored in N. W. Barber, "Self-defence for Institutions" (2013),
72 CLJ 558 as an organic system by which limbs of the state protect themselves: e.g.

There is nothing original about this notion of symbiosis. James Madison wrote in 1788 about the three core functions:

> [U]nless these departments be so far connected and blended, as to give to each a constitutional control over the others, the degree of separation ... essential to a free government can never in practice be duly maintained.[3]

The separation of powers is thus more nearly a descriptive than a normative term. Rather than a doctrine or even an ideal, it is the organic product of a long, uneven and ongoing historical process. It is classically so in the United Kingdom where, as Professor J. A. G. Griffith famously said,[4] the constitution is what happens: if it works, it's constitutional. The separation of powers, in this light and the light of history, represents a principled allocation of core functions among the three central limbs of the state, the legislative, the judicial and the executive. But while these are to an important degree interdependent, are there nevertheless boundaries between them which a polity crosses at its peril? Moreover, does the traditional classification of the state's powers still hold good?

Sovereignty

Within the separation of powers lies the distinct and important question of sovereignty: are the three powers equal in status and, if not, what is their hierarchical relationship? I have contended in the past[5] that sovereignty in the British state is not triangular but bipolar: it resides in the power of Parliament to decide what the law is to be and in the power of the courts to decide, case by case, what the law is. The functions of the executive, while extensive and indispensable, are subordinated to both of these powers: in neither respect does the executive have the last word.

There is, however, an equal and opposite question about sovereignty. Walter Bagehot, writing in the aftermath of the American civil war, contended:

Parliament accords absolute litigation privilege to its own proceedings; the courts will not entertain challenges to the validity of primary legislation; and so forth.

[3] *The Federalist*, No. LXVIII

[4] Chorley Lecture, 1978, 42 MLR 1, 19: "The constitution of the United Kingdom lives on, changing from day to day, for the constitution is no more and no less than what happens. Everything that happens is constitutional. And if nothing happened, that would be constitutional also."

[5] S. Sedley, *Ashes and Sparks* (2011), pp. 270–1, "The Crown in its Own Courts"; and see Ch. 3, n. 8 above.

The splitting of sovereignty into many parts amounts to there being no sovereign.

The Americans of 1787 thought they were copying the English Constitution, but they were contriving a contrast to it . . .

The English Constitution, in a word, is framed on the principle of choosing a single sovereign authority and making it good: the American, upon the principle of having many sovereign authorities and hoping that their multitude may atone for their inferiority.[6]

Looking across the Atlantic today at a state in which President and legislature can be locked in mutual paralysis while the Supreme Court remakes the law, it is hard not to see Bagehot as prophetic. Whether he, like Dicey after him, was justified in according to the United Kingdom's Parliament the state's sole sovereignty requires further consideration.

Where does it come from?

Political theory conventionally traces the idea of the separation of powers to Locke's *Two Treatises of Government,* published shortly after the Glorious Revolution but written, it is now known, about 1680, before the dramatic events of 1688–9 had constitutionalised the British monarchy and constrained the use of prerogative power. It is often convenient to attribute an idea to its first written expression, but it can be misleading to do so. In Locke's case it is doubly misleading, because what Locke described in relation to the separation of powers came close to overlooking the role of the judicial function in the state. What makes his treatise of interest and importance is that it sought to systematise and explain the polity and the political values which were emerging from the historic struggles of the seventeenth century.

Locke's immediate concern, for good reason, was the need to separate elected lawgivers from public administrators:

> . . . it may be too great a temptation to human frailty, apt to grasp at power, for the same persons who have the power of making laws to have also in their hands the power to execute them, whereby they may exempt themselves from obedience to the laws they make . . .[7]

---

[6] W. Bagehot, *The English Constitution* (2nd edn, 1872), pp. 235–6

[7] Book II, Ch. XII, § 143. A classic example was the continuous breach by the bars in the Palace of Westminster of the licensing laws which Parliament had made for everyone else: see A. P. Herbert's unsuccessful challenge, *R v. Graham-Campbell, ex p Herbert* [1934] All ER Rep 681.

It followed in well-ordered societies that an independent executive power was required to carry out the laws made by the parliament. It also followed that a separate power, which Locke called the federative power, was needed to conduct the state's external affairs.

It is probable that, when he spoke of an independent executive power to carry out the law, Locke had in mind judicial as well as ministerial enforcement. A little earlier in the treatise[8] he had accounted for the judicial power as society's delegation to the executive of its power of punishment:

> And so whoever has the legislative or supreme power of any common-wealth is bound to govern by established standing laws, promulgated and known to the people, and not by extemporary decrees; [and] by indiffer-ent[9] and upright judges, who are to decide controversies by those laws ...

Even so, Locke's scheme lacked two essentials of any modern system. First, while it acknowledged the need for an independent and impartial judiciary, it failed to separate the judicial from the executive function. Secondly, and explicitly, it was predicated not on the existence of a democracy but on what Locke called a commonwealth:

> "By commonwealth," he wrote,[10] "I must be understood all along to mean not a democracy, or any form of government, but any independent community which the Latins signified by the word *civitas* ..."

This is no criticism of Locke. As the historian Tony Judt pointed out in his final book,[11]

> If you look at the history of nations that maximised the virtues that we associate with democracy, you notice that what came first was constitu-tionality, rule of law, and the separation of powers. Democracy almost always came last.

To Locke and his contemporaries (as to Burke a hundred years later) democracy was a term of opprobrium: it meant, literally, rule by the mob.[12] It was only in and after the electoral reforms of the nineteenth century that rule by the will of the people came to be regarded as a constitutional norm.

---

[8] Book II, Ch. IX, §§ 128–30   [9] I.e. impartial.   [10] Book II, Ch. X, § 133
[11] Tony Judt with Timothy Snyder, *Thinking the Twentieth Century* (2012)
[12] See the entry "Democracy" in Raymond Williams, *Keywords: A Vocabulary of Culture and Society* (1976).

In any event, a purely descriptive division of the state's powers into the legislative (or deliberative), the executive and the judicial was nothing new. Aristotle[13] had spelt it out two thousand years before Locke. It was Montesquieu rather than Locke who advanced it as a normative condition of civil society, very possibly basing himself not on Locke but on Bolingbroke,[14] whom he had met in England in 1729 and whose anger at ministerial control of Parliament had led him to argue (in anticipation of Madison):

> In a constitution like ours, the safety of the whole depends on the balance
> of the parts, and the balance of the parts on their mutual dependency on
> one another.[15]

Montesquieu was not only extremely well read and travelled; he had served from 1716 to 1726 as a judge in the Bordeaux *parlement*, for most of that time as an assessor to the criminal court. It is likely that it was his own experience, as much as any theory, which convinced him that in a properly ordered society the King cannot be judge in his own cause, and that judges must be both independent of the crown and impartial as between litigants. Unsurprisingly, therefore, it was Montesquieu who developed within the concept of separate powers the idea of an independent judiciary:

> [T]here is no liberty, if the power of judgment be not separated from the
> legislative and executive powers. Were it joined with the legislative, the life
> and liberty of the subject would be exposed to arbitrary control; for the
> judge would then be the legislator. Were it joined to the executive power,
> the judge might behave with all the violence of an oppressor.

He went on, however, to argue for a non-professional judiciary, drawing apparently on Magna Carta:

> The judges ought likewise to be in the same status as the accused, or in
> other words, his peers.[16]

Magna Carta

Does it follow, then, that before the separation of powers was adumbrated by Locke and articulated first by Montesquieu and then by

---

[13] Aristotle, *Politics*, 1297b35ff. "Every state", says Aristotle, "is a form of partnership, requiring a deliberative, a magisterial and a judicial element."

[14] This suggestion is developed in R. Shackleton, "Montesquieu, Bolingbroke and the Separation of Powers" (1949) 3 *French Studies* 25.

[15] *The Craftsman*, No. 208, p. 30   [16] *De l'Esprit des Lois*, Bk. XI, Ch. 6

Madison, it was no more than an idea waiting to be born? On the contrary, by Locke's time political and constitutional development in England and Wales had already brought much of the separation of powers into being. The theory eventually adumbrated in the wake of the Civil War and developed in the course of the eighteenth century had grown out of several centuries of contest, change and eventual constitutional reality in England.

The standing of Magna Carta has gone through a succession of cycles, from adulation in the struggles of the seventeenth century as the primary source of personal liberty to dismissal in the twentieth century as a carve-up of power between a despotic king and his mercenary barons. Although it now risks resuming its former pedestal for no better reason than the coming of its 800th anniversary, Magna Carta was a barometric moment in England's constitutional history. By this I mean that, while it may have played a limited role as hard law, it enunciated and sanctioned a realignment of state power which continues to form part of our constitutional culture, and which arguably set the state on the road to the rule of law.

By 1215 royal undertakings to rule justly were a feature of English governance.[17] Henry I on his accession in 1100 had promised that there should be no more disproportionate penalties and fines. The coronation oath, dating from the late medieval period, still promises both justice and mercy. But, even though the Pope promptly annulled the version signed by King John at Runnymede, Magna Carta was readopted over thirty times by succeeding monarchs, and with each readoption the constitutionalisation of the monarchy became more real.[18] Its fundamental message, Lord Bingham contended,[19] was that no power is absolute. If that is to be a normative proposition, some division of the state's powers among sectors of co-ordinate authority will always be indispensable.

The more specific importance of Magna Carta for the rule of law was the provision it made for professionalising the judicial function and separating it from the other functions of state. By clause 24[20] sheriffs (who were officers of the Crown) were forbidden, save where expressly authorised, to entertain pleas of the Crown – that is to say, to try criminal cases. Clauses 17 and 18 laid down that common pleas – that is, civil

---

[17] See the Introduction.

[18] Thirty-three times, to be exact. The text now regarded as authentic is the one readopted by Henry III in 1225.

[19] T. Bingham, *Lives of the Law* (2011), p. 5   [20] Using the modern numbering.

actions – were no longer to follow the royal court round the country but were to be held in a fixed place, while particular assizes were to be held by justices sent out four times a year (as High Court judges still are) to each county. Even this was not new. Henry II a generation earlier had legislated for the criminal assizes of oyer and terminer and general gaol delivery to be taken by his justices riding out on circuit – as, once again, they still are. By the Statute of Westminster in 1285, it was enacted that lawsuits were to be tried at Westminster on fixed dates unless before the set day the judges reached the locality on assize. The original version of Magna Carta also undertook, by clause 45, to appoint as judges, constables and sheriffs "only men that know the law of the realm and are minded to keep it well".[21]

It is not always appreciated how important the dispersal of justice and its severance from the monarch's person has been over these eight centuries. It is linked to the most celebrated of the promises made by Magna Carta, in what is today tabulated as chapter 29:

> No free man shall be arrested or imprisoned, or be disseised of his property or rights, or be outlawed or exiled, ... nor will we judge him or condemn him, except by the lawful judgment of his equals or by the law of the land. To none will we sell, to none deny or delay right or justice.

This is almost the only survivor of the numerous clauses of Magna Carta that legislators from 1863 onwards have seen fit to repeal as redundant (or possibly embarrassing). In it are the seeds not only of jury trial – the judgment of one's equals[22] – but of an independent and impartial system of justice. Its logical corollary was a uniform system of law and legal principle: a body of judge-made law which, instead of depending on local custom and feudal enforcement, was the same everywhere – a common law.

The division of constitutional labour

In 1489, four years after the Tudor dynasty had assumed the throne, it had been decided by the courts[23] that they would not recognise an act of attainder, nor therefore by implication any other primary legislation, which had not received the assent of the Commons as well as of the Lords. Nobody today would contend that the fifteenth-century House of

---

[21] The provision was dropped from later versions.
[22] Though the majority of the population did not rank as "free men".   [23] YB 4 H.vii 18

Commons was a democratic institution; but its assembly of burgesses, citizens and knights of the shire, themselves elected from 1430 onwards by the forty-shilling freeholders of each county (a franchise which lasted into the nineteenth century), created a potent third estate which, with the clergy and the peerage, came to form a necessary prop of a monarchy in constant need of money for its wars. Coming as it did after the Crown's concession in 1407 that all taxing statutes must pass the Commons, the 1489 decision represented a double constraint on the Crown: without both the assent of the Commons and the recognition of the judges, the monarch's laws were going to be ineffective.

Ironically it was Henry VIII who accelerated the transfer of constitutional authority from the throne to Parliament by his repeated demands for legislation to endorse his repudiation of the papacy. By 1559 John Aylmer, later to be Bishop of London, was describing the state as most truly represented in the parliament house, where the three estates – lords, commons and clergy – governed together. As circumspect a politician as Elizabeth's spymaster Burleigh is said to have remarked that "he knew not what an act of Parliament could not do in England".[24]

I have traced in relation to the royal prerogative[25] how, towards the end of the sixteenth century and into the first quarter of the seventeenth, the successive chief justices of the Queen's and King's Bench – Popham, Fleming, Coke – took control of the prerogative of justice and made it their own, to be administered without regal interference or influence. By then, too, Parliament had established its authority as the primary source of law, largely thanks to the repeated demands of monarchs for legislation not only to raise taxes but – in the case of Henry VIII – to legitimise his power-grabs against the papacy and the monasteries.

> "Henry exalted Parliament," Sir John Baker writes,[26] "by goading it into new feats of sovereignty; and Parliament, in return, magnified Henry."

The 677 statutes passed in Henry VIII's reign displayed a new degree of detail and prolixity, designed, Baker suggests, to restrict the scope for judicial interpretation. If so, the exercise failed: Serjeant Saunders in his celebrated submission in *Partridge* v. *Straunge* in 1553[27] spelt out the case for a purposive interpretation of statutes:

---

[24] G. R. Elton, *England under the Tudors* (1991), p. 396. Cf. Dicey's remark to similar effect: Ch. 7, "Parliament's Powers".
[25] Ch. 6 [26] John Baker, *The Oxford History of the Laws of England* (2003), vol. VI, p. 37
[27] (1553) Plowd, 77v, 82

... things outside the letter thereof shall be taken by the equity thereof...
[T]he efficacy of statutes is not solely in the wording ... but in the
intent ...

Simultaneously, the power of the Crown to rule directly by proclamation
or decree was being marginalised by a judiciary and a legislature which
shared common aims and, to a not insignificant extent, common personnel. Baker[28] has persuasively suggested that even Henry VIII's Statute
of Proclamations 1539 was not a Parliamentary licence to rule by
decree but a confirmation that the king in council was empowered to
regulate certain areas lying traditionally within the prerogative power
(such as foreign relations, which remain today a prerogative matter) or
already legislated for by Parliament; but that, importantly, the statute
went out of its way to exclude any royal power over subjects' life, liberty
or property. Paradoxically, far from turning England and Wales into an
autocracy, the brutal reign of Henry VIII did a good deal to subordinate
the Crown's powers to those of Parliament and the judges. The King, it
was now universally accepted, was subject to the law, even if he was able
to use his power of patronage to secure the laws he wanted.

The separation of the judicial function

This was still a long way from the modern division of state functions.
Judges not only sat in Parliament but were regularly consulted by the
King's ministers, prominent among them Thomas Cromwell, for antici-
patory advice on the law – or rather to ensure that upcoming issues were
going to be satisfactorily decided.

One particular cross-over between the legislative and the judicial
power which was to take centuries to unravel was the use of acts of
attainder, by which Parliament condemned individuals who had
attracted its wrath to death and forfeiture of goods. Although in most
cases some semblance of a trial took place in the House before a bill of
attainder was passed into law, and although it was used only in politically
fraught cases, the practice was a serious encroachment on the judicial
function. There was doubt whether an act of attainder was valid if the
victim had gone unheard; but Henry VIII's judges, when consulted by
Thomas Cromwell, advised that such an act was valid.

---

[28] Baker, *The Oxford History of the Laws of England*, vol. VI, p. 64

The procedure was used against the Gunpowder Plotters in 1605. In reverse form, it was also used at the restoration of the monarchy in 1660, when the Act of Oblivion withheld from forty-nine named participants in the trial of Charles I its general amnesty against trial and execution for treason. What brought about its disuse was probably the development of political parties and ministerial government in the eighteenth century: it was one thing to be able to vote to hang your enemy without a proper trial; it was another that, with a change of government, it was you who might be hanged. The procedure became confined to treasonable acts committed in the course of the Scots risings of 1715 and 1745. It was last used against the Irish rebel leader Lord Edward Fitzgerald in 1798. When finally a lesser penal procedure, a bill of pains and penalties, was moved against Queen Caroline in 1820, the resulting debacle put an end to any notion that Parliament was the proper place in which to conduct a criminal trial.[29]

The judicial role

Nor does the common law tolerate executive encroachments on the judicial function. The claimed power of ministers of the Crown to issue search and arrest warrants, save possibly in cases of treason, was given its quietus in the third quarter of the eighteenth century by the series of cases culminating in *Entick* v. *Carrington*.[30] When in 1909 the Crown, acting through the Governor-General, set up a royal commission with a mandate to make what were essentially judicial findings, the New Zealand court of appeal struck it down as an abuse of the prerogative power.[31] When the legislature of Sri Lanka (then Ceylon) in 1962 passed

---

[29] It has become known from the diaries of the wartime head of counter-espionage, Guy Liddell, that in 1945, as the war drew to a close, the DPP, Sir Theobald Matthew, had "recommended that a fact-finding committee should come to the conclusion that certain people should be bumped off ... that this should be put to the House of Commons and that the authority should be given to any military body ... to ... inflict whatever punishment had been decided on" (*The Guardian*, 26 October 2012): in other words, that there should be an act of attainder. But at Yalta, Churchill, who favoured the proposal, was outvoted by Roosevelt and Stalin: hence the Nuremberg trials. See S. Sedley, *Ashes and Sparks* (2011), Ch. 4.

[30] See Ch. 3.

[31] *Cock* v. *Attorney-General for NZ* (1909) 28 NZLR 405, applying *Clough* v. *Leahy* (1904) 2 CLR at 156; *Case of a Commission of Inquiry* (1608) 12 Co. Rep. 31; cf *McGuiness* v. *Attorney-General of Victoria* (1940) 63 CLR 73; *State of Victoria* v. *Australian Building Federation* (1982) 152 CLR 25, 71. On the justiciability of prerogative acts, see Ch. 1.

an act providing for the trial of eleven individuals allegedly implicated in an abortive *coup d'état,* nominating the three judges who were to try them and setting new minimum penalties, the Privy Council struck it down as an unconstitutional usurpation of the judicial function.[32]

Judicial innovation

There is, however, another and more controversial constitutional cross-over – the power of the judges to declare law where Parliament has not explicitly made law. Is this a breach of the separation of powers or an example of it in action? Dicey, the most vocal of all exponents of parliamentary supremacy, was untroubled by judicial creativity – indeed he claimed that it was the basis of our constitution[33] and devoted a major lecture to the virtues of judicial legislation[34] – though one needs to remember that, to Victorian lawyers, the statute book was no more than an island in the great sea of the common law, where today it forms an entire continent.

While the common law has now disclaimed any power to create new crimes,[35] it has not been able, and never will be able, to avoid adapting old law to new issues such as rape within marriage[36] or assisted suicide.[37] There is no jurisdictional back-burner on which the courts can put an issue while Parliament decides what, if anything, to do about it. It is especially so when the issue is of the kind for which MPs have little appetite: in our own time, the termination of life support;[38] in an earlier generation the outlawing of slavery[39] – issues which garner few new votes but can generate local opposition sufficient to unseat a member. Constitutionally Parliament may be omnipotent, but it is not omnicompetent. Its deliberative role and limited resources require it to delegate a mass of functions to central and local governmental bodies. Correspondingly, it has to rely on the judiciary both to ensure that those bodies stay within

---

[32] *Liyanage v. The Queen* [1965] 1 AC 259

[33] *The Law of the Constitution* (5th edn, 1897), p. 187: "... the general principles of the constitution ... are with us the result of judicial decisions ...."

[34] *Law and Public Opinion in England* (1905), Lecture XI

[35] See the discussion of *Shaw v. DPP* [1962] AC 220 and *Knuller v. DPP* [1973] AC 435 in A. W. Bradley, K. D. Ewing and C. Knight, *Constitutional and Administrative Law* (16th edn, 2014), pp. 464–5.

[36] *R v. R* [1992] 1 AC 599, [1991] UKHL 12   [37] *R (Pretty) v. DPP* [2001] UKHL 61

[38] *Airedale NHS Trust v. Bland* [1993] AC 789

[39] See Sedley, *Ashes and Sparks,* pp. 355–6.

the law and, through the common law, to fill the inevitable spaces in primary and secondary legislation.

These are among the reasons why assisted dying has in recent years had to be addressed, not separately but in concert, by the executive (in the form of the Director of Public Prosecutions[40]) and by the courts.[41] The Supreme Court's message in the *Nicklinson* case that it may have to take its own course in relation to assisted dying if Parliament continues to ignore the human right to autonomy at the end of life was a novel departure, both respecting the separation of the judicial and legislative powers and putting the separation under pressure.

I will not explore here the uncomfortable practice of judges giving evidence to parliamentary committees. From the introduction in 1979 of departmental select committees to the end of 2013, judges had testified to them orally on 262 occasions and had submitted written testimony on a further 145.[42] While it is understandable that parliamentarians want to know how judges' minds work, and perhaps also to give them a piece of their own mind, anything that dilutes the principle that judges speak through their judgments and may not be lobbied or challenged extra-judicially has to be handled with great care.

The monarch and the judges

Let me go back now to one of the pivotal moments in the development of the modern separation of powers, not as a theory but as a reality of political life. Like a number of other such moments in our constitutional and public law, it involves Sir Edward Coke. I have described the plateau (not a very even one) that constitutional law reached in the course of the sixteenth century. From here it was to plunge in the first part of the seventeenth century into the turmoil which erupted in a civil war and was resolved in the historic compromise of 1689.

There were many reasons for the storm that was brewing, but prominent among them was the arrival on the throne of England and Wales in 1603 of a monarch, James I of England, who, as James VI of Scotland, had been accustomed to rule as an autocrat.[43]

---

[40] See Ch. 5.   [41] *R (Nicklinson)* v. *DPP* [2014] UKSC 38
[42] R. Hazell and P. O'Brien, *Meaningful Dialogue: Judicial Engagement with Parliamentary Committees at Westminster* (2015)
[43] Cf. Ch. 6, n. 16

> "Kings are properly judges," he announced in 1616, taking the royal seat in Star Chamber for the first time since Henry VIII, "and judgment properly belongs to them from God ... It is atheism and blasphemy to dispute what God can do; so is it presumption and high contempt in a subject to dispute what a king can do ..."

As to Parliament, James told the Spanish ambassador in 1614 that he was surprised his – James' – ancestors should ever have permitted such an institution to come into existence. But, he said, "I am obliged to put up with what I cannot get rid of".

The 'law of Conveniency'

James died in 1625 and was succeeded by his son Charles, whose belief in his divine right to rule was as entrenched as his father's but who failed to sense the sands shifting under him. Within a year Charles found himself at war with France and in desperate need of money, which he set out to raise without a parliamentary vote. The five knights who, *pour encourager les autres*, were imprisoned for non-payment by the Privy Council acting in the King's name, sued out writs of habeas corpus. In November 1627 the King's Bench, under its new chief justice, held that the monarch had power in an emergency to detain individuals indefinitely without showing cause,[44] but events moved too fast for a final judgment to be reached on the legality of the ship money. The Duke of Buckingham's navy still needed half a million pounds to fight the French; the gentry were still refusing to pay; and soldiers were now to be billeted on civilian homes. Charles had to release the five knights and other imprisoned landowners and to summon a Parliament.

Sir Edward Coke entered the 1628 Parliament[45] as the member for two separate constituencies, Suffolk and Buckinghamshire; the great jurist John Selden, who had argued the case for one of the five knights, took his seat with other leading lawyers; and a twenty-nine-year-old burgess named Oliver Cromwell took his seat as the new member for

---

[44] *Darnel's Case* (1627) 3 St. Tr. 1. Charles had consulted the chief justice of the King's Bench, Sir Ranulph Crewe – a procedure which Coke had told him was improper – and had replaced him with Sir Nicholas Hyde when Crewe refused to endorse the levy. Paul Halliday, *Habeas Corpus: from England to Empire* (2010), pp. 138–9, points out that the decision of the King's Bench in the *Five Knights' Case* represented no more than an affirmation of existing judicial authority. The power of the state, in the name of the Crown, to act arbitrarily in times of emergency is still today a live issue.

[45] He had sat from 1589 as MP for Aldeburgh, and been elected Speaker in 1592.

Huntingdon. A contemporary report recorded a peer's estimate that the Commons could have bought the Lords three times over: these were the men of property without whose support Charles was impotent.

The Parliament of 1628 did not turn the tide of history, but it marked a turning. Four days before its first session, a group which included Coke decided to make personal liberty the focus of debate, using chapter 29 of Magna Carta as their foundational text[46]: "No free man shall be arrested or imprisoned except by the law of the land". In the Commons, Coke, at the age of seventy-six still a potent and respected voice, was confronted by the Attorney-General with one of his own decisions acknowledging an unreviewable prerogative power of detention. I was mistaken, said Coke; I followed precedent rather than principle.

The House drew up four resolutions affirming the right to personal liberty under judicial surveillance and the unconstitutionality of taxation without legislation, and presented the resolutions to the Lords. They also voted the King his taxes; but the big issue – whether the King could levy taxes in his own name – remained unanswered. Coke proposed a petition of right, a standard procedure for soliciting individual redress against the Crown, but in this case one which, if it secured the Crown's assent, would have the force of law.[47] In the end, faced with the unanimous demand of both houses of Parliament, Charles capitulated, using the requisite words: "*Soit droit fait comme il est désiré*" – "let right be done as asked". By an enactment which is still on the statute book, the monarch had had to accept that his prerogative powers were limited by law.

In the debates[48] you can hear the English of the King James Bible in full flow. "Magna Carta is such a fellow," Coke memorably said at one point, "that he will have no sovereign". He also said something less celebrated but today more relevant. Recalling that the reason for the arbitrary royal demands was to wage war, he said:

---

[46] "The debates of 1628 marked the reintroduction of Magna Carta as a major element of English constitutional theory": Eric Schnapper, 84 Colum. L.R. 1675, citing Sir Benjamin Rudyard in debate: "The very point, the scope and drift of Magna Carta was to reduce the regal into a legal power in the matter of imprisonment."

[47] The text of the Petition of Right is accordingly to be found in Halsbury's *Statutes* (4th edn, 2007 reissue) vol. X, p. 34. As Coke put it in debate, "The King may limit himself by acts of Parliament": see next note, vol. V, p. 288.

[48] R. C. Johnson *et al.*, *Commons Debates 1628* (1977) (6 vol.) [Bod. K.10.150], a prodigious work of reconstruction from contemporaneous official, diary and narrative sources. Direct reporting of Parliament's proceedings was punishable as a contempt.

God send me never to live under the law of conveniency or discretion . . ..
Shall the soldier and the justice sit on one bench, the trumpet will not let
the crier speak ... Where the common law can determine a thing, the
martial law cannot.[49]

Star Chamber

Although the Petition of Right represents an important stage in the
history of the royal prerogative, its relevance to the separation of powers
is that it marks a turning point in the long endeavour of the monarchy to
retain a court-based autocracy, governing through favoured aristocratic
ministers and dispensing justice either in person or through a domestic
prerogative court. That court was, of course, Star Chamber, named after
the decorated room in the palace of Westminster in which the Privy
Council had met[50] since the mid-fourteenth century. But it was not until
1487 that a statute conferred on an elite group of counsellors, including
the two chief justices, the inquisitorial powers which came to be used
exclusively for matters of state and which, with the regular use of torture
under James I, became the symbol of the Crown's despotism. Its abolition
by Parliament in 1641, on the eve of the Civil War, was a harbinger of the
coming change; but it also consolidated the centuries-long transition of
justice from the Crown in person to the Crown in independent courts,
administering a law of which Parliament was a principal source and the
judges the sole expositors – a decisive separation of two of the state's
chief powers, and one which was secure before Locke was born.

Although it has had (and in some respects has deserved) a bad press,
Star Chamber was not an English version of the Spanish Inquisition. In
addition to dealing with disputes between individuals,[51] one of its principal functions was to regulate and control the exercise of power by

---

[49] Ibid., vol. II, p. 545: 18 April 1628. I have repunctuated the text, which may have been
misread by the editors. "Shall" is here used conditionally, not interrogatively. "Crier" =
usher.

[50] When not attending the monarch outside London.

[51] Most strikingly, in *Cartwright's Case* (1569) Star Chamber found in favour of an ill-
treated slave who had been brought from Russia, holding that "England was too pure an
air for slaves to breathe in". The dictum (often mistakenly attributed to Lord Mansfield)
was cited in defence of John Lilburne in 1647, and again by counsel for the slave James
Somersett in 1775 (see M. P. Nolan and S. Sedley, *The Making and Remaking of the
British Constitution* (1997), p. 51 n. 9.

officers of the Crown, including justices of the peace. In this respect it was in substance the first court of public law in England.[52]

The Bill of Rights

The seventeenth century embraced a long, complex and bitterly contested era of fundamental change in Britain's polity. Although they lasted only from the execution of Charles I in 1649 to the restoration of his son to the throne in 1660, the ten years of Cromwell's ascendancy[53] saw changes which set English public and constitutional law on the track to the historic settlement of 1689 by which we are still governed.

In 1685 James II, brought up in exile as a Catholic by his French mother, succeeded his brother Charles II and began to dismantle the legal disabilities by which Catholics (who were feared less for their beliefs than as potential agents of hostile states) were denied public office and religious freedom. He had the Declaration of Indulgence, suspending the prohibitions on both Catholicism and Nonconformism, read in Anglican churches.[54] When a second Declaration, invoking a royal power to dispense with the law, prompted mass resistance within the Church of England, James responded by putting seven bishops on trial for sedition.[55] Then, seeking to raise a standing army in the face of threatened invasions, he resorted again to the royal dispensing power in order to commission Catholic officers, and browbeat the judges into endorsing his action.[56] By 1688 it was on the cards that Roman Catholicism might once again be the state religion.

The Protestant Whig establishment responded by organising a *coup d'état*. James II's Dutch son-in-law, William of Orange, was already facing a serious threat of aggression from Louis XIV of France, a Catholic king with whom a Catholic British monarchy might well forge an

---

[52] See J. A. Guy, *The Court of Star Chamber and its Records to the Reign of Elizabeth I* (1985), Ch. 1, cited in C. W. Brooks, *Law Politics and Society in Early Modern England* (2008), p. 12. By the 1630s Star Chamber was attempting to regulate and mitigate the worst effects of enclosure (see Ch. 13) by prosecuting enclosers who had acted outside the law: see R. Powell, *Depopulation Arraigned, Convicted and Condemned* (1636).

[53] See Ch. 4.   [54] See v. 2 of the *Ballad of the Vicar of Bray*, quoted in Ch. 3.

[55] They were acquitted, largely because the crime they were charged with was a misdemeanour, entitling them to be defended by counsel. Had it been felony, they would have had no such right.

[56] *Godden* v. *Hales*: see Ch. 6.

alliance. The birth of a male, and presumptively Catholic, heir to the throne finally prompted a group of Whig politicians to invite William, with his Stuart wife Mary, to assume the throne in James' place. James tried to put his reforms into reverse, but on 5 November 1688 a north European protestant army 15,000 strong landed at Torbay and marched on London. Louis XIV tried to divert it by declaring war on the Netherlands, but the collapse of the Stuart regime was by now irreversible and James fled to France. His fruitless attempt to regain England through Ireland is an enduring part of that country's bloodstained history which still resonates in Ulster's sectarian divide.

I have skittered through the background to the 1689 Bill of Rights because it is treated by conventional legal historiography with a simplistic triumphalism which is as misleading as the negativity commonly accorded to the English Commonwealth and Protectorate. Both were instances of what today is called regime change, each turning on the dethroning of a Stuart monarch by a combination of popular opposition and military force. Each, too, was a reaction to grievances which had become insupportable, and each produced a new constitutional beginning – in 1653 Cromwell's Instrument of Government; in 1689 a Bill of Rights which in significant respects echoed Cromwell's measure.[57] Even so, the Glorious Revolution was in reality a *coup d'état*, conducted within the political establishment.

What matters, however, is that the Bill of Rights which Parliament adopted in the early part of 1689 constitutionalised the British monarchy. It set out the terms on which William and Mary and their successors were to occupy the throne: they were to rule not by divine right, nor by right of conquest, but by popular consent. Together with the Act of Settlement 1700, which granted the judges tenure on fixed salaries subject only to dismissal on a vote of both Houses, it formalised a separation of powers which, although it now carried the imprimatur of political philosophy, had been evolving for the better part of five hundred years.

A constitutional monarchy

The importance of the Bill of Rights in the present context is that it took away for good the power of the monarch, and therefore of the monarch's

---

[57] See Ch. 4.

ministers, to disapply the law.[58] Like the power to raise taxes[59] and the power to maintain a standing army without parliamentary authority, the power to suspend or dispense with Parliament's legislation represented a contested stronghold of Crown authority. The settlement of 1689, by taking these powers decisively from the monarch, resolved one of the fundamental issues of the distribution of state power which had provoked the long crisis of the seventeenth century; but it left a very large tranche of power, notably the conduct of imperial and foreign affairs, in the hands of the Crown's ministers, with consequences reaching down to today.[60]

The soldier and the justice

The similarity of Sir John Anderson's interpretation of his own wartime emergency powers as Home Secretary to the autocratic conduct of the early Stuarts was remarked on by Lord Atkin in his famous dissent in *Liversidge* v. *Anderson*.[61] Today the separation of powers faces much the same pressure – national emergency – as provoked a constitutional crisis under the Stuart monarchs. This is why Coke's remark in the debate on the Petition of Right about what happens if the soldier sits on the same bench as the justice is still relevant. But what does it have to do with what Coke in the same speech called "the law of conveniency or discretion"?

I have traced[62] the containment of arbitrary ministerial power by the judges who in the mid-eighteenth century decided the great series of cases, pivoting on the *North Briton* raids, which not only outlawed general warrants but decisively separated the executive from the judicial

---

[58] Although monarchs continued until early in the eighteenth century to purport to suspend unwelcome legislation.

[59] As I have suggested in Ch. 6, the need for Parliament's authority to raise direct taxes had been acknowledged for centuries: see 45 Edw.3, c.4 (1372). But in *Bate's Case* (1606) 2 St. Tr. 371 the courts conceded an unlimited royal power of indirect taxation, viz import duties; and in *R* v. *Hampden* (1637) 3 St. Tr. 825, the *Ship Money* case, a judicial majority allowed the King to be the sole judge of whether an emergency permitting direct royal taxation for warfare had arisen. However, the Act of 1661 (13 [*sic*] Car. 2 c.4), making a "free and voluntary present" of money to the newly enthroned Charles II, had by s. 5 – which is still on the statute book – declared that "no commissions or aids of this nature can be issued out or levied but by the authority of Parliament", and that the Act was not to be treated as a precedent.

[60] See Ch. 6.

[61] [1942] AC 206. "In this case I have listened to arguments which might have been addressed acceptably to the Court of King's Bench in the time of Charles I."

[62] See Ch. 3.

power of the state. One of the great achievements of modern public law, for which these cases laid the foundation, has been the establishment of the principle that the executive comes before the courts on an equal footing with the individual. It was on this principle that in *M* v. *Home Office*[63] the Home Secretary was found guilty of a contempt of court committed in his official capacity and that the wrongdoing of the state's security services was exposed in the *Binyam Mohammed* case.[64] Conveniency and discretion are useful tools of ministerial government, but they do not constitute law.

Some of what was accomplished in affirming the rule of law has been rolled back by the Justice and Security Act 2013, which allows ministers to keep away from other parties to litigation any evidence on which they propose to rely but disclosure of which they assert would be damaging to the interests of national security.[65] Despite an element of judicial control introduced into the legislation, national security is now a statutory trump card: the soldier's trumpet, as Coke forecast, can drown the voice of justice.

The separation of powers today

A full account of the separation of powers in Britain today could legitimately take in the established church and the media as locations of constitutional power; for each possesses a sufficient measure of autonomy to rank to some degree as a discrete element in the governance of the state. But it is the powers now exercised by the security and intelligence services[66] which raise the question whether the conventional tripartite separation of powers – legislature, judiciary, executive – is any longer an adequate account of the state in this and many other Western democracies. Do the security services now possess a measure of autonomy in relation to the other limbs of the state which requires constitutional recognition? In the United Kingdom, their ability to procure

---

[63] [1994] AC 377

[64] [2011] QB 218. See further Ch. 8, "The Turn of the Tide". Cf. *R (Omar)* v. *Foreign Secretary* [2013] EWCA Civ 118.

[65] See Tom Hickman, "Turning Out the Lights?", UK Constitutional Law Group blog, 11 June 2013.

[66] It may be that the police have now to be included with the security services, not only because their role includes security but because they are acquiring parallel forms of autonomy: see *R (Virgin Media Ltd)* v. *Zinga* [2014] EWCA Crim 52, in which it emerged that a private prosecutor had purchased the services of the Metropolitan Police, esp. §§ 41–6.

legislation which prioritises their own interests over individual rights and even public welfare,[67] to dictate executive decisions, to lock their antagonists out of judicial processes and to operate largely free of public scrutiny seems at least to make the proposition arguable.[68] The argument also invites the further question whether, and to what extent, developments of this kind are now an unpalatable necessity.

At other recent points respect for the separation of powers has promoted worthwhile, or at least defensible, change: the abolition of the Lord Chancellor's judicial functions by the Constitutional Reform Act 2005,[69] for example, and the institution of a supreme court physically divorced from Parliament. The merger of the Lord Chancellor's political role with that of the Secretary of State for Justice, however, has collapsed one of the critical constructs within the separation of powers – the presence in government of a senior minister to guard the interests of a legal system which, on principle, lacks any political clout of its own.

While other constitutions – including those of France and the United States – prohibit any interlocking of church and state, the United Kingdom continues by law to have an established church holding seats in the upper chamber of the legislature, and to authorise religious discrimination by state-funded schools.[70] Few things better illustrate both the historical contingency and the porosity of the separation of powers in the UK than the twenty-six senior bishops of the Church of England who sit by virtue of their spiritual offices on the benches of the upper house of the legislature and who are entitled to speak and vote without restriction – a constitutional anomaly which is not even found in a theocracy such as Iran, but which none of the many governmental proposals of recent years for reforming the House of Lords has made any principled attempt to address.[71]

---

[67] E.g. Regulation of Investigatory Powers Act 2000, s. 17: see Ch. 11, cap. "Security and surveillance".

[68] See L. Lazarus et al. (eds.) Reasoning Rights (2014), Pt. 3, "National security and human rights". The government's expressed satisfaction with the outcome of the Binyam Mohamed litigation (see Ch. 8, fn 34) was overtaken by the 2010–11 report of the Intelligence and Security Committee which recorded US dissatisfaction and asked for an urgent change in the law. Hence the 2013 act.

[69] On the deplorable procedure adopted, see Sedley, Ashes and Sparks, Ch. 10.

[70] Equality Act 2010, Sch. 11, para. 5(g)

[71] For example, the royal commission report A House for the Future (Cmnd 4514, Jan. 2000), on no intelligible basis, proposed replacing them with sixteen elected clerics of the Church of England. Lord Bingham's proposal to replace the House of Lords with a revising chamber of sixty qualified individuals, who might perfectly well include senior clerics, would resolve the issue.

Meanwhile Macaulay's fourth estate – the media – following repeated abuses and intensive scrutiny in the Leveson Inquiry,[72] appears to have reverted to business as usual, setting up a docile regulatory body unable to meet the criteria for recognition under the Privy Council's charter.[73] The fact that the press is a power in the land by default rather than by design may not be a sufficient reason for treating it and its bad behaviour with the same fatalistic resignation as the weather.

Even if the notion of the separation of powers continues to be limited to its traditional three elements, the interlocking of the United Kingdom's parliament, executive and courts since the turn of the last century alone has been a complex and continuously shifting process. For much of the twentieth century the constitutional dominance of the executive was a practical reality which rested on the weakness of Parliament and the acquiescence of the judiciary.[74] That relationship changed radically in the later part of the twentieth century as the judiciary became more interventionist, and there is every reason to think it will go on changing in the twenty-first as government becomes increasingly presidential and a professional civil service grimly watches the repopulation of Whitehall by ministerial placemen and policymakers.

---

[72] *An Inquiry into the Culture, Practices and Ethics of the Press*, HC 780, November 2012
[73] Royal Charter, 25 October 2013; data file 254116   [74] See Ch. 1.

10

Public law and human rights

Human rights are not a recent invention. The common law has recognised many of them for centuries, but the Human Rights Act 1998 put them on a statutory footing. Has this made the common law less or more relevant?

Rights and wrongs

Human rights represent a claim on the state which every individual can make. Some claims, such as the right not to be tortured, are unqualified and, if torture is proved, unanswerable. Others, such as the right to private life or to free expression, are heavily qualified, making their applicability case- and fact-specific. But there is nothing in principle or in practice which confines human rights to the sphere of public law: they crop up daily in family law cases, in libel actions and in criminal trials.

Why then is the intersection of human rights and public law of any particular interest? There are at least two reasons. First, if human rights are legal claims on the state, the legality of state conduct is the business of public law. Secondly, the common law, of which public law is a key component, tends to mimic its environment like a chameleon.[1] The constitutional environment in recent years has included a developing culture of human rights, and public law, without becoming a different creature, has begun to take some of its colour from it.

---

[1] And not always for the best: see Ch. 1. See also the "persons" cases, in which the judges for decades did all they could to block the enfranchisement of women: M. P. Nolan and S. Sedley, *The Making and Remaking of the British Constitution* (1997), Ch. 4. But consider also the opposition of the common law to monopolies (P. Craig, "Constitutions, Property and Regulation" [1991] PL 438) and to slavery (see Nolan and Sedley, *The Making and Remaking of the British Constitution*, pp. 50–1); its creation of crimes of market manipulation, and its abandonment of them as the conventional wisdom of political economy changed (P. S. Atiyah, *The Rise and Fall of Freedom of Contract*, pp. 128–30); and its more recent handling of such issues as rape in marriage (*R v. R* [1991] UKHL 12, [1992] 1 AC 599) and termination of life support (*Airedale NHS Trust v. Bland* [1993] AC 789).

Pretty well the entire substance of English public law is common law. It has been declared, developed, modified and refined over five hundred years and more by the judges, though always with constitutional deference to what Parliament enacts. The minimal primary[2] and slightly more extensive secondary legislation[3] affecting public law has been almost entirely procedural. An attempt by Margaret Thatcher's administration to abolish judicial review was quietly abandoned;[4] so was David Blunkett's threat, as Home Secretary, to take away judicial review and appeal in all asylum cases.[5] But the endeavour to downgrade law returned with the appointment in 2012 of the first legally unqualified Lord Chancellor for three centuries,[6] followed in 2014 by the appointment of two junior barristers as the law officers of the Crown. With the massive reduction of legal aid and the tabloid-led pressure to repeal the Human Rights Act,[7] the future, as I write, is uncertain.

The ECHR and the UK

Although in 1950 the United Kingdom was the first signatory of the European Convention on Human Rights and Fundamental Freedoms, it was fifty years before the rights set out in the Convention became accessible in our domestic law.[8] In the interval, our constitution being dualist, compliance with the Convention remained an international obligation only. It was, however, subject to adjudication by an international court on which each state signatory had a judge, provided the state in question had accorded its citizens the right of individual petition, a step which the United Kingdom took in 1966. This made it possible for

---

[2] Principally s. 81(6) of the Supreme Court Act (now renamed the Senior Courts Act) 1981, a tokenistic attempt by Whitehall to prioritise administrative convenience over justice: see Ch. 5.

[3] In substance, Civil Procedure Rules 1998, Part 54; formerly Order 53, Rules of the Supreme Court (1977).

[4] Hugo Young, *The Guardian*, 9 March 1988

[5] The Asylum and Immigration (Treatment of Claimants etc.) Bill 2004, cl. 11. It is probable, however, that this clause was introduced to distract attention from the comparably unconstitutional clause which slipped through and became s. 8, dictating to immigration judges the facts they were to find in particular circumstances: see Ch. 6, pp. 146–7.

[6] Following the Blair government's reforms of 2003–5, the Lord Chancellorship is now a secondary post for the Secretary of State for Justice.

[7] Impartially described by *The Sun*, in a news story, as "the hated law which frees murderers to kill again".

[8] Human Rights Act 1998, brought into effect from 2 October 2000.

an individual to have the state held in breach of the Convention, but it did not make the Convention part of our law.

In 1998 the new Labour government implemented its electoral pledge to bring the Convention into direct domestic effect. The Human Rights Act 1998, an unusually clear piece of Parliamentary drafting, did this with effect from October 2000. Its effects on the uses of public law were direct. First, the Act by s. 3 required all statute law to be read consistently with the Convention unless to do so was impossible. This meant among many other things that the requirement of article 6 of a fair trial by an independent and impartial tribunal whenever a person's civil rights or obligations were being determined, in addition to being, as it had been for many years, a requirement of the common law, became a statutory mandate to the courts. Secondly, the Act by s. 6 required all public authorities to act compatibly with the Convention save only where primary legislation prevented it. Since the invigilation of the conduct of public authorities is the business of public law, this provision created a whole new area of adjudication for the higher courts.

What I want to look at principally in this chapter, however, is not the statutory content of administrative law but the critical apparatus which public law brings to bear on fundamental rights which come within its range, whatever their origin. Some of this process, of course, derives from the European Convention, but by no means the whole of it.

Telephone tapping

In 1978 an antique dealer named James Malone stood trial with four others in the Inner London Crown Court on a number of charges of handling stolen property. In the course of the trial it emerged[9] that the police had obtained a warrant from the Home Secretary to have Mr Malone's telephone tapped. Mr Malone, having been acquitted on some charges but awaiting a possible retrial on others, issued High Court proceedings for a declaration that the tapping of his telephone was unlawful. His counsel came at the issue from every angle imaginable: property, privacy, confidentiality, human rights as hard law, human rights as soft law, and finally illegality based on want of lawful authority; but all his arguments failed.[10]

---

[9] Today this could not happen: see the Regulation of Investigatory Powers Act 2000, s. 17.
[10] *Malone v. Metropolitan Police Commissioner* [1979] Ch. 344

The Crown made no claim to a prerogative power to intercept phone calls: it simply pointed out that there was no law against it.[11] Article 8 of the Convention, however, declares that everyone has the right to respect for his private and family life, his home and his correspondence. It permits interference with this right only in accordance with the law. In 1978 no law in this country governed telephone tapping;[12] so if article 8 applied, the state was guilty at the very least of failing to regulate phone-tapping by law. Moreover, article 13 of the Convention required states signatories to provide an effective remedy for any breach of the Convention, and the UK had provided none.

The Vice-Chancellor's holding that respect for human rights was a treaty obligation undertaken by the executive, not a legal obligation undertaken by Parliament or the common law, was and still is entirely orthodox. Where he might have been bolder, and a generation later almost certainly would have been bolder, was in being prepared to adapt the common law to the emergent values of confidentiality and privacy. The judgment, still a very a good read, acknowledges that the want of precedent does not count for very much in the common law.[13] But, said the judge, neither the argument for personal privacy running from *Entick v. Carrington*[14] through the Fourth Amendment to the US Constitution and on into modern US case law, nor the law of confidentiality, could furnish a right not to have your phone tapped without statutory authority.

Malone took his case to Strasbourg and, almost inevitably, won.[15] The interception of his phone calls had not been "in accordance with the law" as required by article 8(2) because such regulation as existed was too obscure to amount to law. The United Kingdom was required to regulate telephone interception by legislation. But a common law right to privacy remained unborn, and the law of confidentiality remained in its narrow proprietary cell until the turn of the century. Before we come to that turning point, two other cases deserve attention.

---

[11] Its argument that this is a country where everything is permitted which is not forbidden does not apply to the state: see Ch. 6. The judgment of Megarry V–C is open to criticism for overlooking this.

[12] It was first regulated by the Interception of Communications Act 1985.

[13] Citing Anderson CJ in 1588: "What of that? Shall we not give judgment because it is not adjudged in the books before? We will give judgment according to reason, and if there be no reason in the books, I will not regard them." *Anon*. Goulds. 96

[14] See Ch. 3.   [15] *Malone* v. *UK* (1984) 7 EHRR 14

Gays in the armed forces

In 1995 four members of the armed forces sought judicial review of decisions to discharge them from military service because of their homosexual orientation. All had unblemished disciplinary records. The High Court and Court of Appeal considered themselves unable to find the policy of dismissal irrational at the date when it was operated; they declined to say how the policy would have fared if article 8 had been part of our law; but they did accept the appellants' key proposition of public law that in deciding whether a decision-maker has acted unreasonably, the greater the decision's impact on the individual's human rights, the more the court will require by way of justification.[16]

Sir Thomas Bingham, giving the leading judgment, predicated his acceptance of this proposition on two earlier cases in the House of Lords, both of which had taken a similar approach. In one,[17] an asylum case, Lord Bridge had said:

> The most fundamental of all human rights is the right to life, and when an administrative decision ... may put the applicant's life at risk, the basis of the decision must surely call for the most anxious scrutiny.

In the second, concerning the Sinn Fein broadcasting ban,[18] Lord Bridge had said:

> Any restriction on the right to freedom of expression requires to be justified and ... nothing less than an important competing public interest will be sufficient to justify it.

In this incremental fashion, public law had begun to adapt itself to the Convention concept of proportionality well before the Convention itself had become part of our law.[19] But the most significant manifestation of the process came on the eve of the Convention's entry into domestic force.

---

[16] *R* v. *Ministry of Defence, ex p Smith* [1996] QB 517, 554. Like Mr Malone, these appellants also succeeded in Strasbourg on the ground that the state's lack of respect for their private lives was insufficiently justified by any legitimate objective: *Smith and Grady* v. *United Kingdom* (1999) 29 EHRR 493, *Lustig-Prean and Beckett* v. *United Kingdom* (1999) 29 EHRR 548.

[17] *R* v. *Home Secretary, ex p Bugdaycay* [1987] AC 514, 531

[18] *R* v. *Home Secretary, ex p Brind* [1991] AC 696, 749

[19] In the light of the Court of Appeal's decision, the UK was held in Strasbourg to be in breach of the Convention, the ban being a disproportionate – indeed irrelevant – response to a perceived rather than a real disciplinary problem: *Lustig-Prean and Beckett* v. *United Kingdom* (1999) 29 EHRR 548.

Prison discipline

George Daly, a long-term prisoner, was subjected to repeated cell searches by prison officers. His cell contained privileged correspondence with his lawyers. Although the Home Office accepted that its officers had no right to read such letters, the invariable policy was not to allow the prisoner to be present during the search, so that there was no way of knowing whether the officers were observing the rules. Daly's case,[20] carefully calibrated by his counsel, was that such a blanket policy went further than was necessary in invading a right recognised equally by the common law and by the European Court of Human Rights. There might be particular situations, for example where the prisoner became disruptive, in which exclusion was justified; but what should be an exception was instead the rule.

Lord Bingham agreed:

> The infringement of prisoners' rights to maintain the confidentiality of their privileged legal correspondence is greater than is shown to be necessary to serve the legitimate public objectives [of discipline and control].[21]

He ended by saying this:

> I have reached the conclusions so far expressed on an orthodox application of common law principles derived from the authorities and an orthodox domestic approach to judicial review. But the same result is achieved by reliance on the European Convention.[22]

Lord Bingham then explained how article 8, if it applied, would have produced the same result as the common law. He also pointed out, with possibly a note of self-reproach, that there was no such parallelism in respect to the expulsion of gays and lesbians from the armed services: there the Convention had delivered a protection which the common law had failed to provide.

Lord Steyn, whose reasoning Lord Bingham expressly endorsed, developed the departure from received orthodoxy:

> There is a material difference between the *Wednesbury* and *Smith* grounds of review and the approach of proportionality applicable in respect of review where Convention rights are at stake.[23]

---

[20] *R* v. *Home Secretary, ex p Daly* [2001] UKHL 26; [2001] 2 AC 532 (23 May 2001)
[21] § 19   [22] § 23   [23] § 26

He proceeded to spell out, not from the Strasbourg case-law but from the Privy Council's common law jurisprudence,[24] a three-stage test of proportionality indistinguishable in substance from the European one. Lord Diplock's knowing speculation back in 1985 that proportionality might one day find a home in our domestic law[25] had become flesh. But it was now not confined to the qualified rights for which Strasbourg had developed it: it was to replace the entire straitjacket of *Wednesbury* unreasonableness.

Concurring with these two barometric judgments, the New Zealand public lawyer, Lord Cooke of Thorndon, said:

> ... I think the day will come when it will be more widely recognised that [*Wednesbury*] was an unfortunately retrogressive decision in English administrative law ...[26]

What was happening?

By the time Daly's appeal was argued and decided, the Human Rights Act 1998 was in force; but the searches of his cell and the policy under which they were conducted preceded the Act. His claim therefore had to be a claim at common law. It would not have been difficult for the courts to say (as the Court of Appeal had done in relation to discrimination against gay service personnel) that that was then, and that what happened now must await a more recent event to which the Human Rights Act could be applied. But the law lords had a different goal in view: to make it clear that, irrespective of the introduction of a statutory system of human rights adjudication now directly accessible to UK citizens, the common law itself recognised that fundamental rights were entitled to legal protection in domestic law unless they were defeated by some sufficiently powerful public interest.[27] This was not, the law lords

---

[24] *De Freitas* v. *Ministry of Agriculture* [1999] 1 AC 69

[25] *CCSU* v. *Minister for Civil Service* [1985] AC 374,410: "That is not to say that further development on a case by case basis may not in course of time add further grounds. I have in mind particularly the possible adoption in the future of the principle of 'proportionality' which is recognised in the administrative law of several of our fellow members of the EEC ..."

[26] § 32

[27] See James Maurici [1996] JR 29, listing ten heads under which it was possible to see the incipient operation of the ECHR in our domestic law.

made clear, a manipulation or even an expansion of the concept of irrationality: it was a clean break with it in favour of proportionality.

The words "proportionality" and "proportionate" do not feature anywhere in the text of the European Convention on Human Rights. They are part of the Strasbourg court's interpretative apparatus, borrowed from the courts of Bismarck's Prussia[28] in order to avoid the politically risky enterprise of spelling out, for the purposes of the qualified right set out in articles 8 to 11, what the expression "necessary in a democratic society" means. The court's jurisprudence has determined, in effect, that a democratic society is one which respects qualified rights and will only invade or limit them where the social need to do so outweighs the harm to the individual. As it was put by the Court in *Smith and Grady:*[29]

> An interference will be considered "necessary in a democratic society" . . .
> if it answers a pressing social need and, in particular, is proportionate to
> the legitimate aim pursued.

One question which remained for the common law, however, was which rights were to be regarded by it as fundamental: the Convention rights, the rights tabulated in other international instruments, a selection of these, or a different and possibly longer list? Another was whether the common law, like the Convention, was going to treat certain rights as absolute or was going to allow all of them – even the right not to be tortured – to be restricted so long as the restriction was proportionate.

The street preachers

The process of configuring the common law to Convention values was not confined to *Daly's Case*. In July 1999, in the same interval between the passing of the Human Rights Act and its coming into force, a Queen's Bench divisional court had to deal with a criminal appeal which raised the issue of the limits of free speech in relation to public order. Two women from an evangelical sect were preaching from the steps of Wakefield cathedral. They had gathered a crowd, a few of whom were barracking them. A policeman told them to stop preaching and, when

---

[28] Where it was known as *Verhältnismässigkeit*. See *Klass* v. *Germany* (1979–80) 2 EHRR 214, § 48.

[29] (1999) 29 EHRR 43, § 87

they refused, arrested them for obstructing him in the execution of his duty to keep the peace.

Allowing their appeals against conviction by the local justices and the dismissal of their first appeal to the crown court, the divisional court held that the constable's duties, which were part of the common law, included not only keeping the peace but respecting human rights. The court said:

> Not only is it now accepted that the common law should seek compatibility with the values of the Convention insofar as it does not already share them; executive action which breaches the Convention already runs the risk, if uncorrected by law, of putting the United Kingdom in breach of the Convention ...[30]

Finding that the preachers were not responsible for any threat there might have been to public order, the court turned to prosecuting counsel's submission that the limit of free speech was reached where what was said gave offence, and commented:

> This will not do. Free speech includes not only the inoffensive but the irritating, the contentious, the eccentric, the heretical, the unwelcome and the provocative provided it does not tend to provoke violence. Freedom only to speak inoffensively is not worth having ... From the condemnation of Socrates to the persecution of modern writers and journalists, our world has seen too many examples of state control of unofficial ideas. A central purpose of the ECHR is to set close limits to any such assumed power. We in this country continue to owe a debt to the jury which in 1670 refused to convict the Quakers William Penn and William Mead for preaching ideas which offended against state orthodoxy.[31]

The juxtaposition of the European Convention with one of the seminal cases of the common law – *Bushell's Case*,[32] in which a London jury went to gaol rather than convict two Quaker street-preachers – was designed to stress the continuity of the common law's values with those of the European Convention. The decision preceded the law lords' decision in *Daly's Case* by almost two years, but it was a first step down the same road.

The "gombeen man"

Almost simultaneously with the High Court's decision in the street preachers' case, the law lords had taken their own stride towards

---

[30] *Redmond-Bate* v. *DPP* [2000] HRLR 249, 255–6 (23 July 1999), a decision in which I have to declare an interest.
[31] Ibid., 260   [32] (1670) Vaugh. 135; 124 ER 1006

configuring the common law to the Convention. In a libel action against the *Sunday Times*,[33] a former Taoiseach of the Irish Republic, Albert Reynolds, established to an English jury's satisfaction that he had been falsely accused by the paper of lying to the Dáil and to his cabinet, but was awarded one penny damages, probably because the jury reckoned he had no reputation to lose – the "gombeen man" tag had stuck. The jury also found that the publication had not been malicious; so who was to pay the massive costs of the proceedings turned on whether the publication had been protected by qualified privilege – a category previously confined to interpersonal communications.

In concluding that qualified privilege extended to news publications, the law lords drew directly on the Convention jurisprudence which at that date was not yet part of our domestic law:

> "Freedom of expression," said Lord Nicholls,[34] "will shortly be buttressed by statutory requirements ... The common law is to be developed and applied in a manner consistent with article 10 of the [Convention], and the court must take into account relevant decisions of the European Court of Human Rights (ss. 6 and 2). To be justified, any curtailment of freedom of expression must be convincingly established ... and the means employed must be proportionate to the end..."

Lord Nicholls went on, accordingly, to consider the European article 10 jurisprudence before concluding that the common law of qualified privilege did not require substantial modification; though Lord Hobhouse added:

> There is no human right to disseminate information that is not true.[35]

The Douglas–Zeta-Jones wedding

One of the concerns about introducing the ECHR into our domestic law was that it would be those with the longest purses and the sharpest elbows who would get to drink at the human rights bar. Although events have proved this wrong, among the first customers to come through the door of the court after the Human Rights Act came into force in October 2000 were Michael Douglas and Catherine Zeta-Jones.[36] They had contracted to sell *OK!* exclusive rights to images of their wedding in New York,

---

[33] [2001] 2 AC 127 (28 October 1999)   [34] At 200   [35] At 238

[36] [2001] QB 967 (argued and decided 22–3 November 2000; reserved judgments delivered 21 December). Again I have to declare an interest.

but a pirate photographer disguised as a waiter had sold a set of unauthorised photographs to *Hello!*, which was about to publish them. They sought an injunction to restrain the publication on grounds of breach of confidence.

Two first-instance judges granted the injunction. On *Hello!'s* emergency application to the Court of Appeal to discharge it, the court, albeit taking the view that damages were more appropriate than an injunction, concluded that the claim had a respectable chance of success at trial.[37] The leading judgment[38] took the view that the issue could be dealt with at that stage by applying the special provisions of s. 12 of the HRA concerning prior restraint. The other two judgments took a broader approach, holding that it was no longer necessary to resort to the legal fiction of a confidential relationship between intruder and victim, and that the law should today recognise that privacy was in itself a value entitled to protection.[39]

The road takes a detour

The Douglas–Zeta-Jones wedding litigation wound on through a further series of hearings.[40] We meet it again at the crossroads where the Court of Appeal's proposition that the common law now had a direct role in the protection of personal privacy was advanced in a different case before the House of Lords.

The case was the disturbing case of *Wainwright*, in which the mother and the mentally impaired brother of a prisoner had been strip-searched on a visit in a manner which was unjustified, degrading and harmful. But only a part of what was done ranked in law as an assault. Their claim to damages for the full extent of their humiliation, based on the invasion of their personal privacy, relied principally on the Court of Appeal's reasoning in the *Douglas* case. The House of Lords turned the claim down.[41] It held that there was still no common law tort of invasion of privacy,[42] and that unless and until Parliament legislated there could not be one.

---

[37] It discharged the injunction on the ground that the claim was sustainable but a remedy in damages would be appropriate.

[38] See § 95, Brooke LJ   [39] §§ 125–7; again I have to declare an interest.

[40] They can be picked up at [2008] AC 1, §§ 108 ff. The bottom line was that the Douglases won.

[41] [2004] 2 AC 406 (16 October 2003)   [42] §§ 28–35, per Lord Hoffmann

The decision turned out to be far from the last word. The Wainwrights took their case to Strasbourg and almost inevitably won.[43] They won not only on the ground that their article 8 right to respect for their private life had been unjustifiably infringed, but also on the ground that, in breach of article 13 of the Convention, the UK's law had failed to provide a remedy for it.

Naomi Campbell

The House of Lords, however, had not waited for Strasbourg's judgment. Within four months of delivering their judgment in *Wainwright* they had to consider an appeal which offered them a second chance to take the route they had declined to take in *Wainwright*. The model Naomi Campbell had been followed to meetings of Narcotics Anonymous and surreptitiously photographed outside the meeting place. *The Daily Mirror* published the pictures together with details of her therapy.

This time[44] the law lords held that a privacy right had been actionably infringed:

> "The time has come," said Lord Nicholls in the leading speech,[45] "to recognise that the values enshrined in articles 8 and 10 are now part of the cause of action for breach of confidence ... Further, it should now be recognised that for this purpose these values are of general application. The values embodied in articles 8 and 10 are as much applicable in disputes between individuals or between an individual and a non-governmental body such as a newspaper as they are in disputes between individuals and a public authority."

The passage was a watershed in the legal recognition of human rights. It brought to an end the longstanding debate about whether Convention rights operated on anything except relations between the state and the individual – that is, whether they were solely public law rights. Human rights were acknowledged to be part of private as well as public law.

Lord Nicholls had not been a member of the panel which decided *Wainwright*, but Lord Hoffmann, who gave the second speech in *Campbell*, had been. His judgment contains a measured exposition[46] of the reasons for absorbing the Convention value of respect for personal privacy into the common law. The upshot was that by the time the

---

[43] *Wainwright v. United Kingdom* (2006) 10 ECHR 229 (5 September 2006)
[44] *Campbell v. MGN Ltd* [2004] 2 AC 457   [45] § 17   [46] §§ 46–52

Wainwright case was heard in Strasbourg the House of Lords in *Campbell* had brought the common law into harmony with the Convention.[47]

Did the HRA make the difference?

Does it follow that the law of confidence and privacy would not have developed as it has done without the stimulus of the Human Rights Act? The decision in *Daly* and the earlier sources on which it drew suggest that it might well have done. So does what Lord Hoffmann said on the final lap of the *Douglas and Zeta-Jones* marathon:

> In recent years, English law has adapted the action for breach of confidence to provide a remedy for the unauthorised disclosure of personal information: see *Campbell* v. *MGN Ltd*. This development has been mediated by the analogy of the right to privacy conferred by article 8 of the [Convention].[48]

The phrase "mediated by ... analogy" segregates the process of change from anything as direct or literal as transposition. It aligns the logic of *Campbell*, a private law case, with the public law logic of *Daly*. Above all, it displays the life-force of the common law: the chameleon, simultaneously reactive and proactive, by adapting to its environment equips itself to function more effectively.

The common law and the statute book

Such a history is not only important in itself: it has important implications for a future in which there may not always be a Human Rights Act. The common law's ability to change and to cope will, one hopes, always be there, and with it a concern for fundamental rights that will continue to infuse the body of public law which is one of its greatest achievements. But the statutory content of administrative law also illustrates how profoundly the human rights regime affects the way we are governed and, in turn, how the courts decide cases.

One of the surprises of the Human Rights Act was that s. 19, which was widely thought to be a piece of window-dressing, has turned out to have a material impact on the legislative process. The section provides

---

[47] This does not seem to have been pointed out to the Court of Human Rights when *Wainwright* was eventually argued before it.
[48] [2008] AC 1 § 118

that the minister in charge of any bill must either certify to Parliament that he or she considers the bill Convention-compatible or openly state that the government wants to proceed with it despite the incompatibility. Rather than attempt to secure the passage of incompatible legislation, governments have more than once introduced provisions to make bills compatible. In order to pass the s. 19 threshold, the act which took away all benefits from asylum-seekers who had not applied for asylum on arrival[49] was made Convention-compatible by including a proviso[50] to the effect that the withdrawal of benefits must not be such as to breach the Convention. As a result, the courts were able to intervene on behalf of asylum-seekers who were forbidden by law to work and had become destitute, ill and hungry to a point which violated the article 3 prohibition on inhuman or degrading treatment.[51]

The Belmarsh cases

Probably the most dramatic illustration of the impact of the Human Rights Act on the statute book is the case of the Belmarsh detainees.[52] Following the 9/11 attacks on the United States, the UK government made an order formally derogating from the guarantee of personal liberty contained in article 5 of the Convention, in order to permit the detention of foreign nationals[53] who could neither be charged, because of the want of admissible evidence against them, nor removed or deported, because they would face torture in their countries of origin. The system operated neither against foreign suspects who could be deported nor against suspects who were British nationals.

A nine-judge panel of the House of Lords' appellate committee held that the government's action in derogating from the Convention for this purpose was disproportionate, since it was a response to the situation facing the country which did not rationally address the perceived threat. It was also unlawful since it operated by unjustifiably discriminating against foreign nationals, using immigration controls for what was in reality a security purpose not confined to foreign nationals. The House struck down the derogation order as unlawful and made a declaration that s. 23 of the 2001 Act was not compliant with the Convention.

---

[49] Nationality, Immigration and Asylum Act 2002, s. 55   [50] S. 55(5)
[51] *R (Q) v. Home Secretary* [2003] EWCA Civ 364, [2004] QB 36
[52] *A v. Home Secretary* [2004] UKHL 56; [2005] 2 AC 68
[53] Under s. 23 of the Anti-Terrorism, Crime and Security Act 2001

Reading the judgments, in particular the leading speech delivered by Lord Bingham, you can see the mindset of the Human Rights Act permeating the received categories of public law, amplifying scrutiny for rationality into appraisal of proportionality and gauging the propriety of both secondary and primary legislation by wider and deeper standards than were dreamed of in *Wednesbury*.[54]

Back to the future

Whether or not a domestic rights instrument replaces the Human Rights Act, the common law has now developed the confidence to fill the spaces without requiring a prescriptive tabulation of rights.[55] While the Supreme Court[56] moves towards the concept of a special category of constitutional legislation, the courts have accepted that different rights enjoy differing degrees of fundamentality, starting with the right to life. In this situation it is legitimate to ask whether describing a legal right as a human right adds anything substantive to it.

There may be an answer in one of the oldest judicial review cases in the books, *Rooke's Case*, decided in 1598.[57] The role of the commissioners of sewers in apportioning the cost of maintaining them was an important one, for sewers were not simply foul-water drains: they included the embankment and watercourse works on which the recovery and preservation of agricultural land depended. In *Rooke's Case*, however, the commissioners had levied the entire cost of repairing a river bank on the riparian owner, letting his neighbours benefit from the repair without contributing to its cost. It was said on their behalf – exactly as would be

---

[54] See also *R (Q) v. Home Secretary* [2003] EWCA Civ 364, [2004] QB 36, § 112: "The common law of judicial review in England and Wales has not stood still in recent years. Starting from the received checklist of justiciable errors set out by Lord Diplock in the *CCSU* case [1985] AC 374, the courts (as Lord Diplock himself anticipated they would) have developed an issue-sensitive scale of intervention to enable them to perform their constitutional function in an increasingly complex polity. They continue to abstain from merits review – in effect, retaking the decision on the facts – but in appropriate classes of case they will today look very closely at the process by which facts have been ascertained and at the logic of the inferences drawn from them. Beyond this, courts of judicial review have been competent since the decision in *Anisminic* [1969] 2 AC 147 to correct any error of law whether or not it goes to jurisdiction; and since the coming into effect of the Human Rights Act 1998, errors of law have included failures by the state to act compatibly with the Convention."

[55] This proposition is developed by Lady Hale JSC in "UK Constitutionalism on the March?" [2014] JR 201.

[56] See Ch. 5.   [57] (1598) 5 Co. Rep. 99b

said today – that this was a matter for the commissioners' judgment, whatever the court might think of it. Not so, said Sir Edward Coke –

> notwithstanding the words of the commission give authority to the commissioners to do according to their discretions, yet their proceedings ought to be limited and bound with the rule of reason and law. For discretion is a science or understanding to discern between falsity and truth, between wrong and right, between shadows and substance ... and not to do according to their wills and private affections ...

The point of discretion, Coke wrote in his commentary on Littleton,

> is to discern by the right line of the law, and not by the crooked cord of private opinion ...[58]

Here is the court, more than four hundred years ago, correcting an award because, although it lay within the commissioners' jurisdiction, it was so unfair as to be unreasonable. Is it possible that the common law's antiquity and adaptability will outlive those who want to hobble it, and that it will continue, by pinpointing public law wrongs, to protect what happen at present to be called human rights?

[58] Co. Litt. 227b.

11

The state and the law

The state – Hobbes' *Leviathan* – despite its political and social solidity, is unknown to the common law. Like much else in our constitution, nobody planned it this way: one might say, as Mr Podsnap said to the foreign gentleman, that it was Bestowed Upon Us By Providence.[1] This chapter considers how the law has come to terms with the state in the course of the centuries.

The state as a legal actor

The British state has no legal personality.[2] Although criminal proceedings[3] and judicial review claims are brought in the Queen's name, civil claims cannot name either the Queen or the state as the defendant. This means that the state cannot be directly sued for civil wrongs done by it or in its name.[4] But since 1947[5] the Crown has been vicariously liable for torts committed by its officials (who have always been personally liable[6]), and it is ordinarily bound by contracts entered into on its behalf.[7] So long as some name is available in which to sue it – the Secretary of State for this or that, a nominated department, a corporate public authority, or as a last resort Her Majesty's Attorney-General[8] – does it matter that

---

[1] Charles Dickens, *Our Mutual Friend* (Penguin edn, 1997), pp. 178–9; and see Ch. 14.

[2] The Church of England likewise lacks legal personality, notwithstanding that the canon law which governs it is part of the law of the land: see *Sharpe* v. *Diocese of Worcester* [2013] UKEAT 0243 (Cox J), para. 13 ff. Cf. M. Hill, *Ecclesiastical Law* (3rd edn, 2007), s. 2.01: "The Church of England comprises the provinces of Canterbury and York and is but one part of the Church of God on Earth." For the early history of corporate personality, see J. Baker, *The Oxford History of the Laws of England* (2003), vol. VI, pp. 622 ff.

[3] Save possibly private prosecutions: see *R (Virgin Media Ltd)* v. *Zinga* [2014] EWCA Crim 52, §35–6.

[4] See *Chagos Islanders* v. *Attorney-General* [2004] EWCA Civ 997.

[5] Crown Proceedings Act 1947   [6] *Feather* v. *R* (1865) 6 B&S 257

[7] *Town Investments Ltd* v. *Department of the Environment* [1978] AC 359: see n. 56 below.

[8] Crown Proceedings Act 1947, s. 17

neither the monarch nor the Crown nor the state which they represent can be impleaded by name?

Arguably it does, if only because it illustrates the surprising fact that in the twenty-first century the common law still possesses no solid or unitary concept of the state. Yet, as Janet McLean says:

> There is a state tradition in British legal thought. It is contested, adjustable and complex. These features have given it the flexibility to adjust to changes in state institutions and functions.[9]

The rule of law, in other words, depends in part upon the capacity of the common law to adapt itself to its historical and political environment.

The idea of the state

The word "state" is part of a cluster of English words which describe the way things are: status, stance, static, estate, statue, statute, station, statement.[10] As a term of political science it describes the apparatus by which political power is exercised within a geographically defined community. But as a term of public law it has no meaning at all. It is never used in statutes. Why?

Rather than follow the advice of the King of Hearts to the White Rabbit[11] by beginning at the beginning – the pre-Norman state – and going on till we come to the end – the state we're now in – let me begin in the middle, at the point when, in the upheavals of the seventeenth century, a modern polity began to take recognisable shape and the word "state" began to acquire its present-day meaning.[12] The word generally used for an organised society was "commonwealth", a body which might take the form either of a kingdom or of a republic and which possessed a common set of laws, customs and institutions.[13] But

---

[9] J. McLean, *Searching for the State in British Legal Thought* (2012), p. 310

[10] Blackstone's chapter "Of the Civil State" (*Bl. Comm.*, 1765, I.384 ff), is devoted entirely to social rank.

[11] Lewis Carroll, *Alice in Wonderland*, Ch. 12

[12] See further R. Scruton, *A Dictionary of Political Thought*, and *The Blackwell Encyclopaedia of Political Thought*, "State".

[13] This is the sense in which Aristotle's *Politics* speaks of the state. The OED, *cap.* "State", s. 25, cites Crompton, 1587: ". . . there is no Common wealth, state, or societie of man kind, that can continue, where there is not superiority or preheminence in government"; Bacon, 1625: "Never any State was . . . so open to receive Strangers, into their Body, as were the Romans."

some time before the formal establishment of the Commonwealth, reference was being made to "the State" as a non-partisan means by which Parliament's servants could establish "a corporate identity as the embodiment of their new loyalty".[14]

There is an early instance of this modern usage in Bacon's essay "Of Great Place" (that is, high office), first published in 1612:

> Men in great place are thrice servants – servants of the sovereign or state, servants of fame, and servants of business ...[15]

Earlier still, Sir Edward Coke, prosecuting the Gunpowder Plotters as Attorney-General, had accused them of setting out to

> as it were with one blow, not wound but kill and destroy the whole state.[16]

But it is in Hobbes' *Leviathan*, published in 1651, that the idea is first clearly articulated of the state as an entity distinct from, and greater than, the individuals who compose and administer it.[17] Differing from those who saw the state's powers as derived from the people and therefore as limited by natural law, Hobbes' organic monster, "that great Leviathan called a common-wealth, or state", was more powerful than society itself. If Hobbes is, in Quentin Skinner's words, the first modern theorist of the state,[18] it is no surprise that it was in the years of Britain's republic, albeit that Hobbes himself was in exile with the Court, that his theory crystallised.

---

[14] G. E. Aylmer, *The State's Servants: The Civil Service of the English Republic, 1649–1660* (1973), p. 7. The act of 19 May 1649 which reconstituted the English state (C. H. Firth and R. S. Rait, *Acts and Ordinances of the Interregnum* (1911), vol. II, p. 122) declared it to be "a Commonwealth and Free State" governed by "the representatives of the people in Parliament ... without any King or House of Lords". In consequence, after the Restoration "commonwealth" acquired a republican connotation: see *Smith's Case* (1670) 1 Ventr. 66: ".... to set up uncontrollable jurisdictions below, tends manifestly to a commonwealth; and we shall take care that there be no such thing in our days."

[15] Bacon, *Essaies* (1612 edn). The essay did not feature in the original edition of 1597.

[16] St. Tr. II.177

[17] Few ideas are truly original: much of Hobbes' thinking had been anticipated by the sixteenth-century French philosopher Jean Bodin who, however, believed that the sovereignty of the state was constrained by natural and divine law. And Bodin's concept of the state as an entity had itself been anticipated by Machiavelli, who believed in no such constraint.

[18] Q. Skinner, "The State", in T. Ball *et al.* (eds.) *Political Innovation and Conceptual Change* (1989), p. 90, cited M. Loughlin, *Sword and Scales: An Examination of the Relationship between Law and Politics* (2000), p. 130.

Historians have been divided between those, like G. R. Elton, who see the history of the British state as one of continuous growth from Tudor to Victorian times, and those, like Christopher Hill, who see the republican years of the seventeenth century as a watershed in the professionalising of public administration. Both may have been right,[19] for history tends to accomplish its long-term changes in fits and starts.

The state in reality

Since the time of the Norman kings, government had been conducted not only in the name of the Crown (as it still is) but by it. The Council which Henry VII reassembled after the death of Richard III and the defeat of the House of York grew during the sixteenth century into a powerful oligarchy, though one which, after the dramatic developments of the 1530s, had to defer to Parliament. Parliament, Sir Thomas Smith was able to write in 1565,[20] was "the most high and absolute power of the realm of England", where the nobility and the commons deliberated separately, "every bill or law being thrice read and disputed upon in either House" before the monarch in person gave effect to their advice. But the monarch's own prerogative powers remained vast.

Where, however, Henry VII would personally sign off each page of the royal treasurer's accounts, his successor Henry VIII devolved extensive powers to his administrators, first the astute Cardinal Wolsey and then his protégé Thomas Cromwell. But neither Wolsey nor Cromwell was a viceroy. Prerogative power was exercised on the advice of a royal council composed, in varying numbers, of bishops, office holders such as the Earl Marshal, the Lord Chancellor and the royal treasurer, and favoured nobles, as well as the judges and law officers. It met in one of the two rooms in the Palace of Westminster together known as the Star Chamber, and it dealt not only with public administration but with lawsuits.[21]

---

[19] For a neat summary of the two approaches, see R. Hutton, *The British Republic 1649–1660* (2nd edn, 2000), "Conclusions".

[20] T. Smith, *De Republica Anglorum* (1583), p. 48, cited in G. R. Elton, *The Tudor Constitution: Documents and Commentary* (2nd edn, 1982), p. 240.

[21] These were as often as not civil claims, but by a statute of 1487 (3 Hen.7, c.1) the Council had been empowered to summon suspected wrongdoers before it, to inquire into their acts and to punish them. This was the basis of the inquisitorial criminal jurisdiction, backed by the use of torture, which made Star Chamber notorious. Yet in a case heard in Star Chamber in 1569, "One Cartwright brought a slave from Russia and would scourge him cruelly ... and it was resolved, that England was too pure an air for slaves to breathe

To use members of the hereditary nobility as counsellors and secretaries was a rational way of keeping the nobles where they could be seen and controlled; but it was also of importance to the nobles to have members of their families in the King's confidence and close to his person. Bacon, in his essay "Of Great Place"[22] wrote that the way to it "is by a winding stair" and that those who attain it

> have no freedom, neither in their persons, nor in their actions, nor in their times ... It is a strange desire to seek power and to lose liberty.

As Thomas More, Thomas Cromwell and others found, it was not only your liberty that you could lose in the service of the monarch; but it was a coveted role, and the Tudor state depended on it.

It was Wolsey who hived off the judicial functions of the Council into what became the Court of Star Chamber, and Cromwell who, as Lord Chancellor in the mid-1530s, reorganised its advisory and executive functions into a slimmed-down Privy Council, populated as much by practical men as by aristocrats.[23] In the reign of Henry VIII's ailing son, Edward VI, these functions were divided among five committees, whose secretaries, no longer mere scribes and messengers, continued their slow growth into the Crown's secretaries of state. Despite his fall from favour and eventual execution, Cromwell left a Privy Council which could govern regardless of the competence of the monarch who was its formal head, and which as time went by devolved its work to rudimentary departments: home affairs, revenue, military expenditure and deployment, and – with the break from Rome and the establishment of the Church of England – religion.

Cromwell's work was built on by Elizabeth I's shrewd Secretary of State Lord Burghley. But much of the skilfully managed Tudor state fell apart in the hands of the Stuart monarchs, who sold political and judicial offices as freeholds to raise money and delegated the conduct of government to aristocratic confidants who came into office with their own entourage of subordinates and placemen.

---

in" (cited by Cook, arguendo, in *R v. Lilburne* (1637) 3 St. Tr. 1315, 1352–4. The dictum achieved worldwide currency after *Somersett's Case* (1775).

[22] *Essaies*, 1625; see n. 15 above.

[23] Although the Privy Council then grew in size, Elizabeth reduced it to between twelve and eighteen members, of whom four or five did the bulk of its work, rarely with the monarch herself in attendance: "a very select, and consequently a very powerful, body" (Elton, *The Tudor Constitution*, p. 93).

The state as an entity

In 1649, at the conclusion of the Civil War, Charles I was executed. His Privy Council had already ceased to function, and the House of Lords was now abolished as "useless and dangerous".[24] The vacuum was filled[25] by a combination of three elements: systems inherited from the monarchy; temporary measures of administration developed during the civil war; and parliamentarian and republican structures created under the Commonwealth and Protectorate.

Of these new bodies the most important, both politically and historically, was the Council of State, an appointed body with (usually) forty-one members, which possessed all three features. While the Council was answerable to the House of Commons, its powers were huge. They stopped short of taxation, but they included all the other business of government: foreign relations, deployment of land and naval forces, national security and much else. Although the Admiralty continued to exist, much of its power was transferred to the Council of State's Admiralty Committee, dominated by the eccentric but able Sir Henry Vane, one of an upcoming breed of independent-minded public administrators. Other administrative work – for instance indemnity and compounding – was parcelled out to parliamentary committees. There was as yet no worked-out distinction between the legislative and the executive functions of the state.

The central state

In this and other ways, the Commonwealth was working with the grain of the political culture it had inherited. The old monarchical system, whatever its faults, was a centralised one. Where other European monarchies in the late Middle Ages had dispersed state power to their barons, Magna Carta had as early as 1215 set a different model for England, centralising power in the Crown in return for the King's acknowledgment that he could govern only through his council. The constitution that the Tudors inherited proved pliable enough for Henry VIII's private purposes, but at a significant price: that in return for the legislation he needed to secure his divorces and to break with the papacy, Henry had to acknowledge the supremacy of Parliament. Although Parliament in return, by an act of 1539,[26] gave

---

[24] See Ch. 4.   [25] See Aylmer, *The State's Servants*, pp. 17ff.

[26] 31 Hen.8, c.8: An Act that Proclamations made by the King shall be Obeyed – the origin of the so-called Henry the Eighth clause; repealed by 1 Edw.VI c.12 (1547).

Henry power to issue legally binding proclamations, it specified that these must be made "with the advice of his honourable Council"; and in 1611, in the *Case of Proclamations*[27] Sir Edward Coke held that the monarch's prerogatives were only those which the law of the land allowed him. This did not come out of the blue: it had been established by the mid-sixteenth century that the Crown had no power to raise taxes without parliamentary authority, and by the first decade of the seventeenth century the judges had established that it was not in person but through the courts of law that the monarch dispensed justice.[28]

The monarch's servants

In spite of the growing grip of Parliament and the judges on the royal prerogatives, monarchs in the later seventeenth century still possessed a formidable battery of powers, requiring the services of trustworthy ministers[29] and secretaries. In the fullness of time the King's secretary, a distinct functionary as early as the fourteenth century,[30] was to become a secretary of state – an appointment made to this day by the monarch,[31] though now on the advice of a prime minister who has the support of a parliamentary majority.

How this combination of prerogative and patronage developed into political lawlessness is traced in the great judgment in *Entick v. Carrington*[32] by which, in the mid-eighteenth century, Lord Camden decisively separated the monarch's lawful prerogatives from the justiciable acts of his secretaries of state. But the application of the general law to the Crown's ministers and the restriction of their authority to invade private rights did not conclude the larger question which had been simmering

---

[27] (1611) 12 Co. Rep. 74

[28] See Ch. 9. The monarch as judge is memorably satirised in Ch.11 of *Alice in Wonderland*, where the King of Hearts presides over the Knave's trial wearing his crown (in Tenniel's illustration) on top of a huge wig. Cf. not only the retention of a prerogative judicial power until 1641 by Star Chamber but the continuance today of the legislative powers of the Privy Council: see Ch. 6.

[29] The word "minister" means servant.

[30] See J. F. Baldwin, *The King's Council* (1913), pp. 73–4.

[31] Many ministers are still unelected peers, and at least two in modern times (Patrick Gordon-Walker and Frank Cousins) were members of neither House.

[32] (1765) 2 Wils. K.B. 275; 19 St. Tr. 1030. See Ch. 3.

since the late sixteenth century: were there powers of government which lay outside the rule of law?

Law and government

Elizabeth's reign had seen some subtle interweaving of statutory, judicial and prerogative powers. As described by the American legal historian James Hart,

> Her conception of the modern state was one which operated within accepted legal constraints, when and where it could safely do so, but which also had the power and flexibility to respond decisively to crisis when that too proved necessary. If she managed to meld medieval and modern it was by cultivating the art of ambiguity, by exercising both kinds of power while never publicly acknowledging a distinction between the two.[33]

By the time her successor, James I of England and VI of Scotland, had ascended the throne, the common lawyers were powerful enough,

> not to deny the king a role in the making of law [but] to move him slightly off center, to challenge the notion of his sovereign control.[34]

John Selden, writing in 1610, claimed that sovereignty had always been shared in England between the monarch, through statute law, and the people, through customary law. Thus, says Hart, for Selden

> Parliament itself represented the most important principle of the common law – the subjects' right not to be concluded by laws to which they had not given their consent.[35]

Yet in 1636 Justice Berkeley, in dismissing a challenge to the legality of ship money, declared:

> There is a rule of law and a rule of government, and things that might not be done by the rule of law might be done by the rule of government.[36]

---

[33] J. S. Hart, *The Rule of Law, 1603–1660* (2003), p. 10.   [34] Ibid., p. 15.

[35] Ibid. p. 16, citing J. Selden, *Jani Anglorum*.

[36] *Chambers v. Wentworth*, Rushworth, *Historical Collections*, 2.323 (June 1636). See further Ch. 14. Chambers was a London merchant who refused to pay Ship Money. His claim for false imprisonment against the Lord Mayor of London, who had gaoled him, was dismissed by a court which included Berkeley J on the ground that the legality of Ship Money was not justiciable. See p. 274 below.

The dichotomy of law and government as separate locations of sovereignty was to characterise four centuries of constitutional conflict and development.

The state's servants

Both prerogative bodies, the Privy Council and Star Chamber, became seen as instruments of tyranny in the hands of the first Stuart monarchs, and both fell to the first wave of republicanism: Star Chamber was abolished by the Long Parliament in 1641, and the Privy Council sank with the monarchy in 1649. What then happened illustrates Aylmer's account of continuity and discontinuity. The Privy Council became the Council of State, and Oliver Cromwell its first president. When after four years the republican impetus faltered and Cromwell was made Lord Protector, he continued to govern with an advisory council.

> "Taken collectively," Aylmer wrote of the republic's administrators, "their work and careers do indicate that a new kind of public service, in some ways a new administrative system, was coming into existence in republican England until its development was retarded, if not reversed, by the events of 1660."[37]

At the Restoration, state officials became once more the King's servants, appointed by patronage or by purchase, with the fees and perks that they had enjoyed before 1642 but now with the enhanced salaries of the republican years. Star Chamber never returned: it stood in such odium that no attempt was made to revive it.[38] But as the state now grew in power with the re-establishment of the Stuart monarchy, and as the use of the royal prerogative expanded, the courts of common law found themselves having to take sides between the state and the individual.

The Crown and the courts

The entitlement of citizens to sue the Crown in equity was established by the courts in *Pawlett v. Attorney-General* in 1667[39] and extended in the

---

[37] *The State's Servants*, p. 341

[38] With the result that when the Restoration rake and dramatist Sir Charles Sedley was charged with drunken behaviour which offended against public morality, his counsel was able to argue, albeit unsuccessfully, that the abolition of Star Chamber meant that there was no longer any court with jurisdiction over public morals: *R v. Sidley* [sic] (1663) 1 Sid. 168.

[39] *Pawlett v. Attorney-General* (1667) Hardres 465.

Bankers' Case[40] to claims against the Crown for breach of contract. Pawlett had mortgaged his land to a man whose heir was attainted of treason, with the result that his property, including the mortgage, was forfeit to the Crown. But the Court of Exchequer allowed him to redeem his mortgage:

> "It would derogate from the king's honour," said Baron Atkyns with no more than a hint of irony, "to imagine that what is equity against a common person should not be equity against him."

The present relevance of the complex *Bankers' Case*,[41] which arose from debts incurred by the Stuart monarchy to a number of bankers, is that in the Court of Exchequer Chief Justice Holt, basing himself on a sixteenth-century case,[42] held that debts owed by the Crown could be recovered by action against the responsible Crown servant – here the Treasurer and Chamberlain – who became debtors on the judgment.[43]

In this way, the courts of common law and equity, by personalising liability in the Crown's servants rather than the monarch, had begun by the end of the seventeenth century to create a set of civil remedies against the state, though never by name. The historic series of tort actions which in the mid-eighteenth century drove ministers out of the administration of justice and limited their power to suppress criticism,[44] were all brought against individual ministers or officers of the Crown, from the King's Messenger Nathan Carrington to his Secretary of State Lord Halifax. Even when in 1947 Parliament finally legislated by the Crown Proceedings Act[45] to permit tort claims to be brought against the state, it did so not by investing the state with legal personality but by making the Crown[46] vicariously liable *as if* it were

---

[40] (1700) 14 ST 1

[41] For a full account of the case, see W. S. Holdsworth, *A History of English Law* (1938), vol. IX, pp. 32–99.

[42] *Wroth's Case* (1573) Plow. 452

[43] Petitions of right, if sanctioned by the Attorney-General, had become the regular means before the passing of the Crown Proceedings Act of enforcing contracts against the Crown, albeit by declaration rather than by money judgment.

[44] See Ch. 3.

[45] The Act superseded the previous means by which a claim could be made against the Crown, the petition of right, a cumbersome procedure which required the Crown's own fiat.

[46] The Crown is in law a corporation, though whether a corporation sole (viz. the monarch) or a corporation aggregate (viz. the state apparatus) remains contentious. See Holdsworth *History of English Law*, vol. IV, p. 203; *R (Bridgeman) v. Drury* [1894] 2 IR 489. Janet McLean has pointed out to me that boroughs were historically common law corporations

"a private person of full age and capacity",[47] and authorising the publication of a list of departmental and ministerial names in which it could be sued.[48]

Habeas corpus, long established as the means by which the courts required other limbs of state to justify any deprivation of liberty, became in the later seventeenth century a focus of contest. The Habeas Corpus Act 1679 consolidated the principle that any detention is prima facie unlawful and requires a justification recognised by law. It also established an advanced rule – reflected today in the Fourth Geneva Convention – that no prisoner was to be held outside the realm. Perhaps its most striking impact came in its first two years of life, when the Commons resolved to imprison Thomas Sheridan, a suspect in the Popish plot. Lawyer MPs unashamedly argued that the Habeas Corpus Act was never intended to bind Parliament itself, and judge after judge prevaricated and declined to intervene,[49] until one of the barons of the Exchequer, Sir Richard Rainsford, took the bull by the horns and ordered the serjeant-at-arms to release Sheridan. There was no stand-off: Sheridan was released and the authority of the common law within the state confirmed.[50]

Conflict within the state

The state, as many such episodes illustrate, is not and never has been a unitary or homogeneous entity. Within it, interests and power-bases jostle and compete for influence and dominance. One can think, in

with inherent powers and fraternal traditions which the Municipal Corporations Act 1835 severely restricted, not least by inhibiting the expenditure of funds on food and drink. See p. 225.

[47] S. 2(1)

[48] See Crown Proceedings Act 1947, s. 17 and the list in the Annual Practice. Even after the passage of the 1947 Act this remained, in almost parodic form, the means by which the Crown submitted to judgment in criminal proceedings for putting unsafe government vehicles on the road. Starting with the Lights on Vehicles Act 1907, legislation – latterly the Road Traffic Act 1972, s. 188(8) – required Crown to nominate a person to be treated as responsible for any infringement for which the driver alone was not responsible. The civil servant nominated to take the rap every time a government vehicle was caught with a bald tyre or a defunct light bulb finally took exception to having the longest criminal record in history: see Barnett v. French [1981] 1 WLR 848.

[49] There was no rule (in fact there was none until the 1990s) preventing a prisoner from applying to judge after judge for either discharge or bail.

[50] See Paul Halliday, Habeas Corpus: from England to Empire (2012), pp. 237ff.

the late sixteenth and early seventeenth centuries, of the wresting of the administration of justice from the hands of the monarch and the prerogative courts; in the mid- and late seventeenth, the corralling by Parliament of the prerogative powers of the Crown; in the eighteenth, the repudiation by the courts of the claimed ministerial power to issue general warrants designed to stifle free speech; in the nineteenth, the steady devolution of power from Parliament to a burgeoning executive; in the twentieth, the dominance of the executive over Parliament and its eventual control by the courts.[51] In the twenty-first century, the conflict may be taking the form of an endeavour by ministers to restrict judicial review of executive government.

The most dramatic example of conflict within the state, as opposed to conflict about it, was the *coup d'état* of 1688–9. The Catholic James II's repeated and partisan use of the royal prerogative[52] had provoked the Protestant political class to rebel; and it was in offering the crown to William of Orange and his British wife Mary that Parliament was able to impose terms of tenure which made the British state the constitutional monarchy which it still is. The Whig ascendancy was quick to claim it as a revolution of a very different character from that of 1649 – a glorious revolution. But its present interest is that, unlike the Cromwellian revolution, it was conducted principally within and by means of the state apparatus. This is not to ignore the advance through southwest England of a large Protestant army under James' son-in-law William of Orange; but it was there by way of collusion with the domestic opposition to James II, who had prorogued Parliament in November 1685, leaving a group of statesmen, following the acquittal of the Seven Bishops in the summer of 1688, to invite William to assume the throne. The impending battle of Salisbury fizzled out when James' generals defected, and James first retreated to London, then fled to France. The revolution may not have been particularly glorious, but it was at least bloodless.[53]

---

[51] For a conspectus, see Martin Loughlin, *The British Constitution: A Very Short Introduction* (2013).

[52] It would be agreeable to see James as an exponent and practitioner of religious tolerance; but neither he nor his opponents saw it that way, despite his extension of public office to dissenters as well as Catholics. "The use of his prerogative enabled James [II] to pose an almost limitless threat to the established order": J. R. Western, *Monarchy and Revolution: The English State in the 1680s* (1972), p. 203.

[53] James' subsequent attempt to retake England through Ireland was a very different story.

The status of the state

The story I have outlined makes no pretence at completeness. Its purpose is to illustrate how, by the end of the seventeenth century, England – shortly to become part of Great Britain – possessed not only the organisational elements but the intellectual concept of the state as an entity distinct from and greater than the individuals who ran it. Today the state, represented by the icon of the Crown, brings both criminal and judicial review proceedings in its own name. It is when the state is being held to account, whether in tort or in public law, that it dissolves into ministers and public corporations (in other words, natural and artificial persons) rather than face proceedings as a distinct Hobbesian entity.[54]

This, as we have seen, is the product of a long process of history which, by collapsing the Crown into its ministers and servants, has held these individuals personally liable, by virtue of their office, for the state's wrongs. If the Crown remains an entity which is unable in legal theory to do wrong, it is arguably because all its functions apart from the purely formal and ceremonial ones are performed by one accountable limb or another of the state: the executive is accountable (in principle at least) to both Parliament and the courts; Parliament (at least the Commons) is accountable to the electorate; and the judges, despite the enduring allegation that they are unaccountable, have to publicly justify every decision they make, are subject to multiple layers of appeal and can have their decisions overset in the last resort by legislation. What accountability does not mean is making judges subject to removal if their decisions are resented by the vocal or the powerful.

The distinction between the Crown and its servants as potential wrongdoers is not, however, simply a deferential shield for the monarchy.[55] The landmark decision of the House of Lords in *M* v. *Home Office* broke this barrier by holding the Home Secretary liable for contempt of court, not as a private individual (which was how Lord Halifax had been made to pay damages to John Wilkes[56]) but in virtue of his office. In doing this, it stopped carefully short of holding the

---

[54] In international law, by contrast, the United Kingdom, like every state, is a legal entity: C. McLachlan, *Foreign Relations Law* (2014), s. 10.09.

[55] See Janet Maclean, *Searching for the State in British Legal Thought* (2012), pp. 309–10: "When distinctly public law norms of obligation and duty did emerge in the twentieth century, they did not attach to a personification of the state but were rather in the nature of a system of rules applied to public authorities on behalf of the public ..."

[56] *Wilkes* v. *Halifax* (1769) 19 St. Tr. 1406

Crown itself liable.[57] Whether this is to be ascribed to a historic habit of deference or to a realistic recognition that coercive orders against an abstract entity do not work, it continues to delineate the reach of public law.[58]

What can the state lawfully do?

Thus the possibility that the state may incur private law liabilities by owing debts, breaking contracts or negligently injuring people is now catered for by processes which, with few exceptions, bring the state and the individual before the courts on an equal footing.[59] But the state cannot contract out of its public law functions.[60]

Central to this proposition is the question of the state's lawful powers. In the Somerset stag-hunting case[61] Mr Justice Laws put it this way:

> For private persons the rule is that you may do anything you choose which the law does not prohibit ... But for public bodies the rule is the opposite ... It is that any action taken must be justified by positive law ... A public body has no rights properly so called ... Where a public body asserts claims or defences in court, it does so, if it acts in good faith, only to vindicate the better performance of the duties for whose fulfilment it exists ... The rule is necessary in order to protect the people from arbitrary interference by those set in power over them.

---

[57] [1994] 1 AC 377. See Lord Woolf at 425: "In accord with tradition the finding should not be made against the 'Crown' by name but in the name of the authorised department (or the Attorney-General) or minister."

[58] I made this point in "The Crown in its Own Courts" in C. Forsyth and I. Hare (eds.), *The Golden Metwand and the Crooked Cord* (1998), p. 257, going on to ask whether we have nevertheless reached a point at which the state in the name and right of the Crown should be able to be directly impleaded. However, that is not yet the law: see *Chagos Islanders* v. *Attorney-General* [2004] EWCA Civ 997, § 20.

[59] In *Town Investments Ltd* v. *Department of the Environment* [1978] AC 359 it was held that a lease taken by the Secretary of State "for and on behalf of Her Majesty" made the Crown a contractual tenant. See W. Wade and C. Forsyth, *Administrative Law* (10th edn, 2009), p. 40 n. 6 for a sharp critique of the failure to distinguish the Crown from its ministers. It can be cogently suggested that while public law seeks to distinguish the Crown from its ministers, contract law for its own purposes seeks to assimilate them: Janet McLean, "The Crown in Contract and Administrative Law" (2004) OJLS 1219. See generally Janet McLean (ed.) *Property and the Constitution* (1999).

[60] *Rederiaktiebolaget Amphitrite* v. *R* [1921] 3 KB 500

[61] *R* v. *Somerset CC, ex p Fewings* [1995] 1 All ER 513,524; upheld on appeal [1995] 1 WLR 1037

Thus the private individual has the right, although it may be subject to legal limitations, to spend money or dispose of property capriciously or maliciously or irrationally. The state cannot lawfully do any of these things. But the corollary is not that the state may do only what the law explicitly says it can do. It is that it may do anything which is reasonably incidental to the performance of its lawful functions. This is a common-sense proposition in public law, as it is in contract and company law, and it both explains and immunises from challenge a huge range of govern-mental and official acts for which no express authority exists. What is reasonably incidental cannot be comprehensively defined, but it is limited, like all public law acts, to those done – in Wade's formulation – "reasonably and in good faith and upon lawful and relevant grounds of public interest".[62] This is why the search for a distinct or "third" source of governmental power is a hunt for a mare's nest.[63] Government, as the courts have constantly recognised, already has power to do whatever is reasonably necessary to its work.[64]

The local state

The state at local level operates under different rules from the central state. Local authorities are statutory corporations, governed by similar broad principles to those governing other corporate bodies. But because the extent of their powers was sometimes in doubt, s. 111 of the Local Government Act 1972 confirmed that a local authority had power to do anything calculated to facilitate or conducive or incidental to the dis-charge of any of its functions. Then, because of further doubts which had arisen,[65] greater specificity was provided by s. 2 of the Local Government Act 2000, which gave local authorities power to do anything they con-sidered likely to assist the economic, social or environmental wellbeing of their area.

---

[62] Wade, *Administrative Law* (6th edn, 1988), pp. 399–400, cited by Laws J *ante*.

[63] See the discussion of this in Ch. 6.

[64] See *R (New London College)* v. *Home Secretary* [2013] UKSC 51, § 28: "... the statutory power of the Secretary of State to administer the system of immigration control must necessarily extend to a range of ancillary and incidental administrative powers not expressly spelt out in the Act ..." As to the supposed third source of power, see ibid., § 34. See also Ch. 6.

[65] See *R v. Richmond LBC, ex p McCarthy Developments* [1992] 2 AC 48; *Crédit Suisse* v. *Allerdale BC* [1997] QB 306.

Although subsequent litigation confirmed the breadth of this range of powers,[66] in 2009 the Department of Communities and Local Government launched a consultation on further reform. The Local Government Association responded with a draft Bill which the coalition government adopted. According to the Department's *Plain English Guide* to the Bill:

> The new, general power gives local authorities more freedom to work together with others in new ways to drive down costs. It gives them increased confidence to do creative, innovative things to meet local people's needs. Councils have asked for this power because it will help them get on with the job.

This is what s. 1(1) of the Localism Act 2011 actually says:

> A local authority has power to do anything that individuals generally may do.

As I have pointed out,[67] individuals are generally free to live their lives and dispose of their money or property profligately, recklessly, stupidly or spitefully. Public authorities, on first constitutional principles, are not free to do any such thing.

But nothing that follows in the Localism Act modifies the licence apparently given by s. 1(1). Indeed s. 1(2) makes it clear that the power extends to acts which are unlike anything a local authority could otherwise do and unlike things other public bodies may do, while s. 1(4) permits the exercise of the power in or outside the UK, commercially, or otherwise than for benefit of the authority or people in its area. Apart from a requirement[68] that a commercial purpose is permissible only where same thing could be done for a non-commercial purpose, and must be done through a company, the only limits are those (if any) imposed by statute.[69] As to these, however, the Secretary of State "may by order amend, repeal, revoke or disapply" any statutory provision which he "thinks ... prevents or restricts local authorities from exercising the general [s.1] power".[70]

---

[66] *R(J)* v. *Enfield LBC* [2002] EWHC 432 (Admin); *R (Theophilus)* v. *Lewisham LBC* [2002] EWHC 1371 (Admin); cf. *Brent LBC* v. *Risk Management Partners Ltd* [2009] EWCA Civ 490.

[67] Ch. 6   [68] S. 4   [69] S. 2

[70] S. 5, subject to limitations in s. 6 and procedures laid down by s. 7. Such debate as there was is in Hansard, 17 January 2011, vol. 521, col. 562, and 1 February 2011, cols 175–193. See Woolf *et al.*, *De Smith's Judicial Review* (7th edn 2013), §§ 5–102.

There is a lawyer's tale[71] that, in the course of getting an interminable and unreadable local Bill through Parliament in the days when divorce was hard to come by, the town clerk slipped in a provision, which duly became law, that "The marriage of the town clerk of X is hereby dissolved". It looks as if the Local Government Association has achieved something similar but grander.

The courts have no desire to micromanage local government, but they have been there, as required, when local government has overstepped the mark. They were there when, in 1894, the Dublin councillors challenged the disallowance by the district auditor of the cost of the picnic which accompanied their annual inspection of the Vartry waterworks.

> "I have before me," said Sir Peter O'Brian CJ, giving judgment, "the items in the bill. Amongst the list of wines are two dozen champagne – Ayala 1885, a very good branch, at 84s a dozen; one dozen Marcobrunn hock – a very nice hock; one dozen Chateau Margaux – an excellent claret; one dozen fine old Dublin whiskey – the best whiskey that can be got; ... six bottles of Amontillado sherry – a stimulating sherry; and the ninth item is some more fine Dublin whiskey ...
>
> There is an allowance for brakes; one box of cigars, 100; coachmen's dinner; beer, stout, minerals in syphons, and ice for wine. There is dessert and there are sandwiches, and an allowance for four glasses broken – a very small number broken under the circumstances.
>
> The Solicitor-General in his most able argument ... appealed pathetically to common sense ... He represented that the members of the Corporation would traverse the hills in a spectral condition unless they were sustained by lunch. I do not know whether he went so far as Ayala, Marcobrunn, Chateau Margaux, old Dublin whiskey and cigars. In answer to the Solicitor-General, we do not say that the members of the Corporation are not to lunch. But we do say that they are not to do so at the expense of the citizens of Dublin.[72]

So where tea and biscuits, like paperclips, may fall within the ordinary ancillary powers of the state, champagne and caviar will not; and it is not very helpful to the rule of law to create a power by which public administration can attempt to evade these principles.

---

[71] R. E, Megarry, *Miscellany-at-Law* (1955), pp. 344–5

[72] *R (Bridgeman)* v. *Drury* [1894] 2 IR 489. Until the passing of the Municipal Corporations Act 1835, local government was conducted by common-law corporations without statutory restrictions on their powers. Like the friendly societies which were bureaucratised by the National Insurance Act 1911, local corporations had a fraternal character not wholly inconsistent with convivial picnics.

Security and surveillance

Even so, the legitimate ambit of central government's implied ancillary powers is a serious and growing question. It extends today to the state's security and surveillance activities, once conducted entirely under the broad prerogative but now authorised and partially governed by statute and – thanks to recent revelations[73] – highly controversial.

The result of *Malone's Case*,[74] was the Interception of Communications Act 1985. This was replaced in 2000 by the Regulation of Investigatory Powers Act (RIPA), which forbade unauthorised telephone tapping but went on to permit any interception authorised by a minister's warrant on grounds of national security, serious crime or the nation's economic wellbeing. It is arguable that the handing of such powers to ministers – meaning, in substance, their advisers – without any prior judicial filter and with limited opportunities for effective checks by the statutory commissioner and tribunal, is a reversion to the years before the historic decision in *Entick* v. *Carrington* put an end to the ministerial practice of issuing general search and arrest warrants,[75] setting in its time a worldwide standard for the rule of law.

One particular section of RIPA stands out as a source of injustice – bearing in mind that justice is for the benefit not only of the accused but also of the public. Section 17, in elaborate detail, forbids the introduction in court of any evidence which may reveal the use of intercepts. This bar, designed to shield the interests of the security services, has serious consequences for the rule of law. It obstructs or prevents the prosecution of many individuals for terrorist, narcotics or other offences which have been detected by intercepts, and it has resulted in a series of alternative measures which deny suspects the benefit of due process and allow the unilateral use of intercept evidence before closed tribunals. Parliamentarians of all parties, and numerous others, have called for it to be repealed or modified, but the security services have succeeded in resisting reform.[76]

---

[73] Edward Snowden's revelations, reported in 2013 in the London *Guardian* and the US *New York Times*.

[74] *Malone v. Metropolitan Police Commissioner* [1979] Ch. 344, discussed in Ch. 10.

[75] See Ch. 3; A. W. Bradley and K. Ewing, *Constitutional and Administrative Law*, Ch. 22D.

[76] The *Report of the Privy Council review of intercept as evidence* (J. Chilcot *et al.*, Cm 7324, February 2008), advised that an ECHR-compliant use of intercept evidence in criminal trials was both desirable and feasible. In 2014, after lengthy consultations, a differently constituted committee under the same chairman decided that the committee's proposal, in addition to being costly, was not reconcilable with MI5's, MI6's and GCHQ's

I have suggested in relation to the separation of powers that it may be necessary to recognise that the security services now constitute an autonomous limb of the state.[77] What is relevant to the present topic is that both the functioning of a national security service and the practice of covertly intercepting private communications developed without any statutory authority or, therefore, parliamentary approval. The use of infiltrators and informers is as old as the state itself, but the origins of the modern security service lie in the run-up to the First World War.[78] From then until, in 1989, they were placed on a statutory footing, the security services were authorised, protected and paid for by governments, using the prerogative power without recourse to Parliament.[79] This was the situation at the time of the GCHQ litigation[80] in 1984. The prime minister decided to bypass the established machinery for negotiating terms and conditions with the civil service staff unions at GCHQ and to impose new ones by means of an instruction issued under a prerogative Order in Council made in 1982 for the regulation of the civil service. The law lords made it clear that they would have imported into these prerogative regulations a duty to consult before deciding, had it not been for the government's last-minute invocation of national security as its reason for not doing so.

Some conclusions

National security furnishes a series of critical instances of the difficulty of reconciling the modern state with the rule of law. The rule of law requires every state function to be legal and to be lawfully conducted, while the

---

requirement that they alone "should be able to determine how intercept material is transcribed and selected for retention" and so was unacceptable.

[77] Ch. 9

[78] See generally Bradley and Ewing, *Constitutional and Administrative Law*, Ch. 25.

[79] The problem of finally giving statutory authority to an officially non-existent institution was elegantly solved by the opening words of the Security Services Act 1989: "There shall continue to be a Security Service ... under the authority of the Secretary of State": Security Services Act 1989, s. 1(1). The same formula was used in the Intelligence Services Act 1994 to regularise the secret intelligence service (s. 1(1)) and GCHQ (s. 3(1)). The principal functions of the security service were spelt out as the protection of national security and the safeguarding of the nation's economic wellbeing. The functions of the intelligence services were spelt out in the Intelligence Services Act 1994 as "to obtain and provide information relating to the actions or intentions of persons outside the British Islands" in aid of the same functions as the security service. Both were additionally tasked with helping to combat serious crime.

[80] *Council of Civil Service Unions* v. *Minister for the Civil Service* [1985] AC 374

state requires certain of its functions and activities to be beyond the reach of the law. The courts in the course of the later twentieth century have accepted that there are some decisions which they are not equipped to make, ceding the terrain of national security to ministers and to the security services which advise them. But the state also requires adjudications against individuals accused or suspected of acts which jeopardise national security, and to this end it has repeatedly had to manage or modify the judicial process.[81] It is odd that in this situation it should be the courts which sometimes find themselves accused of undue interference in the business of government.

The insubstantiality of the state itself in public law reflects the fact that the state has never been a monolithic entity. The constitutional unity of an iconic Crown elegantly disguises the heterogeneity of the state which it represents. For centuries the state has been, as it still is, a site both of collaboration and of conflict among its separate but interdependent powers – the legislature, the judiciary, ministers and their executive departments, and today arguably the security establishment. All of these now function in the name of a monarch whose throne since 1689 has been in the gift of Parliament. Unlike the many states in which power flows down from a written constitution, power in the United Kingdom flows up from the state's component elements, making the Crown its receptacle, not its source.

[81] See Ch. 9.

Standing and "sitting"

"It has been the practice," said the chief baron of the Exchequer in 1835,[1] "which I hope never will be discontinued, for the officers of the Crown to throw no difficulty in the way of any proceeding for the purpose of bringing matters before a court of justice, where any real point of difficulty that requires judicial decision has occurred". Who can bring a public law claim? Who answers for the state? These are not merely technical questions: the effectiveness of the rule of law depends on the answers.

The privy counsellors

In 1916, when anti-German feeling was running high and anti-semitism was no less than it had been for centuries, Sir George Makgill, a Scottish baronet of extreme right-wing views, who as well as being a writer of boys' fiction was the secretary of the Anti-German Union,[2] brought judicial review proceedings to disqualify from membership of the Privy Council two Jewish financiers of German origin, Sir Ernest Cassel[3] and Sir Edgar Speyer,[4] both of them British subjects and major philanthropists. Makgill's application, although it failed both in the Queen's Bench[5]

---

[1] *Deare* v. *Attorney-General* (1835) 1 Y & C Ex 197, 208, per Lord Abinger CB

[2] He was a nephew of Lord Haldane LC.

[3] Who had in fact converted to Catholicism. See A. Lentin, *Banker, Traitor, Scapegoat, Spy?: The Troublesome Case of Sir Edgar Speyer* (2013)

[4] See ibid.

[5] *R* v. *Speyer; R* v. *Cassel* [1916] 1 KB 595 (Lord Reading CJ, Avory and Lush JJ). The issue was not straightforward, since s. 3 of the Act of Settlement 1700 provides that "no person born out of the kingdoms ... (although he be made a denizen) ... shall be capable to be of the privy councill". It was held that a later statute providing for naturalisation impliedly repealed this provision *pro tanto*, a conclusion which may no longer be open in the light of *R (HS2 Action Alliance Ltd)* v. *Secretary of State for Transport and another* [2014] UKSC 3. The claim was in substance for a writ of quo warranto, by which a person's entitlement to an office which he claimed to hold could be tested – a remedy still available by way of injunction under s. 30 of the Senior Courts Act 1981 and 54 CPR 2(d).

and in the Court of Appeal,[6] is of considerable legal interest for more than one reason.

First, the courts at both levels accepted that the prerogative power of the King to appoint whom he chose to be a privy counsellor was justiciable, and that it was arguable – though incorrect – that it did not extend to appointing naturalised counsellors.[7] Secondly, and more directly material to the present topic, the divisional court rejected the submission of the Attorney-General, F. E. Smith QC, that the claim should be dismissed because Makgill had no standing to bring it. Only the Attorney-General, as guardian of the public interest, Smith argued, could bring such a question as this before a court of law.[8]

> "No", said Lord Reading CJ; "Sir George Makgill appears to have brought this matter before the court on purely public grounds without any private interest to serve, and it is to the public advantage that the law should be declared by judicial authority. I think the court ought to incline to the assistance, and not to the hindrance, of the applicant in such a case . . ."[9]

He cited a much older case on standing in which Lord Kenyon CJ had said of a similar claim:

> I do not mean to say that a stranger may not in any case prefer this sort of application; but he ought to come to the court with a very fair case in his hands.[10]

Mr Justice Avory, concurring, made a critical link between the procedural question of standing and the substantive issue of justiciability:

> Section 3 of the Act of Settlement must in my opinion be regarded as an abridgement or curtailment of the prerogative right of the Sovereign to

---

[6] [1916] 2 QB 858 (Swinfen Eady, Phillimore and Bankes LJJ).

[7] See Ch. 6. Act of Settlement 1700, s. 3: "no person born out of the kingdoms of England Scotland or Ireland or the dominions thereunto belonging (although he be . . . made a denizen . . .) shall be capable to be of the privy council or a member of either House of Parliament . . .". It was held that naturalisation overcame this bar.

[8] The use of relator actions – proceedings brought in the name of the Attorney-General – is dealt with below.

[9] At 613

[10] *R* v. *Kemp* (1789) H.29.G.3: note appended (1 East 46n) to the dictum of Kenyon CJ in *R* v. *Clarke* (1800) 1 East 38: "The Court have indeed on several occasions said, and said wisely, that they will not listen to a common relator coming . . . as a mere stranger to disturb a corporation with which he has no concern." In *Kemp* Kenyon CJ had said of the relator, immediately before the passage cited by Lord Reading CJ: "He comes here as a perfect stranger to the corporation, prowling into other men's rights . . ."

appoint whomsoever he pleases to be of the PC . . . It is therefore a statute which necessarily binds the Crown . . .

. . . [I]t is conceded that if the remedy by quo warranto does not lie in this case there is no other remedy, so if the contention of the Attorney General prevails so much of s. 3 of the Act of Settlement as relates to the Privy Council was and is of no effect.[11]

Mr Justice Lush added:

The process is enforced for the benefit of the community, and is the only available remedy if the office is either abused or usurped.[12]

When Makgill took his case to the Court of Appeal, the Crown dropped its challenge to his standing.

The legal rules

In 1916 there was no prescribed test of standing for judicial review in the High Court rules, although a number of statutes gave "persons aggrieved" a right of appeal to the courts from administrative decisions. The courts administering public law had worked out over time whom they were prepared to hear on different issues.[13] So when in 1883 the first modern procedural rules for the High Court were promulgated, they simply provided[14] that "proceedings on the Crown side of the Queen's Bench Division" should continue to be heard by divisional courts.[15] Who could be heard on either side would remain, as it had always been, a matter for the judges.[16]

This remained the case when, in 1977, the name "judicial review"[17] was conferred by the court rules[18] on the procedure for obtaining what

---

[11] At 618, 619   [12] At 628

[13] According to Robertson, *Civil Proceedings by and against the Crown* (1908), "though prerogative practice has progressed, it still remains, for many purposes, in the condition in which the general practice of the Courts was before the Judicature Acts [of the 1870s] . . ."

[14] Rules of the Supreme Court 1883, O. 59 r. 1

[15] I.e. courts consisting of two or more judges of the Division.

[16] Until the *IRC* case, the conventional wisdom was that, while a successful applicant with a personal interest was entitled to a remedy as of right, any remedy for a public interest applicant was discretionary: *R v. Thames Magistrates Court, ex p Greenbaum* (1957) 55 LGR 129.

[17] Derived, it would seem, from the title of the first specialist textbook on public law, Professor S. A. de Smith's *Judicial Review of Administrative Action* (1959) – a rare accolade for an academic work.

[18] Rules of the Supreme Court (Amendment No. 3) 1977

were by now called prerogative orders.[19] Following the recommendation of the Law Commission, permission to apply for these was to be given only if the court considered that the applicant had "a sufficient interest in the matter to which the application relates". Deliberately, no attempt was made to constrict or to define what amounted to a sufficient interest. In parallel, it was also provided that "all persons directly affected" must be served,[20] giving such persons a near-automatic right to be heard. In 1981 the "sufficient interest" test was adopted by statute,[21] and there it has so far remained without elaboration or qualification, continuing to depend on what the court itself considers a sufficient interest in the issue before it.

The Woolf reforms in 1999 opened further doors by enlarging the obligation to serve the proceedings on any "interested party" (not merely persons directly affected), and by providing that

> Any interested *person* may apply for permission (a) to file evidence or (b) make representations at the hearing of the judicial review.[22]

Today, therefore, there exists not only a catholic concept of standing for the purpose of bringing judicial review proceedings, and a corresponding obligation to serve every interested party, but a power in the court to accept third party interventions – in American terms, amicus briefs – on whatever terms the court considers likely to be helpful.[23]

Reliance on judicial experience and judgment to determine who is entitled to be heard has thus been consistent and longstanding, and has worked well. But it is an aspect of judicial independence which has come under scrutiny and stress as the volume and scope of judicial review have grown.

The *Fleet Street Casuals* case

The principles by which the courts accord standing in judicial review are not and have never been arbitrary: they are the product of a long process

---

[19] Administration of Justice Act 1938, s. 7. They were formerly, for centuries, prerogative writs.

[20] O. 53 r. 5(3); initially in the 1938 amendment of the Rules.

[21] Supreme Court Act [renamed the Senior Courts Act] 1981, s. 31(3)

[22] Civil Procedure Rules 1999, 54.17(1)

[23] This has now been constricted by new rules on third party interventions: CPR 54.17; 54 APD 13.

of history, some of which I have sketched. Lord Diplock recognised this in the *Fleet Street Casuals* case in 1982:

> The rules as to standing for the purpose of applying for prerogative orders,[24] like most of English public law, are not to be found in any statute. They were made by judges, by judges they can be changed; and so they have been over the years to meet the need to preserve the integrity of the rule of law . . .[25]

He was dealing with an application by the National Federation of the Self-Employed to bring the Inland Revenue before the court for its failure to stop tax evasion by casual workers in the then near-anarchic newspaper industry. To describe the issue is practically to predict the outcome: the Federation was angered at the contrast with the rigorous taxation of its own members, but these would gain nothing, apart from moral satisfaction, even if the litigation succeeded; and their claim that the Revenue was not doing its job was barely litigable even if it was true. The Federation's position was more nearly that of a busybody.

The courts not infrequently show busybodies the door. To take one of many examples, when a Church of England cleric applied to the High Court to stop the ordination of women by the Church in Wales, the court held him to be

> a busybody . . . a stranger to the organisation, whose affairs, since disestablishment, were governed by the Welsh Church Act 1914 [which] cut the church free from the jurisdiction of the temporal courts in relation to any questions of doctrine.[26]

Less uncivilly, Nolan LJ said of another applicant:

> It would be inaccurate as well as discourteous to describe [her] as a busybody, but her attempt to intervene is at best quixotic . . .[27]

The *Fleet Street Casuals* case is significant not only for its confirmation of the judicial doorkeeper role but also for the variant reasoning of the five law lords who finally decided it against the Federation. While a majority held that the sufficiency of the claimant's interest depended in large part on the substantive merits of the case, the two most knowledgeable public

---

[24] The name given at the time to remedies in judicial review.
[25] *R v. Inland Revenue Commissioners, ex p National Federation of the Self-Employed Ltd* [1982] AC 617, 639
[26] *R v. Dean and Chapter of St Paul's Cathedral* [1998] COD 130
[27] *R v. Legal Aid Board, ex p Bateman* [1992] 1 WLR 711, 718

lawyers on the committee, Diplock and Scarman, took different approaches. Scarman rejected the Federation's standing for want of substantive merits – in other words the Federation lacked standing because the Revenue had done nothing obviously wrong. Diplock, perhaps more logically, held (as the Court of Appeal had done) that the Federation had standing but that it failed on the substantive issue.

What principle?

It is little wonder that, in the years following that decision, first-instance judges (among them Schiemann J in the *Rose Theatre* case, to which I am about to come) had trouble distilling the principles to be applied in the search for a single point of entry. You could reduce them to the proposition that the courts will entertain any public interest challenge if they think the nature of the issue and the identity of the challenger warrant it. But this is elliptical. The principle that emerges from the cases is that the courts will entertain a claim of abuse of public power if the claim appears sound and the challenger has good reason to advance it. But this too has its delphic side.

The Rose Theatre

Fast-forward to 1989. Foundations are being excavated in Southwark for a new building in which millions of pounds held by the Post Office pension fund are invested. The contractors find that they have uncovered the remains of an old timber structure, and archaeologists, rapidly on site, realise that these are the remains of the Rose Theatre, where many of Marlowe's plays were performed and two of Shakespeare's plays were first staged – a priceless piece of our national heritage. But the Secretary of State for the Environment, Nicholas Ridley, refuses to use his statutory power to protect the site by scheduling it as a national monument. So the Rose Theatre Trust Company, formed by a swiftly convened group of scholars and actors, brings judicial review proceedings against the Secretary of State (who does not dispute that the site is of national importance) to force him to protect it.

I need to introduce here some detail which does not appear in the law report. The application[28] came before Mr. Justice Schiemann, a judge

---

[28] R v. *Secretary of State for the Environment, ex p Rose Theatre Trust* [1990] 1 QB 504

with extensive experience of planning and public law.[29] The developers were represented as an interested party by Peter Goldsmith QC; I represented the pension fund as another interested party. We took the point that a limited company (one which had seemingly been formed simply as an insurance against a costs order) had no sufficient interest and could not generate a sufficient interest by writing the issue into its objects. In response, counsel for the trust sought and obtained leave to disaggregate the company and to substitute as applicants the individuals behind it. They included the actors Peggy Ashcroft and Laurence Olivier and the leading historian of the Elizabethan stage Andrew Gurr; but in my view both then and now, their personal distinction was irrelevant: any citizen of this country had a sufficient interest in the remains of the Rose Theatre to try to preserve them by legal action from demolition or burial.[30] I considered that the objection on standing had been overcome, but Goldsmith maintained his challenge to the individual applicants' standing. I was duty bound to my own clients to adopt his submission, and it succeeded.[31]

For the theatre itself, the outcome of the case was not wholly negative: the developers and their architects redesigned the new building[32] to place it on stilts, leaving much of the remains intact and visible. But in law the *Rose Theatre* case became a low-water mark for the concept of standing in judicial review.

On the subject of standing, Mr. Justice Schiemann said:

> There is no doubt that, in the early part of this decade [the 1980s], the High Court was fairly liberal in its interpretation of who had "a sufficient interest" to be able to apply for judicial review.[33]

He turned to the *Fleet Street Casuals* case, distilling from the speeches in the House of Lords the reasoning that, since to allow everyone to complain of any breach of statutory duty would rob "sufficient interest" of all meaning, a sufficient interest, while it did not require

---

[29] Later a lord justice of appeal and the UK judge on the European Court of Justice.

[30] This was the basis on which, for example, the court had heard Raymond Blackburn MP's claim that the GLC was failing to use its power of censorship to ban pornographic films: *R v. GLC, ex p Blackburn* [1976] 1 WLR 550: he and his wife were held to have standing "as citizens, ratepayers and parents within the council's jurisdiction" to apply for an order of prohibition.

[31] The judge had first decided the case on its merits in favour of the government, making the provisional assumption that the applicants had standing.

[32] At 56 Park St.

[33] Citing *Covent Garden Community Association Ltd v. GLC* [1981] JPL 183 (Woolf J).

a direct financial or legal interest, required more than a simple assertion of concern, whether by one or many persons or by a corporation.[34]

So far as it went, there was nothing to criticise in this. The problem was that the judgment went no further. It concluded:

> Applying the approach [set out in *IRC*], it seems to me that the decision not to schedule is one of those governmental decisions in respect of which the ordinary citizen does not have a sufficient interest to entitle him to obtain leave to move for judicial review.

The judge recognised that this could leave an unlawful act uncorrected, but considered that it followed from the terms in which the material power had been conferred on the minister by Parliament.

> The court will look at the matter to which the application relates ... and the statute under which the decision was taken ... and decide *whether that statute gives that individual expressly or impliedly a greater right or expectation than any other citizen of this country to have that decision taken lawfully*. We all expect our decision makers to act lawfully. We are not all given by Parliament the right to apply for judicial review.

The problem with the passage I have italicised is that it conflates public law wrongs with private law rights. If the judge, in doing this, was seeking to regulate the liberalisation of standing which he had identified earlier in his judgment, his reason was the perfectly intelligible one that, taken to its logical conclusion, to give everyone standing to challenge the legality of any governmental act would mean that any interest was a sufficient interest.[35] But did it follow that nobody's standing could be sufficient in the absence of personal harm or a statutory right? Standing was an intermediate question which public law was answering, in the manner of the common law, case by case rather than by devising blanket principles.[36]

One example is Mr. Justice Otton's conclusion, in 1994, that Greenpeace should be allowed to challenge the legality of authorisations granted by the pollution inspectorate. Greenpeace was, he held,

---

[34] I.e. unless one or more individuals had standing, aggregation or incorporation could not confer it on them.

[35] For a helpful discussion of the issues, see Sir Konrad Schiemann, "Locus standi" [1990] PL 342.

[36] The riskiness of rigid principles of standing was brought home, following the law lords' decision in *O'Reilly* v. *Mackman* [1980] 2 AC 237 that all public law issues must be resolved by way of judicial review, by *Wandsworth LBC* v. *Winder* [1985] AC 461, where a private law claim had been met with a public law defence.

an entirely responsible and respected body with a genuine concern for the environment ... who, with its particular experience in environmental matters, its access to experts in the relevant realms of science and technology (not to mention the law), is able to mount a carefully selected, focused, relevant and well-argued challenge.[37]

Whitehall strikes back

It is not surprising that government would prefer not to have to face such challenges; but if they cannot be brought, it is the rule of law which will be the loser. So let me fast-forward again, this time to the government's September 2013 consultation paper on further reforms to judicial review – further, because the Ministry of Justice had already consulted on proposals to starve judicial review claims of legal aid and to intensify the filtering process. The subsequent paper[38] proposed among other things to limit standing to persons with a "direct and tangible interest" in the outcome: in other words, to wipe out two or more centuries of legal history in the course of which the judges had adjusted the gateways of judicial review to meet the needs of the rule of law. The blinkered determination which was being brought to bear on the issue can be seen in the consultation paper's treatment of the Pergau Dam litigation.[39]

The Pergau Dam

The Foreign Secretary, Douglas Hurd, was proposing for political reasons to go ahead with a subvention of £316m to Malaysia for a hydro-electric project which the government's Overseas Development Administration had advised would be uneconomic, an abuse of the overseas aid programme and "a very bad buy". The World Development Movement challenged the legality of the proposed grant. The Foreign Secretary contested its standing.

Taking the question of standing in the context of the substantive issue, the divisional court held that the rule of law, the importance of the issue, the probable want of any other source of challenge, the nature of the

---

[37] R v. HM Inspectorate of Pollution, ex p Greenpeace Ltd (No 2) [1994] 4 All ER 329, 350 (Otton J, declining to follow Rose Theatre)

[38] Cm. 8703, September 2013

[39] R v. Secretary of State for Foreign and Commonwealth Affairs, ex p World Development Movement [1995] 1 WLR 386

breach of legality and the prominent and responsible character and role of the World Development Movement,[40] combined to create a sufficient interest. On the substantive issue, the court held that the power in s. 1(1) of the Overseas Development and Co-operation Act 1980 to provide assistance "for the purpose of promoting the development ... of a country ..." did not include promoting unsound development, which this undisputedly was. They struck down the decision. There was no appeal. It later became known that the Foreign Secretary had not sought the advice of his own lawyers, which would have been that the funding was illegal.

Would it have been better had the World Development Movement not been allowed to bring this challenge before a court, leaving over £300m of public money to be squandered? The Ministry of Justice's consultation paper[41] cited the *Pergau Dam* decision as a prime example of challenges which ought not to be brought – especially since such challenges are "relatively successful compared to other judicial review cases".[42] In other words, the validity and utility of challenges like the *Pergau Dam* decision were a reason for stopping them.

One further piece of conjuring in the consultation paper is worth noting. The paper announced[43] that the basis of its proposal about standing was

> The principle that Parliament and the elected government are best placed
> to determine what is in the public interest.

The implication that the judges had been substituting their own view of the public interest for that of the elected government was misleading. Public interest litigation does not mean litigation about what it is and is not in the public interest; it means litigation which reflects the interest of the public in seeing the law upheld. Departments of state have sometimes welcomed public interest challenges as a means of clarifying the law. In 1990, for instance, when a consortium consisting of the Child Poverty Action Group, two London borough councils and the National

---

[40] The WDM was a company limited by guarantee, with cross-party governance, concerned with the provision of overseas aid and having consultative status with UNESCO.

[41] Cm 8703, para. 76

[42] Cm 8703, para. 78. The Secretary of State for Justice eventually withdrew the proposal to abolish public interest standing and announced: "I believe in protecting judicial review as a check on unlawful executive action ..."

[43] Para. 80

Association of Citizens Advice Bureaux challenged the way the social security legislation was being interpreted and administered by the Department and by independent adjudicators,[44] the Department did not contest their standing.[45]

Relator proceedings

In addition to powers given to the Attorney-General by statute to bring proceedings in his or her own right (for example the power used in 2013 to get the original Hillsborough inquest verdicts quashed[46]), the Attorney-General possesses a common law power both to bring proceedings in the public interest where no individual has standing to do so and to authorise individuals who lack standing to bring such a challenge in the Attorney-General's name. The procedure, which derives not from the royal prerogative but from the judges' control of the right of audience,[47] is known as a relator action: the Attorney-General acts at the relation of the citizen or corporation, lending his or her name to guarantee their standing but leaving them to be responsible for the conduct and the costs of the proceedings. While the decision to do this rests with the Attorney-General, the decision whether to grant the order which is sought in his or her name rests, as always, with the court.

The process can be illustrated by Manchester Corporation's relator action, brought in 1960 in the name of the Attorney-General, for an injunction against a couple who at weekends sold flowers at the gate of a municipal cemetery and went on doing so in spite of a succession of fines for highway obstruction. The first-instance judge, Mr. Justice Salmon, thought the whole thing was trivial and probably instigated by local

---

[44] *R* v. *Secretary of State for Social Services, ex p Child Poverty Action Group* [1990] 2 QB 540

[45] It sought, however, to reserve the right to challenge standing in analogous cases. The Court of Appeal (Woolf LJ at 556) considered this unacceptable, since standing went to jurisdiction and could not be conferred by silence or consent.

[46] Coroners Act 1988, s. 13. Although the Coroners and Justice Act 2009 prospectively repealed this provision and instead introduced an appeal to the new office of Chief Coroner, there appears to be nothing to prevent the Attorney-General, or indeed any individual with a sufficient interest, from challenging a decision of the Chief Coroner if it is erroneous in law.

[47] According to counsel for the plaintiffs in *Gouriet* v. *Attorney-General* [1978] AC 435, 462, the relator action probably derived from seventeenth-century Chancery and Exchequer practice. Much learning on its history can be found in the judgments of the Court of Appeal in *Gouriet* v. *UPW* [1977] 1 All ER 696, 706 (CA).

shopkeepers, and refused an injunction.[48] The Court of Appeal, reversing him, held that the Attorney-General's status as guardian of the community's "larger and wider interest in seeing that the laws are obeyed"[49] made it incumbent on the court to grant an injunction in all but exceptional circumstances.

Although relator actions are today very rare, they are still available; and, if the proposal to restrict public interest standing is revived, they may become more prominent. This makes it relevant to touch on one particular aspect of the power: the Attorney-General's discretion to authorise or to refuse to authorise the use of his or her name. It is a discretion which has been traditionally said to be absolute – in other words, beyond the reach of the courts;[50] but, like the royal prerogative,[51] it may no longer be so.

In 1977 John Gouriet and his associates in the Freedom Association attempted to sue the Union of Post Office Workers for an injunction to halt a postal boycott of the South African apartheid regime. Since the union was not a public authority, this had to be done by way of a civil action rather than judicial review, where public interest standing might have come to Gouriet's aid. His lawyers recognised that he therefore needed the Attorney-General's consent. The Attorney, Sam Silkin QC, refused to grant it, coming in person before the Court of Appeal and submitting that his discretion was absolute and unreviewable.[52] The Court of Appeal rejected his application to strike out the proceedings for lack of his consent and granted Gouriet an interim injunction. Denning's judgment, one of his judicial classics and worth reading for that reason alone,[53] suggested that if the Attorney-General refused his consent without good reason, the court could proceed without it. The other members of the court reached a similar conclusion by more circuitous means.

When the case reached the House of Lords, the issue was dropped: it was accepted that Gouriet had to succeed either without the Attorney-General's support or not at all.[54] But Denning's questions still invite answers: what if the Attorney-General's refusal were dictated by party

---

[48] *Attorney-General v. Harris* [1960] 1 QB 31   [49] [1961] 1 QB 74, per Pearce LJ at 95

[50] *LCC v. Attorney-General* [1902] AC 165 – per Lord Halsbury *obiter*; but followed in *Attorney-General v. Westminster City Council* [1924] 2 Ch 416.

[51] See Ch. 6   [52] *Gouriet v. UPW* [1977] 1 All ER 696, 706 (CA)

[53] It was neatly parodied by Marcel Berlins in *Not The Times*: see S. Sedley, *Ashes and Sparks* (2011), pp. 203–4.

[54] [1978] AC 435

politics or a desire to protect members of his own government from criticism? One answer might be Denning's: to ignore his refusal and let the challenge proceed regardless. A less dramatic one, more consonant with constitutional reality, would be to recognise that the Attorney-General has two inconsistent roles: one as a member of the government with collective responsibility for its policies and decisions; the other as the government's independent legal adviser, with an obligation to ensure that ministers and their departments abide by the law. The Commons Constitutional Affairs Committee in 2007 advised that this double role was unsustainable and should be split, but nothing has been done or seems likely to be done to follow their advice. In this situation, there would appear to be nothing to stop the courts satisfying themselves that any refusal of the Attorney-General's fiat for a relator action was based exclusively on the maintenance of the rule of law and not affected by governmental or party political considerations. If the court were not satisfied of this, a mandatory order might follow, requiring either reconsideration of the Attorney-General's refusal or – in a strong case – the grant of his or her fiat.

Third party interventions

There is, at least in theory, a risk in all public interest litigation – and indeed in conventional private interest litigation too – that relevant points of view will go unheard. I have mentioned the introduction in the modern rules of a power to hear appropriate third parties. But how wide can such a power go? Ought climate change denialists to be given a chance to be heard in a case about the need to reduce atmospheric pollution? If supporters of General Pinochet had asked the House of Lords for a right of audience in opposition to Amnesty International's intervention, should they too have been given permission to intervene in the argument?[55]

Although there are theoretical problems of this kind, and although the power to hear third parties might be thought to be open-ended and vulnerable to abuse, it has in fact been well managed and helpful to the process of justice.[56] There have been a number of judicial review cases in

---

[55] *R v. Bow Street Magistrate, ex p Pinochet Ugarte* [1998] 3 WLR 1456; [1999] 2 WLR 272; [1999] 2 WLR 827.

[56] This has not stopped the Secretary of State for Justice manipulating the costs rules so as to deter interveners: see n. 22 above.

which, for political or tactical or financial reasons, the named defendant decides not to oppose the claim, and central government has been allowed to step in to contest the case.[57] There have been others – many more in fact – where an intervener has given at least as much help to the court as either party:[58] the Mental Health Act Commission,[59] the Refugee Legal Centre,[60] the UN High Commissioner for Refugees,[61] the Ramblers' Association[62] and many others. They have been admitted not under the modern rules of procedure but under the court's inherent power to determine rights of audience.[63]

Standing in historical perspective

It is clear from the early reported cases that by the beginning of the nineteenth century there was a body of judicial authority and practice about the scope of standing. One such dictum is quoted at the head of this chapter. To make a violation of private rights a necessary condition of public law standing is to misunderstand what public law is about, for it is elementary that a public authority may break the law without invading any individual rights. As Lord Reed said in the *Axa* case,[64] sufficiency of interest

> cannot be based upon the concept of rights, and must instead be based upon the concept of interests.

Another way to put it is that public law is not about rights, though these often turn out to be engaged, but about wrongs – that is to say, abuses of public power.[65] Once this is understood, the appropriateness of

---

[57] E.g. *Backhouse* v. *Lambeth LBC*, Times, 14 October 1972

[58] For a conspectus, see Fordham *Judicial Review Handbook* (6th edn) §22.2.5

[59] *R* v. *Bournewood NHS Trust, ex p L* [1999] 1 AC 458, 481

[60] *Horvath* v. *Home Secretary* [2001] 1 AC 489. 493

[61] *R* v. *Home Secretary, ex p Sivakumaran* [1988] AC 958, 992

[62] *R* v. *Secretary of State for the Environment, ex p Kent CC* (1995) 93 LGR 322, 334

[63] See generally Justice, *To Assist the Court: Third Party Interventions in the UK* (2009), §§ 9–24, esp. § 20.

[64] *Axa General Insurance Ltd* v. *Lord Advocate* [2011] UKSC 46 [170]. See also Lord Diplock in the *NFSE Case* [1978] AC 644: "It would ... be a grave lacuna in our system of public law if a pressure group ... or even a single public-spirited taxpayer, were prevented by outdated rules of locus standi from bringing the matter to the attention of the court to vindicate the rule of law ..."

[65] *R* v. *Secretary of State for the Environment, ex p Kirkstall Valley Campaign* [1996] 3 All ER 304, 325; *R* v. *Somerset CC, ex p Dixon* [1998] Env LR 111, 121; *R (Corner House*

considering challenges based on public rather than private or personal interests becomes plain.

***

"Sitting"

The less often studied counterpart of standing is what I have, for want of a better word, called sitting. That is to say, *against* what individuals or bodies can judicial review proceedings be brought?

The answer is not affected by the fact that the common law does not recognise the state,[66] since what the law does instead is recognise the responsibility of the state's officers and institutions. But it is one thing to recognise that the Home Secretary is answerable for the legality of the conduct of immigration control. It is another to decide whether the commercial companies which run its detention facilities are also amenable to judicial review.

How do the courts decide – and how, historically, have they decided – where the reach of public law ends? The answer they have arrived at, in principle at least, is that judicial review reaches, but reaches only, acts or omissions which involve the performance of public functions. This was the governing concept which emerged from a series of cases starting in 1987 with the *Datafin* case. It was enshrined from 2000 in the Civil Procedure Rules, which define a claim for judicial review as a claim concerning

> a decision, action or failure to act in relation to the exercise of a public function.[67]

Manifestly not everything which affects the public is a public function: the contractor who digs up the road and then goes off to do something else may deserve to be put out of business but is not liable to a mandatory order from the Administrative Court.

How then do you identify a public function? Part of the problem today is that the concept of public functions has itself changed over the last few decades in response to deep-lying changes in the political terrain. Seeking to give guidance at a relatively early stage, 1987, when the question arose in the *Datafin* case of the amenability of the City of London's Panel on

---

Research) v. *Secretary of State for Trade and Industry* [2005] EWCA Civ 192; *R (Kay)* v. *Chief Constable of Northumbria* [20110] EWHC 31 (Admin).
[66] See Ch. 11.   [67] 54 CPR 1(2)(a)(ii)

Takeovers and Mergers to judicial review, the Court of Appeal,[68] while accepting that the panel was a voluntary self-regulatory body with no statutory or prerogative underpinning, concluded that in a proper case it would nevertheless be susceptible to judicial review. Among its reasons was the likelihood that if the panel did not exist the state would have to invent it. There was therefore, said Lloyd LJ, "an implied devolution of power".

Two and a half decades later, such a proposition may no longer be self-evident. The dominant ideological premise (stubbornly resistant to experience) is that markets are self-adjusting, with the consequence that self-regulation is seen as the norm and the state as an unnatural inter-loper. In such a situation it may no longer be easy to reason from an omnicompetent state to an implied devolution of power, or to character-ise the functions of private psychiatric hospitals,[69] farmers' markets[70] or horse racing associations[71] as public functions.

As with a sufficient interest to confer standing, so with a public function sufficient to generate "sitting", in all but clear cases the outcome depends more on the feel of the issue in its context than on any tick-list of features. Clear cases will include, on the one hand, exercises of power conferred directly by statute, and on the other relationships which are purely and voluntarily contractual. But the margins of both categories are soon eroded. Statutory recognition was not enough to make the functions of either the Chief Rabbi[72] or the Football Association[73] public functions. And contractual relations may not be enough to divest functions of their public character where there has been no option but to join a body, such as the Jockey Club,[74] which has monopoly control of an activity.

This is unavoidable in a mixed economy and a diverse polity.[75] What is avoidable is mistaking the effect of standing on "sitting".

---

[68] R v. Panel on Takeovers and Mergers [1987] QB 815

[69] R (A) v. Partnerships in Care Ltd [2002] EWHC 529

[70] R (Beer) v. Hampshire Farmers' Markets Ltd. [2003] EWCA Civ 1056

[71] Mullins v. Jockey Club Board of Appeal [2005] EWHC 2197 (Admin)

[72] R v. Chief Rabbi, ex p Wachmann [1992] 1 WLR 1036

[73] R v. Football Association, ex p Football League Ltd [1993] 2 All ER 833

[74] Datafin at 846; cf. R v. Jockey Club, ex p Aga Khan [1993] 1 WLR 909

[75] See esp. Hoffmann LJ in Ex parte Aga Khan [1993] 1 WLR 9009, 932–3: "In a mixed economy, power may be private as well as public. Private power may affect the public interest and livelihoods of many individuals. But that does not subject it to the rules of public law. If control is needed, it must be found in the law of contract, the doctrine of restraint of trade … and all the other instruments available in law for curbing excesses of private power."

The Insurance Ombudsman Bureau was set up by the insurance industry to give direct redress to members of the public. Because its relationship with the insurance companies was entirely contractual, the High Court halted a judicial review claim against the Ombudsman by one of the insurance companies. But did it follow, as the court held it did, that the Insurance Ombudsman Bureau was "not ... a body susceptible to judicial review"?[76] A member of the public in dispute with his or her insurer, unlike the insurer itself, has no contractual relationship with the ombudsman. Unless judicial review is available to the private individual, an error of law or due process by the ombudsman will go without redress. In other words, the amenability of a public or semi-public body to judicial review – its "sitting" – may in some cases depend on the claimant's standing.

There is an analogy, if not a perfect fit, between the judicial test of a public function and the statutory category of a public authority. S. 6(1) of the Human Rights Act 1998 declares:

> It is unlawful for a public authority to act in a way which is incompatible with a Convention right.

The section goes on to include in the meaning of a public authority

> any person certain of whose functions are functions of a public nature

except in relation to private acts.[77] The meaning and implications of these formulae have not been fully worked out, but the leading case so far has decided that a parochial church council, although invested by law with power to compel persons unconnected with the church to contribute large sums of money to its upkeep, is not a public authority for Human Rights Act purposes.[78] Some may find that surprisingly restrictive. The subsequent majority decision of the House of Lords[79] that a care home funded principally by local authorities to discharge their statutory obligation to care for the elderly was also not a public authority was so egregious that Parliament swiftly legislated to reverse it.[80]

---

[76] R v. *Insurance Ombudsman Bureau, ex p Aegon Life Assurance* [1994] CLC 88, 93–4
[77] S. 6(3)(b); s. 6(5)
[78] *Aston Cantlow PCC* v. *Wallbank* [2003] UKHL 37; [2004] 1 AC 546
[79] *YL* v. *Birmingham City Council* [2007] UKHL 27; [2008] 1 AC 95
[80] Health and Social Care Act 2008, s. 145

History and law

As public law woke in the later twentieth century from the long sleep it had fallen into after World War I, it had to work out the logic of what it was now required by the rule of law to do. Who was entitled to draw the court's attention to a possible abuse of public power? Must they have something personal to gain by it? Which officials and bodies could they bring before the courts? If it could only be those performing public functions, what was a public function?

The courts of public law have worked on these questions over the last three decades, starting from the way their predecessors handled public law challenges in the eighteenth and nineteenth centuries. In particular they have aimed, as Lord Diplock thirty years ago suggested they must, to keep pace with changes in the nature and functioning of the state, which have carried some activities out of the public domain and have generated new ones within it. Both standing and sitting have changed accordingly, and they will go on changing.

13

Law without courts: the tribunal system

There are more ways than one of resolving legal disputes. Are tribunals second-class courts or an innovative part of the legal system?

Dispute resolution

When people talk about the law, they are almost invariably talking, consciously or unconsciously, about the law administered in law courts. Yet there is nothing – or very little – to stop people agreeing to have their disputes settled either according to some extraneous system of law or by a person or tribunal bound by no particular system of law. The courts still hold the ring: it is they who will decide whether such agreements are enforceable and whether they have been properly followed. But within that perimeter many other kinds of law and practice prevail. The tabloid indignation which greeted the Archbishop of Canterbury's acknowledgment in 2008 that it might be acceptable for people to have their disputes settled according to the *shari'a* law was testimony enough to the widespread unawareness that this had been possible for centuries. Every golf club or bridge club committee which is given power by the rules to adjudicate on allegations of cheating constitutes what is sometimes called an Alsatia – a place where the royal writ does not run.[1] But even here the law holds a watching brief, for the club rules generally form a contract between the members, and into it the courts will imply (if they are not already spelt out) rules of procedural fairness.[2]

---

[1] The former sanctuary at Whitefriars, located between the Thames, the Fleet River, the Temple and Fleet Street, was until 1697 a refuge for debtors and criminals. It was named after the province of Alsace, which was fought over for centuries and became a place where no state's writ ran. Its modern equivalent is the Sinai Peninsula.

[2] See Ch. 8, n. 6. See further M. Freedland, "The Impact of Public Law on Labour Law 1972–1997" (1997) 26 ILJ 311; J. Laws, "Public Law and Employment Law: Abuse of Power" [1997] PL 455; S. Sedley, "Public Law and Contractual Employment" (1994) 23 ILJ

Public law claims

These are – at least in theory – voluntary or elective jurisdictions dealing with private law relationships. Relationships between the individual and state, which are the business not of private but of public law, cannot be dealt with in this way. If a dispute arises between state and citizen, either it has to go before a court or some other means has to be found of reaching a binding decision according to what may well be an arcane body of law.

There are two immediate problems in letting such decisions go before the regular courts of law. One is sheer volume. By the beginning of the twenty-first century, almost a million disputes of this kind were being decided each year,[3] a number which had been growing steadily for well over a century.[4] The other is expertise. A judge who has to turn from a steady diet of crime and commerce to the effect of innocent non-disclosure on a means-tested social security benefit is likely not only to take several times as long as a specialist adjudicator to grasp the relevant law but either to get the answer wrong or – almost as bad – to reach the right answer by deficient reasoning. This is, and has for two centuries been, the essential case for adjudication by specialist tribunals.

Tribunals and the law

At the same time, specialist tribunals can fail to act fairly or get the law wrong themselves. This is the case for eventual recourse to the courts. Historically it has taken two forms. One is the supervisory jurisdiction which the High Court has exercised for many hundreds of years over what are rather disparagingly called inferior – that is to say subordinate – tribunals and courts, to ensure that their processes are fair and their decisions lawful, and to quash any that are not. The other is an appellate jurisdiction, which has to be created by statute and which gives the High Court the last word on questions of law which have come before the tribunals. By the latter part of the twentieth century[5] there were

---

201. In relation to commercial arbitration, see *Scott* v. *Avery* (1856) 10 ER 1121, *Czarnikow* v. *Roth, Schmidt* [1922] 2 KB 478.

[3] *Tribunals for Users* (the Leggatt Report), HMSO, March 2001, § 2

[4] It has now been cut back by the simple expedient of raising the fee for lodging an employment claim to £1,200, causing an estimated drop of about 79 per cent in such claims (TUC report *At What Price Justice?*, June 2014).

[5] See the list, as at 1992, in Annex 2 to Law Commission consultation paper No. 126 (1993).

almost a hundred such statutes, giving rights of appeal against tribunal decisions on topics ranging from salvage awards in the Cinque Ports[6] to state pensions,[7] from the registration of architects, dentists, audiologists, solicitors and farriers[8] to copyrights,[9] cycle lanes[10] and forfeiture of obscene articles.[11] Here, without doubt, questions of law could arise, some of which needed to be answered by the highest courts; but it did not follow that they all needed to go there. As we shall see, the reshaping of the tribunal system has sought not only to keep as many as possible of these questions of law "in-house" but to draw a growing number of judicial review issues away from their natural home in the High Court and into the ambit of the tribunal system, a transition which has been characterised as "non-judicial review".[12]

In the course of this process, one tsunami-sized wave passed through the system of public law. In 1969 the decision of the House of Lords in *Anisminic*[13] swept away the historic distinction between unreviewable errors of law within the jurisdiction of subordinate tribunals and reviewable errors going to their jurisdiction, replacing them by susceptibility to review for all errors of law. One effect was to make statutory appeal on points of law largely redundant, save where the principle was invoked that judicial review, being a remedy of last resort, would not be granted if a statutory appeal on the same point was available.

But the Leggatt Report, or more precisely its legislative and judicial aftermath, changed all this. Although the reforms based on the report were ultimately enshrined in legislation, the legislation itself left some big questions of public law unanswered, and it has been falling to the courts to make fuller sense of the new order. But before I look at this history in the making, I want to look back at how we had arrived at the situation which confronted Sir Andrew Leggatt when, in May 2000, he and his panel were set to work, with ten months to review and report on the UK's entire tribunal system: seventy different administrative tribunals in England and Wales (there were others in Scotland), only twenty of which heard more than five hundred cases a year and some of which had ceased to function altogether; many of them inefficient and cumbersome; and

---

[6] Cinque Ports Act 1821, ss. 4, 5   [7] Pension Appeal Tribunals Act 1943, s. 4
[8] See n. 5, *passim*.   [9] Copyright, Designs and Patents Act 1988, s. 152
[10] Cycle Tracks Act 1984, s. 3   [11] Obscene Publications Act 1959, s. 3
[12] P. Cane, "Judicial Review in the Age of Tribunals" [2009] PL 479
[13] *Anisminic Ltd* v. *Foreign Compensation Commission* [1969] 2 AC 147. See the Introduction.

critically, as Leggatt stressed in his opening paragraph, "not independent of the departments that sponsor them".

Private law claims

In addition to resolving public law disputes between the individual and the state, use has in places been made of non-court forums to decide private law claims. The modern paradigm is the system of employment tribunals, which has grown out of the industrial tribunals first established in 1964.[14] But many other private law issues, such as patents and copyrights,[15] now fall into this mould.

This is not a haphazard allocation of functions. It reflects both an area of legal specialism and a need, or at least a desire, to relax the formal rules of court procedure. But the distinctions between tribunal procedure and court procedure are not nearly as sharp or clear as they were. Whether this is a cause or an effect of modernisation, it is part of a long-term assimilation of two formerly distinct roads to justice which is altering our constitution.

Tribunals in history

The idea of having individuals' rights and obligations decided by a body which, while empowered to make binding decisions, is not a court of law, is not by any means recent. Anybody venturing into this field of legal history and theory rapidly comes to know the work of two particular authors: the Canadian scholar Harry Arthurs and the British legal historian Chantal Stebbings. Stebbings[16] has mapped the topography and development of the tribunal system in England during the greatest period of the central and local state's growth.[17] Arthurs[18] has argued persuasively that the courts need to recognise the law developed by these tribunals and the justice administered by them as a valid system parallel and not inferior to lawyers' law.

---

[14] Their initial role was to hear appeals against industrial training levies; then from 1965 to adjudicate on redundancy payments; and from 1971 to hear claims for the newly created tort of unfair dismissal.

[15] Though these, and others, have arguably a public law dimension.

[16] C. Stebbings, *Legal Foundations of Tribunals in Nineteenth-Century England* (2006)

[17] See Ch. 2.

[18] H. W. Arthurs, *Without the Law: Administrative Justice and Legal Pluralism in Nineteenth-century England* (1985)

The dichotomy of tribunal justice and doctrinal law is far from abstract. The central achievement of the 1957 Franks Report,[19] consolidated in prompt legislation,[20] was a broad alignment of tribunal justice with legal justice. The central achievement of the Leggatt Report over forty years later was the restructuring of the United Kingdom's entire tribunal system.[21] But structural reforms, as we shall see, have again thrown open the relationship of tribunal justice to conventional legality.

Adjudicative non-court bodies, often with life-changing powers over individuals, go back for centuries, and with them the supervisory jurisdiction of the courts of law. It is the use of the name "tribunal" for such bodies that is relatively modern. Until the twentieth century the word, at least to lawyers, connoted a court of law[22] (as in modern French it still does). In consequence, any name but tribunal was used for newly devised dispute-resolution bodies: commission, board, inspectorate, but not tribunal. Confining the name "court" to those bodies empowered to exercise the judicial power of the state, as Lord Scarman was classically to do in the late twentieth century,[23] is impressively tidy – but what is an employment tribunal or an immigration tribunal doing if it is not exercising the judicial power of the state?

The knot is untied only by recognising that the state has historically given adjudicative powers to a great variety of bodies and individuals. Some of these are true courts of law, characterised above all by their constitutional independence from government; but the old idea that tribunals, by contrast, are agencies of the executive was always constitutionally suspect and now is – or ought to be – defunct.[24] The more significant distinction is between tribunals which make binding adjudications, whether between the state and the individual or between one citizen and another,[25] and tribunals (such as the Chilcot Inquiry into the Iraq war or the Leggatt commission itself) which inquire and report but make no legally conclusive determination.[26] The large number of

---

[19] Cmnd. 218 (1957)

[20] Tribunals and Inquiries Act 1958, replaced by the Tribunals and Inquiries Act 1972

[21] Tribunals, Courts and Enforcement Act 2007

[22] See *Royal Aquarium etc.* v. *Parkinson* [1892] 1 QB 431, 446, per Fry LJ.

[23] *Attorney-General* v. *BBC* [1981] AC 303

[24] See G. Richardson and H. Genn, "Tribunals in Transition: Resolution or Adjudication?" [2007] PL 116.

[25] There are some tribunals which do both: e.g. the Lands Tribunal, which deals both with compulsory purchase and with restrictive covenants.

[26] See S. Sedley, "Public Inquiries: A Cure or a Disease?" (1989) 52 MLR 469 for a historical conspectus of forms of inquiry.

bodies now empowered to make binding adjudications spans a plethora of courts and tribunals whose procedures, and even whose personnel, have tended steadily to converge. The amalgamation in 2011 of the courts' and tribunals' administration into a single Courts and Tribunals Service was a formal recognition of this. It may have been prompted by nothing more lofty than the Treasury's desire to save money, but it gives legal form to what has been in substance a constitutional realignment of the machinery of justice, and has made it possible to create a single Judicial College for training personnel.

Judicial control of tribunals

The early history of the prerogative writ of certiorari is in significant part the history of the supervision by the central courts of the proceedings of such tribunals as the Courts of the Forests, the courts merchant, the Commissioners of Sewers and even the Court of Admiralty, not with the purpose of retaking their decisions but with the purpose of ensuring that they did not exceed their jurisdiction.[27]

Rooke's Case, reported by Sir Edward Coke,[28] is a classic instance, not only because it spells out principles of review which are still applicable but because it illustrates how slim the divide always has been between law and merits. The commissioners of sewers had levied the entire cost of repairing a river bank on the riparian owner, letting his neighbours benefit from the repair without contributing to its cost. It was said on their behalf – exactly as would be said today – that this was a matter for the commissioners' judgment, whatever the court might think of it. Not so, said Coke –

> notwithstanding the words of the commission give authority to the commissioners to do according to their discretions, yet their proceedings ought to be limited and bound with the rule of reason and law.

The Commissioners of Sewers were not the only early tribunal, but they were among the more reputable. In 1660, when the newly restored Crown was badly in need of revenue, a board of Commissioners of

---

[27] S. A. de Smith, "The Prerogative Writs" (1951) 11 CLJ 40, 46

[28] (1598) 5 Co. Rep. 99b. For a fuller account of the case see Ch. 2, n. 60. The decision would be classed today as an intervention for irrationality. See also *Keighley's Case* (1609) 10 Co. Rep. 139.

Customs and Excise was set up by statute,[29] their decisions appealable to justices of the peace but their independence widely doubted. Dr Johnson in his *Dictionary*, described them as "wretches hired by those to whom excise is paid".[30]

Professor Wade[31] took the view that the modern tribunal template was created in the years before World War I by the administrative machinery set up in 1908 for old age pensions[32] and in 1911 for national insurance.[33] But there is an arguable continuity between these statutory bodies (and others[34] of the same period) and the boards, inspectorates and commissions which proliferated in the course of the nineteenth century. One has only to recall what happened when the Wandsworth Board of Works demolished Mr Cooper's building without notice[35] to realise how much of the twentieth-century tribunal system had been prefigured both by the development of statutory tribunals of various kinds during the Victorian years and by the expansion of judicial review to monitor them.[36]

The enclosures

Possibly the most important non-judicial tribunals between the seventeenth and twentieth centuries were the inclosure[37] commissioners who were given the task of allocating to private ownership what had till then been common or waste land, while preserving or rerouting highways and rights of way. Thanks to local historians we know a great deal about how millions of acres were enclosed by the great landowners, evicting commoners in their thousands to join the swelling population of the industrial slums.[38] The Statute of Merton 1235 had authorised "the great men of England ... to make their profit of their lands, waters, woods and pastures" so long as they left their tenants enough pasture for their own

---

[29] 12 Charles II, c.23, s.3 1(5)

[30] Samuel Johnson, *Dictionary* (5th edn, 1696), "Excise": "A hateful tax levied upon commodities, and adjudged not by the common judges of property, but wretches hired by those to whom excise is paid." It is now known that the Attorney-General, William Murray (later Lord Mansfield), advised that Johnson could be prosecuted in respect of this entry for seditious libel.

[31] See now W. Wade and C. Forsyth, *Administrative Law* (10th edn, 2009), p. 771.

[32] Old Age Pensions Act 1908   [33] National Insurance Act 1911

[34] E.g. the Local Government Board at the centre of *Arlidge's Case*: see Ch. 1.

[35] *Cooper v. Wandsworth Board of Works* (1863) 14 CB(NS) 180   [36] See Ch. 2.

[37] The word was spelt this way until the late nineteenth century.   [38] See Ch. 2.

needs. But no major enclosure movement followed until the Black Death had halved the rural population and the sale of the dissolved monasteries' lands had let in a new type of commercial landowner. By the mid-sixteenth century Thomas More was saying that the sheep were eating up the men, and Bishop Latimer, denouncing "inclosers and rent-raisers", described a land in which,

> where there have been many householders and inhabitants, there is now but a shepherd and a dog.[39]

A rising in Oxfordshire in 1596, in the wake of a series of bad harvests verging on famine, demanded the restoration of access to common land and an end to the conversion of arable land to pasture.[40] Although Coke, as Attorney-General, succeeded in deploying the full weight of the law against the leaders (they were first tortured for information about their collaborators, then convicted of treason and hanged within sight of the Enslow Hill enclosures which had prompted the rising), prosecutions before Star Chamber of unlicensed inclosers were stepped up, and Parliament in 1597 legislated to restrict the use of inclosure to convert arable land to pasture.[41]

During the seventeenth century a practice developed of making collusive applications for inclosure decrees in the Chancery or Exchequer court.[42] It was not until the eighteenth century that enclosure by statute became, in effect, industrialised.[43] Private inclosure acts were passed in increasing numbers, each of them authorising the

---

[39] The wider problems of land tenure and common right are summarised by Stebbings, *Legal Foundations of Tribunals*, pp. 12–17, including the case for enclosure, in spite of its huge human cost.

[40] See J. Walter, "A 'Rising of the People'? The Oxfordshire Rising of 1596", 107 *Past and Present* (1985), 90. Oxfordshire, Northamptonshire and Buckinghamshire were particularly heavily affected by Elizabethan enclosures. The eventual legislation in 1597 to restrict enclosure was supported by Bacon as well as (ironically) by Coke himself.

[41] 39 Eliz, c.1 & 2, respectively An Acte against the Decayinge of Towns and Howses of Husbandrye and An Acte for the Maintenance of Husbandrie and Tillage.

[42] The process is described in W. E. Tate, *The English Village Community and the Enclosure Movements* (1967), p. 47. It might start with a meeting at which the commoners, the manorial lord and the incumbent would appoint commissioners to represent their respective interests. Following a survey and a draft award, proceedings would be launched claiming that the lord refused to consent; the lord would deny this; and thereupon the court would decree the enclosure. The commoners will have been bought out; other objectors had to acquiesce or face heavy bills of costs.

[43] Beginning in 1773, general provision was made by statute for enclosures. The Inclosure Acts 1845–1882 created a template which made recourse to Parliament unnecessary.

inclosure of the lands of which the promoters owned the subsoil together with the extinction of rights of common, and appointing commissioners to lay out the reapportioned lands. To this end, the act would appoint a number of individuals, usually three but sometimes a dozen or more, each representing a named interest but all nominated by the bill's promoter. They would be serviced by a surveyor and a clerk in mapping, dividing and allocating the land with its roads, paths, ponds, lakes and watercourses.[44]

Since the commissioners were entirely creatures of statute, sworn on appointment to do their work "without favour or affection, prejudice or partiality", the legality and integrity of their proceedings and determinations was unquestionably a matter for the courts. Moreover, what is known of the individuals who served as inclosure commissioners makes it probable that some of them were idle or corrupt or both.[45] The lacuna in the appointing statutes, which never laid down any procedural standards or methods, was one which the common law would have been ready to fill. But despite the magnitude of their effects on rural populations and on the tenure and ownership of land, there seems to have been little litigation about enclosure awards, and what there was concerned their enforcement rather than scrutiny of their validity.[46] Here, nevertheless, was a major forum with binding adjudicative powers, divorced from the court system but set up and sanctioned by the state.

---

[44] Tate, The English Village Community, notes an act of 1545 (37 Hen.VIII, c.2) which appointed commissioners to partition Hounslow Heath and therefore antedates the act of 1603 (for enclosing lands at Radipole in Dorset) which was conventionally taken to be the first inclosure act. By the time of the last one, in 1914, a total of about 2,400 inclosure acts had been passed (Tate, The English Village Community, p.108) and perhaps 5 million acres of England enclosed (see Ency. Brit. 1911 edn, "Commons", p. 783). But by the 1870s the inclosure movement had substantially been halted by the litigation brought by commoners to block the inclosure of Epping Forest, and by the work of the Commons Preservation Society which in 1876 secured the passing of the Commons Act.

[45] Tate, The English Village Community, pp. 108–12, records commissioners such as John Burcham, who sat on sixty-nine inclosures between 1801 and 1840 and died worth £600,000. But the majority appear to have been one-off appointments.

[46] Cf Digest, 3rd reissue, vol. 11(1), No. 64–117. Thus the Court of Chancery, which had assumed the power to order dissentient freeholders to consent to an inclosure, in 1613 ordered Magdalen College, Oxford, to give its consent to the inclosure of lands to which the college had, presumably, freehold rights which it was unwilling to give up (Hide v. Prebends and Scholars of Magdalen College Oxford (1619) Toth. 110; 21 ER 138).

The personnel of tribunals

The venality of many of the inclosure commissioners was only one aspect of the perennial problem of bias. The Victorians had a visceral regard for status. They tended to measure this by an individual's prosperity and social standing rather than, as in an earlier age, by birth;[47] but they frequently had difficulty in separating status from impartiality. The history of the railway and canal tribunals, which had to try to harmonise the operations of numerous fiercely competitive enterprises into a national transport system, shows perhaps the sharpest swings in the state's attempts to get things right. The railways had initially been regulated directly by the Board of Trade, but in 1846 regulation was devolved to a Railway Commission[48] which had power to resolve a considerable variety of disputes but possessed no legal expertise. In 1854[49] Parliament went to the opposite length of making the Court of Common Pleas the tribunal for regulating competition between rail and canal companies and preventing the abuse of their statutory monopolies. The court was to sit if necessary with expert engineers to advise it,[50] but the judges even so felt increasingly uncomfortable with a jurisdiction that depended at least as much on technical knowledge as on law. In 1873 the system was therefore abandoned in favour of a commission of experts.[51] This too had its critics: the commission itself lacked legal expertise, but it was infested and browbeaten by highly paid specialist barristers whom the railway companies had increasingly used ever since the 1854 Act redirected disputes into a court of law.[52]

One result in the years which followed was a reluctance to let any lawyers into tribunal proceedings. Another, more benign, was a deliberate simplification of procedures to ensure that unrepresented individuals could cope. A third, which did not crystallise until the later twentieth

---

[47] The sharpest example was the local justices of the peace, qualified only by the possession of property of a minimum value and selected by their social peers. Blackstone, in an earlier era, had considered nobility alone a sufficient qualification to sit as a judge.

[48] Commissioners of Railways Act 1846

[49] Railway and Canal Traffic Act 1854, promoted by the President of the Board of Trade, Edward Cardwell, with the principal object of preventing railway companies from abusing their local and regional monopolies.

[50] A procedure familiar then and now in the appointment of Trinity House Elder Brethren to advise admiralty courts in collision cases.

[51] Railway and Canal Traffic Act 1873, s. 6

[52] See Stebbings, *Legal Foundations of Tribunals*, pp. 226–7 for some examples.

century, was to have tribunals chaired by lawyers trained in the specialised work of the tribunal, together with lay members trained in the
essential elements of substantive law and fair procedure – a model which
seems to work well.

The transition

Until 1991, illegal parking was a criminal offence.[53] Parking tickets were
issued by police officers, and if you contested one you had to go to court.
It wasted countless hours of police, motorists' and magistrates' time,
despite the practice of listing parking appeals for hearing on Saturday
afternoons so that attending court to dispute a ticket meant missing the
football match. Starting in 1992, the London boroughs, followed by the
rest of England and Wales, decriminalised parking offences and, for
contested cases, introduced an adjudication system.

The parking and traffic adjudication system forms a transitional
model, antedating the Leggatt reforms and now continuing alongside
them.[54] It is a single-tier system, using qualified lawyers as independent adjudicators.[55] Before it was set up, the first (and subsequently
chief) adjudicator, Caroline Sheppard, visited the US to study the
potential for using IT as the basis of an appeal system.[56] The time
and money were well spent, and the system became a model of its
kind.

Parking adjudication is not a law to itself. Panels of adjudicators are
assembled to decide issues of wider significance, and all adjudicators'
decisions are open to judicial review for error of law or failure of due
process. Not many such challenges succeed, but this is a simple and
classical tribunal structure which works well – at least if a measure
of its quality is that more than half the appeals it deals with are
allowed.

---

[53] The power to decriminalise parking offences was created by the Road Traffic Act 1991.
[54] Although Leggatt wanted to incorporate it (see para. 6.41 and Table C), parking control is
not within the new structure, partly because it is a self-financing system needing no
support from public funds, and partly because the adjudicators themselves do not want to
be absorbed into a more complex structure.
[55] Independence has seemingly not proved an issue in practice, but the fact that adjudicators' salaries come out of a pool funded by fines might be thought to be a breach of the
principle of *Dr Bonham's Case* (see Ch. 7). Cf Leggatt, p. 165, para. 14.
[56] See the 1993–4 report of the Parking Committee for London, p. 10.

The new tribunal system

The Leggatt report was followed in 2004 by a forward-looking white paper[57] and in 2007 by legislation[58] which, unusually, adopted and enacted the substance of the report. From November 2008 the new structure began to materialise. The Act, by its first section, extended to all tribunals the guarantee of independence given to the judiciary by s. 3 of the Constitutional Reform Act 2005. The general mandate contained in s. 2 – that the tribunals should be accessible, quick and efficient, with members knowledgeable in their fields of law and a preparedness to innovate in methods of dispute resolution – could have formed a mandate for the courts were it not for the last element.

The new structure[59] was to be both horizontal and vertical. Horizontally, the tribunals were to operate at two levels: a first-tier tribunal with fact-finding powers, empowered to make binding determinations, and an upper tribunal to sit on appeal, in appropriate cases, from decisions of the first tier. On any important point of principle or practice, onward appeal to the Court of Appeal, and potentially the Supreme Court, was provided for.[60] But nothing at all was said in the act about judicial review of these tribunals, despite the fact that they had all been historically subject to the supervisory jurisdiction of the High Court. If it was assumed that statutory appeal would in practice replace judicial review, the parliamentary drafters were mistaken.

The tribunals were to be divided into chambers, initially six in number but since added to, each representing a specialist jurisdiction. The first six chambers were social entitlement; health, education and social care; war pensions and armed forces compensation; tax and duties; land, property and housing; and general regulatory matters. These were to be funnelled, on appeal, into a smaller number of upper tribunal chambers, each presided over by a High Court judge. The list of chambers gives only a rudimentary idea of the magnitude and variety of jurisdictions which

---

[57] *Transforming Public Services: Complaints, Redress and Tribunals*, HMSO, Cm 6243. Brooke LJ had convened a tribunal presidents' group, which had a significant input into the white paper. The white paper in turn proposed a new and informal approach to dispute-resolution across the board.

[58] Tribunals, Courts and Enforcement Act 2007

[59] A diagram can be found at p. 3 of the 2013 report of the Senior President of Tribunals, www.judiciary.gov.uk/publications-and-reports/reports/Tribunals/spt-annual-report-2013.

[60] S. 13; Appeals from the Upper Tribunal to the Court of Appeal Order 2008 (SI 2008/2834), art. 2.

they embrace. The social entitlement chamber contains tribunals which deal with social security, child support, asylum support and criminal injuries compensation. The centuries-old functions of the Commissioners of Sewers are now part of the land drainage jurisdiction of the property chamber. The tax chamber contains the oldest extant tribunal, the general commissioners of income tax, set up when the tax was first introduced in 1799. The general regulatory chamber contains a dozen or more jurisdictions ranging from charities and gambling to information rights and consumer credit.

There remains one major bystander: the employment tribunal system, which has – so far successfully – resisted incorporation. It is accordingly described not as a chamber but as a pillar of the tribunal system – a good metaphor, since, like Trajan's column, it stands in splendid isolation, neither receiving nor offering support. The chief ground on which the first-instance and appellate employment tribunals resisted incorporation in the Leggatt structure was that, unlike other tribunals, they dealt with party-and-party disputes rather than with rights and remedies against the state. But other tribunals – for example the property chamber – handle private law rights, and Leggatt considered this an insufficient reason for separation. The true reason may have more to do with a sense that the employment tribunals, both first-instance and appellate, formed a cohesive and self-governing system which did not need outside regulation.

Inquisitorial or adversarial?

The procedural needs of the various tribunals differ considerably, and with them the components of administrative justice. Cheapness, friendliness and informality may be the watchwords for assessing disability benefit, but the amounts and issues at stake before the Lands Tribunal or the tax commissioners, probably with the parties represented by counsel, often call for a measure of formality not very different from that of a court.[61]

A good deal of attention has been given to whether modern tribunals are, or ought to be, inquisitorial bodies rather than simply forums for adversarial contests on the model of the courts. The answer is probably that tribunals need to adapt their procedures to the particular issue and

---

[61] See R. Carnwath, "Tribunal Justice – A New Start" [2009] PL 48, 53.

the parties before them. Some claimants may have a worked-out case which can be presented and contested much like an issue in litigation. Others may be at sea from the start or lose their bearings in the course of the hearing: if so, they will need some help from the tribunal. The problem for a tribunal is that if it offers too much help it will appear to be taking sides, and that if it raises issues which neither side has raised it may be accused of taking charge instead of listening. But the proposition that tribunals may have to investigate and not merely adjudicate is today well established.[62] It is arguable that the courts of law should be willing to do the same.

Independence

What is, or ought to be, less controversial is that tribunals need to be independent of the executive. The Franks Committee in 1957 was firm in its view that tribunals belonged not to the machinery of administration but to the process of adjudication.[63] Not only does the 2007 Act guarantee their independence; all the judges of the High Court and Court of Appeal are *ex officio* members of the tribunals. Although it has been suggested that independence, like orality, is not an essential characteristic of adjudication,[64] in the common law tradition it is central. The fact[65] that one cannot find any point of origin for the requirement of independence is, if anything, an illustration of its fundamentality.[66] It may be true that it is possible for a decision-maker to be impartial without being institutionally independent, but a contrary perception is likely to be irresistible. It has been said that the two things are closely linked,[67] but they are significantly different from one another: impartiality is a state of mind; independence is a state of being; and both are as necessary in a tribunal as in a court.

This is why it is unfortunate that the old vocabulary of departmental "sponsorship"[68] of individual tribunals has in places been retained. The

---

[62] See *R v. Medical Appeal Tribunal, ex p Hubble* [1958] 2 QB 228, 240, per Diplock J; *Hooper* v. *Secretary of State for Work and Pensions* [2007] EWCA Civ 495.

[63] *Report of the Committee on Administrative Tribunals and Inquiries* (1957) Cmnd. 218, §40.

[64] G. Richardson and H. Genn, "Tribunals in Transition: Resolution or Adjudication?" [2007] PL 116, 119, n. 19

[65] See ibid., 120.   [66] See generally Ch. 3.

[67] *Gillies* v. *Secretary of State for Work and Pensions* [2006] UKHL 2, per Lady Hale, § 38

[68] Also sometimes called "parenting".

notion, which belongs to an earlier phase of the managerial state,[69] has no proper place in an independent tribunal system. If administrative law has had one quiet success in the last fifty years, it has been to dissolve the proprietorial attitude of departmental government to the tribunals which stand between it and the public, a process now consolidated by the Leggatt reforms.[70] In relation to the employment tribunals, remarkably, Leggatt received submissions from the CBI, the TUC and the Law Society all supporting their policy link with the Department of Trade and Industry,[71] despite the fact that central government was not infrequently a litigating party. But the link has been severed, and the employment tribunals, while still not formally part of the tribunal structure, are now within the tutelage of the Courts and Tribunals Service.

Most problematical have been decision-making structures which actually make the minister the final tribunal, making it likely that adjudication will simply be collapsed into policy. This has notoriously been the case with town and country planning, a system in which ministerial policy is also filtered down to inspectors. In the *Alconbury* case[72] it was found necessary, in order to avoid having to condemn the entire planning system as fundamentally unfair, to hold that the availability of judicial review – a system axiomatically divorced from merits adjudication – was sufficient to assure objectivity and independence in planning. The decision is a strained one; it might be better for public law to accept that its principles cannot work in areas of decision-making where policy and objectivity are inextricably entangled.

---

[69] See Ch. 2. The Legatt report, Table C, listed sixty–four tribunals alongside the government departments responsible either for their administrative support or for their policy. The fact that administration and policy had to be conflated in this way was itself disturbing. The Lord Chancellor's Department, which should have been responsible for all of them, managed only the immigration tribunals and the appellate citizen-and-state tribunals.

[70] When the employment appeal jurisdiction was transferred in 1975 from its temporary home in the Law Courts to the new Employment Appeal Tribunal in St James' Square, it was staffed by clerical officers from the Department of Employment. One of them, an usher with no legal training, rapidly worked out that once he had seen the notice of appeal and the name of the judge listed to preside at the hearing, he could generally predict the outcome. He took quite a lot of money in small bets from the barristers who came to the EAT. The success of his technique did not say a great deal either for departmental involvement or for judicial impartiality.

[71] See p. 145 para. 13.

[72] *R v. Secretary of State for the Environment, ex p Holdings and Barnes plc* [2001] UKHL 23

Fairness

Informality and briskness are capable, as they have always been, of producing injustice. The problem of being visibly fair has historically been bedevilled both by the functions and by the practices of different tribunals. Some have sat in public, others in private. Some have adopted a court-like approach to evidence, refusing to admit unproven documents and insisting on formal examination and cross-examination of sworn witnesses; others have been willing to look at documents or take unsworn testimony for what these may be worth, or have required questions to be put through the chair. Some gave reasons, others did not, until legislation required them to do so.[73]

Status

With its elevation to a largely self-contained structure, but one located within the justice system, the constitutional status of tribunals has begun to be of more than academic interest. I want to consider here two aspects of this development: judicial review *by* tribunals and judicial review *of* tribunals. The bare coexistence of these two apparently incompatible functions points up one of the anomalies still to be resolved: how can a judicial body be both a forum of judicial review and itself amenable to it?

Judicial review of tribunals

If a question of law arises out of a first-tier decision, the upper tribunal is expected to give permission to appeal to itself. But what if it takes the view that there is no worthwhile point of law, and the losing party disagrees? There is nothing to take to the Court of Appeal. The only remedy, if there is one, is judicial review of the upper tribunal. But is this legally possible?

The 2007 Act got off to a shaky start by declaring the Upper Tribunal to be a superior court of record.[74] This had previously been done by the legislation setting up the Employment Appeal Tribunal, and had been thought to have the purpose and the effect of immunising it from judicial review by the High Court.[75] But in Scotland, to which the 2007 Act

---

[73] Tribunals and Inquiries Act 1958, s. 12; Tribunals and Inquiries Act 1971, s. 12
[74] S. 3(5)
[75] See *R (Cart)* v. *Upper Tribunal* [2009] EWHC 3052 (Admin) § 61; *mea culpa* – see n. 76.

applies equally with England and Wales, the concept of a superior court of record is unknown. And it has become clear on fuller consideration that even in England and Wales it is a status which does not necessarily carry immunity from judicial review.[76]

So it was inevitable that the amenability of the upper tribunal to judicial review would arise early in the life of the new system. In the event it arose in Scotland and in Wales almost simultaneously – and serendipitously too, because Scottish and English (and therefore Welsh) public law have developed differently and are capable of producing different answers to the same question. Both the English and the Scottish courts were satisfied that the upper tribunal was not immune to the supervisory jurisdiction of the central courts. But where the Court of Appeal in London took the view that, to give effect to Parliament's prescription, it was necessary to restrict the ambit of review to acts done without jurisdiction and to outright denials of due process,[77] the Inner House of the Court of Session in Edinburgh considered itself unable to impose any such restriction and concluded that the upper tribunal must be open to judicial review for all errors of law.[78]

The courts thus had a multiple choice: to deny all judicial review of the Upper Tribunal; to confine judicial review to securing the boundaries of the system; to accord judicial review on all known grounds; or to do this provided the point at issue was sufficiently significant.[79] An uninstructed observer might have thought the last of these was a non-starter, because it made it almost impossible to know in advance what would and would not qualify. The Court of Appeal, concurring with the judgment of the divisional court, had rejected both this solution and the even larger one of unrestricted judicial review, for reasons which may yet prove to have been sound:

---

[76] *R (Cart)* v. *Upper Tribunal* [2009] EWHC 3052 (Admin) §§ 43–75 sets out a full historical account of the concept.

[77] *R (Cart)* v. *Upper Tribunal* [2010] EWCA Civ 859; [2011] QB 120. These were, of course, the pre-*Anisminic* categories of judicial review, but none the worse for that, since they represented stark forms of error which Parliament could not possibly have intended to stand, but left error within jurisdiction alone (apart from regular second appeals).

[78] *Eba* v. *Advocate General* [2011] SC 70

[79] Viz. by adopting as the gateway for judicial review the test laid down by the Access to Justice Act 1999, s. 55(1) for second appeals to the Court of Appeal, namely is there an important point of principle or practice or some other compelling reason for judicial review? Dyson LJ had adumbrated this solution in *R (Wiles)* v. *Social Security Commissioner* [2010] EWCA Civ 258.

> [T]he new tribunal structure, while not an analogue of the High Court,[80] is something greater than the sum of its parts. It represents a newly coherent and comprehensive edifice designed, among other things, to complete the long process of divorcing administrative justice from departmental policy, to ensure the application across the board of proper standards of adjudication, and to provide for the correction of legal error within rather than outside the system ... with recourse on second-appeal criteria to the higher appellate courts ... While [the system] could no doubt cope with any of the models of judicial review which we have described, the one which seems to us to implement Parliament's intent in enacting the Leggatt reforms is one which secures the boundaries of the system but does not invade it.[81]

The Supreme Court, which took both cases together,[82] had to find a solution which would work equally well north and south of Hadrian's Wall. By now the government had abandoned the contention that judicial review was barred and was arguing for the solution arrived at by the High Court and the Court of Appeal – review confined to excess of jurisdiction and failure of due process. But the Supreme Court decided to adopt a different solution – the fourth option – for both English and Scottish[83] public law. Whether it was right to do so will only emerge from experience, but it seems a pity that a sharp-edged and historically principled test was not adopted.

Judicial review by tribunals

The 2007 act also made unequivocal provision[84] for certain judicial review claims to be transferred from their natural home, the High Court, to the Upper Tribunal. The transfer is subject to two important conditions. One is that only cases falling into classes approved by the Lord Chief Justice can qualify. The other is that they must be heard by a tribunal in which a High Court judge is presiding.

Judicial conservatives were disturbed by the dilution of the centuries-old monopoly of public law by the High Court and its predecessors, but the first Senior President of Tribunals, Sir Robert Carnwath, was upbeat

---

[80] The Court of Appeal had differed on this point alone from the divisional court.
[81] *R (Cart)* v. *Upper Tribunal* [2011] QB 120, 162 (CA), §42, a judgment in which I have to declare an interest.
[82] [2011] UKSC 28 and 29
[83] The Supreme Court took the opportunity to lay to rest the suggestion in *Watt* v. *Lord Advocate* 1979 SC 120 that judicial review in Scotland was not affected by *Anisminic*.
[84] S. 15(1)

about it, arguing that it would now be possible for the tribunals to develop their own forms and standards of justice, in parallel but not in competition with the Administrative Court of the Queen's Bench.

Administrative justice

This brings the wheel round to the issue flagged up by Arthurs and still demanding attention: ought the tribunal system to be allowed, even encouraged, to resume developing law and procedure in ways which may not chime with the culture of the courts but which still deliver justice?

Introducing his historical study of the law of public administration, Arthurs wrote:

> The very fact that lawyers tend to equate administrative law with the law of judicial review shows how deep-rooted is the assumption that law is a thing external to, apart from, even poised against whatever goes on within the administration . . .
>
> [H]owever, it was by no means clear that Alsatia always recognised the king's writ. Sometimes, it is true, administrative regimes devoted to important public purposes were frustrated, inhibited, and intimidated by reviewing courts. But in many instances the effects of judicial review were either dispelled by subsequent amending legislation or obfuscatory manoeuvres or allowed to spend themselves in single instances without affecting the ongoing activity of the administration.[85]

The long contention between administrators and judges about who is to have the last word has swung between the audacious seizure of the commanding heights by the House of Lords in *Anisminic*[86] and the enactment by Parliament, at the instigation of the Department of Social Security, of an unconstitutional provision requiring adjudicators to ignore judicial rulings.[87] But this is another story. What does require attention today is the fact that tribunal judges are in no true sense administrators: they stand between the administrators and the judges.

This has come about slowly and painfully. The departmental sense of proprietorship of tribunals has died hard. The Supplementary Benefits Commission during the 1960s and into the 1970s had a policy document

---

[85] Arthurs, *Without the Law,* pp. x–xi   [86] See Ch. 1.

[87] Social Security Act 1990, Sch. 6 para. 7(1); *Bate* v. *Chief Adjudication Officer* [1996] 1 WLR 814. See M. Nolan and S. Sedley, *The Making and Remaking of the British Constitution* (1997), p. 62, and Ch. 7 above.

known as the A Code, purportedly protected by the Official Secrets Act, by which all its discretionary and evaluative determinations were guided. The lay tribunals to which appeals came knew that it existed – they were clerked by departmental officials – and were correspondingly reluctant to interfere with officers' decisions. But this began to change. Lay chairmen were phased out in favour of qualified lawyers, and wing members were given training in adjudication.[88] The A Code had meanwhile been replaced by published regulations, and a final appeal now lay to the well-qualified and independent Social Security commissioners.[89]

These were the kinds of change which Leggatt was to consolidate. But with change came the danger against which Arthurs had warned: the judicialisation of adjudication and the shrinkage of constitutional pluralism. In the 1830s there still existed, in addition to the central courts, a plethora of local courts established by custom, feudal grant, royal charter or act of Parliament, all of them administering "the internal law of a particular place or trade".[90] Although these steadily went out of existence, there were some four hundred local courts of requests by the time the establishment of county courts in 1846 made them redundant; and the law administered by the forest courts was not finally repealed until 1971.[91] Arthurs' argument was not an exercise in nostalgia. It was that the old pluralism had been replaced by a new pluralism, as administrative tribunals of different kinds were brought into being by Victorian and Edwardian legislatures,[92] so that the old case for recognising that there can be more than one kind of justice was still alive and well.

Administrative pluralism

It is a case which is seemingly acquiring credence within the new structure.

Gareth Jones was driving a gritting vehicle on the M25 near the Dartford crossing when a lorry coming in the other direction skidded in a vain attempt to avoid a man who deliberately ran into its path. In the ensuing crash Mr Jones suffered catastrophic injuries, but he was refused compensation by the criminal injuries compensation tribunal, which is now part of the social entitlement chamber, because suicide itself is no

[88] Health and Social Services and Social Security Adjudication Act 1983
[89] Social Security Act 1980   [90] Arthurs, *Without the Law*, pp. 19–20
[91] Wild Creatures and Forest Laws Act 1971
[92] See Lord Haldane's speech in *Arlidge* v. *Local Government Board*, discussed in Ch. 1.

longer a crime and the suicidal act did not, in the view of the compensation authority, constitute the reckless infliction on Mr Jones of grievous
bodily harm.

The first-tier tribunal upheld this decision on the ground that
Mr Jones had not in their judgment been the victim of a crime of
violence. The Supreme Court[93] held that what amounted to a crime of
violence, despite its legal components, was an issue for the tribunal's
judgment, not a pure question of law. Lord Carnwath rejected the notion
that it was "a jury question". He said:

> Where, as here, the interpretation and application of a specialised statu-
> tory scheme has been entrusted by Parliament to the new tribunal system,
> an important function of the Upper Tribunal is to develop structured
> guidance on the use of expressions which are central to the scheme, and
> so as to reduce the risk of inconsistent results by different panels at the
> First-tier level.

He cited Lord Hoffmann's earlier dictum:

> it may be said that there are two kinds of questions of fact: there are
> questions of fact; and there are questions of law as to which lawyers have
> decided that it would be inexpedient for an appellate tribunal to have to
> form an independent judgment.[94]

Lord Carnwath went on:[95]

> The idea that the division between law and fact should come down to a
> matter of expediency might seem almost revolutionary. However, the
> passage did not attract any note of dissent or caution from the other
> members of the House. . ... [I]t was intended to signal a new approach . . .

It is a self-denying approach which many lawyers will find it difficult to
adjust to. It is also an approach which has to have known limits. Whether
these will be located in *Wednesbury* – by interfering only where, for
example, the decision as to the occurrence of a crime of violence is
beyond the bounds of reason – or at some point closer to the everyday
work of the law courts, remains to be seen. What can be predicted is that
the mapping of the line is itself going to give rise to uncertainty. Where in

---

[93] *R (Jones)* v. *First-Tier Tribunal* [2013] UKSC 19

[94] *Moyna* v. *Secretary of State for Work and Pensions* [2003] 1 WLR 1929, § 28. Compare,
however, the firmer line taken on fairness – a pre-*Anisminic* issue – in *R* v. *SW London
Supplementary Benefits Appeal Tribunal, ex p Bullen* (1976) 120 Sol. Jo. 437, discussed in
the Introduction.

[95] At 46, quoting from his article "Tribunal Justice, a New Start" [2009] PL 48.

the last few decades we have finally shuffled off the arid distinctions between the void and the voidable and between the administrative, the quasi-judicial and the judicial, we may find that we have acquired a whole new industry of distinguishing issues of law not only from issues of fact but from questions of law that the courts choose to leave to tribunals of fact. Relative autonomy for tribunals may well have strong cultural and historical antecedents; it may also have much to be said for it today; but it evidently comes at a price.

14

The rule of law

The idea of the rule of law – in fact the expression itself – comes from
Dicey. What Dicey meant by it was historically flawed and juridically
incomplete. But although what it means today is still contentious, the
rule of law in one form or another is a criterion of civilisation.

Dicey and the rule of law

Everybody believes in the rule of law, but few people could tell you what
it means, and for everyone who could tell you, there would be two others
to say they were wrong. But we at least know, or think we know, that the
concept originated with Albert Venn Dicey's *Introduction to the Study of
the Law of the Constitution*, first published in 1885.

Dicey's book was divided into three parts. The first was "The Sovereignty of Parliament", something which Dicey took to be fundamental,
total and beyond challenge. As Brian Simpson wrote:[1]

> Dicey announced that it was the law that Parliament was omnicompe-
> tent,[2] explained what this meant, and never devoted so much as a line to
> fulfilling the promise he made to demonstrate that this was so.

Moreover, when some three decades later Irish home rule returned to
Parliament's agenda, Dicey changed his mind about its omnipotence.[3]

---

[1] "The Common Law and Legal Theory" in A. W. B. Simpson, *Legal Theory and Legal
History* (1987) p. 378

[2] In fact Dicey's word was "omnipotent". Even he recognised that Parliament had to devolve
many of its functions because of its limited competence.

[3] "If the Government, without any dissolution of Parliament, avail themselves of the
Parliament Act to transform the Home Rule Bill into the Home Rule Act 1914, it will
be in form a law but will lack all constitutional authority, and the duty of Unionists will be
to treat it as a measure which lacks the sanction of the nation ... The Act will violate the
principle that no Bill which changes the foundations of the Constitution should pass into
law until it has obtained, directly or indirectly, the assent of the electors. This principle has

In the final edition of *The Law of the Constitution* in 1915 he lamented that parliamentary sovereignty had fallen prey to the party system – something that political scientists both before and after Dicey's time were well aware of.[4]

Dicey's second section was "The Rule of Law". His third dealt, much more briefly, with constitutional conventions.

A number of features of Dicey's extensive treatment of the rule of law deserve attention. He links it with what he calls "the omnipotence or undisputed supremacy" not only of Parliament but of central government, by which he means the Crown both in and out of Parliament. The failure to distinguish between the executive and the legislative limbs of the state is of a piece with Dicey's persistent denial that Britain had, or needed, any system of administrative law. This was not simple myopia; it was driven by Dicey's xenophobic antipathy to France and to civil law systems, which he regarded as autocratic and Napoleonic.[5] When, later in his account of the rule of law, he describes the amenability of the executive, when deploying delegated powers, to "the supervision, so to speak, of the Courts", he declines to recognise that this was precisely because we did by his day have a developed system of administrative law, operated through the prerogative writs of certiorari, mandamus, prohibition and quo warranto. To have recognised this would have been to puncture his inflated assertion that there was a single system of law in England.

When Dicey turned in his treatise to the components of what he took to be the rule of law, he listed them as follows: first, that there could be no punishment or penalty save for a proven breach of the law; secondly that the same law applied to everyone and was administered in the ordinary courts; and thirdly that it was from decisions of the courts, and not from any fixed constitution, that these principles sprang. Although Dicey continues to be credited with having both identified and articulated the concept of the rule of law, no modern account of it comes anywhere near adopting these as its defining components.

---

been tacitly but practically recognised by statesmen and by the country for at least eighty years." A. V. Dicey, *A Fool's Paradise* (1913) p. 117.

[4] See W. Bagehot, *The English Constitution* (1865), Ch. 6; Tony Wright, *Citizens and Subjects* (1994) *passim*.

[5] The attitude was not unprecedented: Fortescue's *De Laudibus Legum Angliae* (c. 1470) was "blatantly nationalistic in comparing English legal institutions with those of France" (C. W. Brooks, *Law, Politics and Society in Early Modern England* (2008), p. 23.

One striking feature of Dicey's thesis, so obvious that it is commonly overlooked, is that it is not couched in theoretical or normative terms at all: it is a partial and Panglossian account of the English legal system at the height of its Victorian self-assurance, as disparaging of foreign systems as it is vain about our own, reading more like a pamphlet than a textbook. It is difficult not to be struck by the similarity of Dicey's prose to that of the pompous Mr Podsnap in Dickens' *Our Mutual Friend*. But where Mr Podsnap considered that our constitution was "Bestowed Upon Us By Providence", Dicey insisted that it was "a judge-made constitution". He dismissed as "absurd" the notion that the British constitution "has not been made but has grown", seemingly oblivious of the complex mass of historical forces – political, legislative and prerogative, as well as judicial – which had gone into the making of a constitution which contained far more than his account of it allowed.[6]

After Dicey

Dicey has now been debunked many times,[7] but he is still taught in law schools because the rule of law continues, for good reason, to have a totemic importance. Yet it is hard to dispute Ferdinand Mount's appraisal of him:

> It seems extraordinary that such an erratic and violent thinker could ever have achieved such monumental status as a constitutional authority.[8]

Critics of the rule of law

There was for many years a left-wing critique of the rule of law as a theory which legitimised class domination. Behind it lay a spoken

---

[6] Cf. H. Lauterpacht, *International Law and Human Rights* (1950, 2nd edn. 1968), p. 128: "... the English constitutional practice of safeguarding the rights of the subject by statutory enactment, beginning with Magna Carta and its successive confirmations, continuing through the Habeas Corpus Act and the Petition of Right, and ending with the Bill of Rights and the Act of Settlement – a practice which, contrary to the current view, was not altogether alien to English political doctrine."

[7] Starting with W. A. Robson, *Justice and Administrative Law* (1928); see also H. W. Arthurs, *Without the Law: Administrative Justice and Legal Pluralism in Nineteenth-century England* (1985) and "Rethinking Administrative Law: A Slightly Dicey Business" (1979) 17 *Osgoode Hall LJ*.

[8] Ferdinand Mount, *The British Constitution Now* (1992), p. 56

or unspoken suggestion that a workers' state would not need such constraints on its power.

> Although this pragmatic approach to the legal system has been the predominant theme within the Marxist tradition ... [i]t is wondered whether or not there may be some intrinsic value to individual rights and the requirement that the state apparatus be constrained by its own rules.[9]

The question had already received an affirmative answer from the Marxist historian E. P. Thompson in a celebrated passage in his study of the origins of the Black Act[10]

> I am insisting only on the obvious point, which some modern Marxists have overlooked, that there is a difference between arbitrary power and the rule of law. We ought to expose the shams and inequities which may be concealed beneath this law. But the rule of law itself, the imposing of effective inhibitions upon power and the defence of the citizen from power's all-intrusive claims, seems to me to be an unqualified human good.[11]

Bingham's contribution

Lord Bingham, in the few years between his retirement and his death, wrote a short but influential book on the rule of law.[12] He acknowledged Dicey's weaknesses but argued that the concept of the rule of law was now so solidly entrenched in national and international instruments and jurisprudence that it had to be accorded a meaning. It is used, for instance, in the preambles to the Universal Declaration of Human Rights ("human rights should be protected by the rule of law") and the European Convention on Human Rights ("a common heritage of political traditions, ideals, freedom and the rule of law"). Even more pressingly for the UK, it now features as hard law in the Constitutional Reform Act 2005, which in its first section announces that it does not adversely affect "the existing constitutional principle of the rule of law" and which goes on, in s. 17, to prescribe an oath of office for the Lord Chancellor by which he or she promises to respect the rule of law and defend the

---

[9] H. Collins, *Marxism and Law* (1982), p. 144
[10] 9 Geo. I c.22 (1723), criminalising with severe penalties a variety of acts associated with poaching or civil insurrection.
[11] E. P. Thompson, *Whigs and Hunters* (1975), p. 266
[12] Tom Bingham, *The Rule of Law* (2010)

independence of the judges. That these provisions were the outcome of a standoff between the heads of the judiciary and a government which was set on pulling down the inherited constitutional edifice does not reduce their potency. What matters more is that the Constitutional Reform Act has left it to the judges to determine what the rule of law means. This at least is welcome.

Lord Bingham spelt out his view of what the rule of law means under eight heads:

1. The law must be accessible, intelligible and predictable
2. Rights and liabilities should be determined by law rather than discretion
3. Laws should apply equally to all, save where objective differences justify differentiation
4. Public powers must be exercised in good faith, fairly, reasonably and for their true purpose
5. The law must adequately protect human rights
6. There must be accessible courts for the resolution of disputes
7. Adjudicative procedures must be fair
8. The state must comply with its international legal obligations

Bingham's list, while uncontentious, is interesting for what it does not contain: a democratic polity; separation of the state's powers; an independent judiciary. All of these, it is manifest from his commentary, he takes for granted. But not everybody does.

Political democracy and the "rule of government"

Take democracy. Where Dicey took it that the popular will (albeit derived from what was still a heavily restricted franchise and operating on a partly unelected legislature) was enough to keep Parliament in check, Nazi Germany and apartheid South Africa were to demonstrate the capacity of elected parliaments to enact legislation which denied fundamental human rights to entire sectors of the population. It has accordingly become necessary for rule of law theory to pose limits to what even an elected legislature can do.

This is one of the places where the concept of the rule of law starts to come under stress, for it is here that the structural requirement of a political system responsive to popular wishes finds its scope limited by a doctrine of natural law which became prominent in the English conflicts of the mid-seventeenth century. The doctrine was that, contrary to what

Hobbes postulated in *Leviathan*, the state was not an entity distinct from and greater than the individuals who were its subjects but was their creature and their delegate, with no more right to tyrannise over others than individuals possessed. The farsighted radical John Warr wrote in 1649:

> it is possible for a society to exercise tyranny as well as a single person.[13]

The authoritarian view – that the state (like the heart[14]) has its reasons of which reason knows nothing – has never gone away. In recent years it has been emerging from the law and economics movement in the US, where critics[15] point to the endemic failure of modern democracies to curb executive power. They argue from this not to the need for a renewal of representative democracy or an intensification of judicial review of executive action but to a need to accelerate the trend towards executive autonomy, brushing aside what they call tyrannophobia and trusting public opinion, much as Dicey did, to control a technocratic presidential executive. In the American context of a directly elected presidency, the proposal may be doing little more than conferring intellectual respectability on what is already happening.[16] For parliamentary rather than presidential democracies, the idea is arguably retrogressive and even dangerous – but that does not mean that we shall not hear more of it.

I have said that this viewpoint has never gone away. Let me give an example of what I mean. In 1636, a few years before England's Civil War broke out, a London merchant named Richard Chambers brought an action for false imprisonment against the Lord Mayor of London, who had had him gaoled for refusing to pay the Ship Money, a tax levied by the King without the consent of Parliament. The judges refused to hear argument on the legality of the tax. Justice Berkeley, evidently speaking for the court, said:

> There is a rule of law and a rule of government, and things that may not be done by the rule of law may be done by the rule of government.[17]

---

[13] John Warr, "The Privileges of the People" (1649) in S. Sedley and L. Kaplan (eds.), *A Spark in the Ashes: The Pamphlets of John Warr* (1992), p. 77

[14] Pascal, *Pensées*, iv. 277

[15] E.g. E. Posner and A. Vermeule, *The Executive Unbound: After the Madisonian Republic* (2010)

[16] Though the Obama administration's bruising encounters with the obstructive power of the Senate suggest that the US's elected legislators still have some shots in their locker.

[17] Rushworth, *Historical Collections of Private Passages of State*, vol. II, p. 323

The fact that five years later Berkeley was impeached by the Long Parliament, along with the rest of the high court bench, for high treason – he was eventually convicted of a lesser offence and fined[18] – does not diminish the significance of his pronouncement. First, he uses the expression "the rule of law" not in the limited sense of some specific proposition (e.g. that it is a rule of law that you may not profit by your own wrong) but in the generic sense in which, three and a half centuries later, Dicey was to use it.[19] Secondly, he counterposes the rule of law to the rule of government. This is a subtlety which was to escape Dicey; yet the dichotomy is critical, because it points up the risks inherent in a separation of powers – a topic to which Dicey devoted very little attention – unless each of the powers is itself checked by the others or (in the case of Parliament) by a free electorate.

Democratic legitimacy

What is it that links the rule of law to political democracy and the separation of powers? Is it inconceivable that a dictator or a hereditary monarch might make laws which respect basic freedoms (other than the right to vote) and which are administered by independent judges and implemented by a conscientious executive? The answer has to come not from the rule of law but from political morality: no adult owes allegiance to a regime which they have had no voice in choosing. This is one reason why the rule of law has come to signify not only a state in which and by which law is respected, but one which is democratically governed, with an independent judiciary empowered to enforce recognised human rights and competent and uncorrupt public administration. Such a set of attributes is less a good conduct medal than a platonic ideal.

The moral authority of legislation in a democracy, like the presumption of parliamentary supremacy, depends on one of the underlying premises of the separation of powers: that the legislative power rests in the hands of a parliament chosen at intervals by a popular vote and thereby possessing what is customarily called democratic legitimacy. In the United Kingdom, we tend to assume that we have a clean bill of health on this score: is ours not the Mother of Parliaments? Other nations look in astonishment at a democracy whose unelected upper

[18] James Hart, *The Rule of Law 1603-1660* (2003), pp. 148ff

[19] The expression, as used by Dicey, is apparently his own invention. I have been able to find no antecedent use of it apart from this one telling instance.

legislative house contains ninety-two hereditary peers, twenty-six bishops of the Church of England and several hundred political appointees, many of whom contribute little or nothing to the deliberative process. The promise contained in the preamble to the 1911 Parliament Act that it was only the first step towards democratising the upper chamber remains unfulfilled.

But there is a paradox within the paradox. Alongside the political loyalists with which each major party tries to fill its allocated seats are a good number of able and experienced politicians, historians, lawyers, social, political and natural scientists, and others who bring a disinterested and acute mind to bear on issues which, in the lower house, may have undergone perfunctory debate and been voted on according to the dictates of the party whips by MPs who barely know what they are voting on. Recent and less recent history has shown the capacity of the unelected House of Lords to save parliamentary democracy from itself.

I am describing this bizarre situation not because it offers a model to any other states but because it throws up one of the big questions about the rule of law: how undemocratic does a society have to be before it forfeits its rule of law badge? I have suggested that it reaches that point if the democratic mandate is used to deny the fundamental rights of individuals or minorities. But what those rights are understood to be varies radically from one generation, and one society, to the next. While no other state in the world had laws as vicious as the Nuremberg laws, plenty of other states, Britain among them, at that time tolerated overt racial (and gender) discrimination in employment, education, the professions and elsewhere. Indeed Britain continues by statute to allow overt religious discrimination in its publicly funded schools.[20]

I have also suggested that the point of demotion is reached if the franchise by which the legislature is elected unjustifiably excludes significant sections of the governed. But here too I suspect that there are few states which can claim a clean bill of health. The United Kingdom, for example, has still not complied with the judgment of the European Court of Human Rights which held that the legislative withdrawal of the right to vote from all prisoners, regardless of the length of their sentence or the reason why they are in gaol, is disproportionate and therefore contrary to the Convention. The ban is particularly bizarre when by law anyone in gaol for up to twelve

---

[20] Equality Act 2006, Part 2, s. 50(1)(a).

months is entitled to stand for Parliament.[21] Nor is it easy to explain why at sixteen a young person, although still legally a child, is old enough to fight and die for his or her country but not mature enough to vote.

The fuzzy edges

There are other things that a theory of the rule of law needs to be able to account for.

It seems straightforward enough that the rule of law must mean acting according to and not contrary to the law. But injustices can occur not only despite, but sometimes because of, adherence to the law. There can be few judges who cannot verify this from their own experience. What space, then, is there for justice in the rule of law?

A second question is how much law there should be. A state which is over-governed to the point where individuality is stifled may be able to claim observance of the rule of law but does not have a lot to boast about. Nor, however, does a state which leaves individuals free to harm others. The same is arguably true of a state which fails to govern itself; a state, in other words, which has no or inadequate means by which the executive, and the legislature too if the constitution permits, can be called to account before independent courts for the legality of what they do.

Given these and many other fuzzy edges, there may be some force in the sceptical view that the rule of law is simply a form of self-congratulation – a badge which a society or a legal system awards itself, or which scholars award it, for good behaviour. This may not matter if it opens up the question whether the recipient deserves the award; in fact this is where it gets interesting. If South Africa under apartheid and Nazi Germany were to be stripped of the badge, it had to be by adding some further conditions to the rule of law. Hence the modern consensus that institutional respect for fundamental rights is an essential ingredient of the rule of law. But this too is more difficult than it seems: which rights are to rank as fundamental?

Discrimination and the contingency of human rights

Take the human right not to be subjected to unwarranted discrimination. A century ago it was by no means obvious to everyone, even to liberals in

---

[21] Representation of the People Act 1981, s. 1. A similar bar applies in European elections. For local elections a sentence of three months or more disqualifies.

developed societies, that women were equal to men or black people to white. Discrimination against children is still legal: the law, at least in the UK, permits assaults on children which would be crimes if committed against an adult,[22] and denies them autonomy and citizenship in a variety of forms. The justification for these things still seems to us obvious. But obviousness is a dangerous substitute for logic. Dicey warned that if women were given the vote, the next thing would be women in the jury box and on the bench. Happily he was right. When I was called to the Bar in 1964 it was perfectly legal in Britain to refuse to let accommodation or give employment to foreigners or people with black or brown skins: property rights – which continue to feature in most modern lists of fundamental human rights – trumped all others.

Our common sense of what is acceptable in these and many other fields has gone through a social and political metamorphosis which has revolutionised not only our concept of human rights but their relationship to one another. The right not to be subjected to discrimination on grounds of gender or race, whatever its impact on private property and contract, is now beyond civilised contest. But, recalling that fifty years ago the converse was largely the case, we would be fooling ourselves if we imagined that the process was now over – that we had somehow arrived at the end of history. In fifty years' time, people will look back in surprise at some of the things we took for granted and the (to them) obvious things we failed to comprehend.

How does this affect the rule of law?

What implications does this have for the meaning of the rule of law? Does it mean that Dicey was talking nonsense when he claimed, at a time when race and sex discrimination were embedded in law, that Britain was an exemplar to the world of the rule of law? Does it mean, now that we forbid both these things, that the rule of law is finally established? To take either stance would be blinkered and ahistorical. But it has more than these merely negative implications: it sheds some light on the possible meanings of the rule of law.

If you are going to be rigorous about its meaning, either you have to accept that the rule of law is an ideal which few if any states can claim to have attained, or you have to cut back its meaning so as to exclude all but

---

[22] Children Act 2004, s. 58; *R* v. *H (Assault on child: reasonable chastisement)* [2001] EWCA Crim 1024

the true pariah state. If you want to be less rigorous and more inclusive, you can legitimately do both – that is to say, you can accept that what the French call *l'état de droit* (a state of legality) is a badge of merit which few states will ever truly deserve but which ought to be denied only to those which deliberately turn their backs on its essential components.

Judicial independence

One of those essential components is the uniform and dispassionate application of the law: the endeavour (in the words of the judicial oath) to do justice according to law without fear or favour, affection or ill-will.

It's perhaps useful first to recall what it is that distinguishes independence from impartiality. Impartiality is a state of mind – in the vocabulary of the judicial oath, the absence of affection or ill-will. Independence is a state of being – freedom from what the judicial oath calls fear or favour. When critics of the bench describe judges as unaccountable, they cannot mean that judges do not account for their decisions, for judges uniquely have to give full reasons in public for everything they do. They mean that judges are unable to be removed from office even if their decisions displease those in power, including a vociferous and opinionated press. A judiciary which goes in fear of offending the politically powerful is antithetical to the rule of law. Lord Bingham's list includes the right to a fair-minded adjudication – that is to say a decision by an impartial judge; but it is necessary to add that if judges could be forced from office for giving unpopular decisions – if, in other words, judges were not truly independent – unpopular minorities would go unprotected, demagogy would subvert democracy and the rule of law at its most basic level be undermined.

Bingham himself had no doubts on this score. Judges, he wrote,

> must be independent of anybody or anything which might lead them to decide issues coming before them on anything other than the legal and factual merits of the case as, in the exercise of their own judgment, they consider them to be.

This, however, requires qualification. Judges may become, or show themselves, unfit for office in other ways. Every bench has had such judges at one time or another, and a fair and objective disciplinary or vetting system for terminating the tenure of unfit judges is a necessary part of the rule of law. Bingham was attracted by the old convention that the judges must seek reappointment on the death of the monarch; but a formal complaints system such as the UK now has is less arbitrary. The 2010 Kenyan constitution set up an independent inquiry into judicial corruption; and while the panel which vetted the judges of the court of appeal found no proof of corruption, it nevertheless decided that four of the court's nine judges should stand down from their office because of unjudicial behaviour on the bench. Such a process, far from diminishing judicial independence, can secure it. But the risk of having unfit judges on the bench is a risk which each society needs to balance against the misuse of dismissal to placate criticism.

Conclusion

The rule of law is an elusive and protean concept. It has no fixed meaning. It certainly no longer has the anglocentric self-assurance with which its originator, Dicey, clothed it. What it signals today is a shared ideal that individuals and society should not be subject to the whim of the powerful, and that their rights and obligations should be determined by laws made by an elected legislature which respects fundamental rights, administered without discrimination by independent and competent judges, and enforced by an uncorrupt executive. To this extent the rule of law is egalitarian, though it cannot make the poor richer or the rich less opulent. But so long as it can contribute to Amartya Sen's project of minimising injustice in the world,[23] it will still be an ideal worth pursuing.

[23] A. Sen, *The Idea of Justice* (2009)

INDEX

Notes on the indexing of cases

Legal cases are by and large indexed under the name by which they are most easily identified, not necessarily the strictly correct citation form.

For reasons of space, cases are indexed only where there is significant comment on their content and/or relevance to a given topic.

Where a plaintiff's name is indexed the case name is not given separately.

Lightning Source UK Ltd.
Milton Keynes UK
UKOW06f1113210117

292578UK00015B/936/P